THE LEGENDS OF
WEST BROMWICH ALBION

First published in Great Britain in 2010 by The Derby Books Publishing Company Limited, 3 The Parker Centre, Derby, DE21 4SZ.

ISBN 978-1-85983-799-3
Printed and bound by DZS Grafik, Slovenia.

THE LEGENDS OF
WEST BROMWICH ALBION

TONY MATTHEWS

ACKNOWLEDGEMENTS

I would like to thank the following who, in their own way, albeit on a small or large scale, have assisted me with this book: Dave Baxendale (Ashton-under-Lyme, Lancashire), former Albion director Joe Brandrick (Wombourne), Jonathan Eden (Solihull), the late 'Wayne' Gwynne (Rowley Regis), John Hickling (Dudley), James Hodge (Luton), David Instone (Newport, Shropshire), Gill Keys (from Stockport, the great-grand-daughter of Major H. Wilson Keys), Colin Mackenzie (Solihull Lodge), Barry Marsh (London), Eddie Miller (Morden Park, Surrey), Nick Oldham (Football Trader), Peter Owen (Quinton, Birmingham), Charlie Poultney (Brierley Hill), Terry Price (Yew Tree, Walsall), Laurie Rampling (Albion's official photographer from Essex), Neil Reynolds (Bedworth), Keith Simcox (Wednesbury), Marc Soulsby (Dudley, grandson of Harold Pearson and great grandson of Hubert Pearson), Dean Walton (Leamington Spa), Terry Wills (Stirchley, Birmingham) and last but by no means least, from DB Publishing, Derby, Steve Caron, Alex Morton and Jonathan Hoggard.

And I mustn't forget my darling wife Margaret, either…I bet she's fed up to the teeth, hearing me tapping away on the computer keyboard, my head buried in programmes, magazines, books and magazines, day after day, week after week. Don't worry Love, I still have a few years – and books – left in me yet!

Tony Matthews

CONTENTS

INTRODUCTION

Choosing 100 legends for any club which is over 125 years old is not easy.

This is not the first time I have had to select a century of great Albion players. In fact, I have done it twice before and each time there have been people who have criticised my choice, for one reason or another. That begs the question – who do you select and who do you omit?

In the past I received help from several loyal and dedicated Baggies supporters and I also took into consideration the views of several ex-players, a handful of club officials, past and present, a couple of directors, two former secretaries, a trainer and two managers. This time round I have liaised with just three people, one of them an ex-player.

I can only say, with reservations, that as time goes by, more and more 'superstars' (heroes, if you like) will appear on the scene and give Albion great service…and that will make the task of selecting the top 100 for a future book a lot harder.

Even now I am certain I will get some detrimental feedback from a handful of critics, and I know the main question a lot of people will be asking is simple: 'Why isn't so and so included in the 100?' And that means, without doubt, that at least another 25 players, maybe 50, have not been mentioned – players who, in certain people's minds, should have been included among the legends.

The 100 former players I have chosen this time around are my personal choice, and obviously if I had more space then the write-ups on each one would have been far more extensive. I have tried to cram as much onto one page as I could.

I have included several players from the late 1880s and early 1890s; virtually all the team that won the League Championship in 1920; the main XI who achieved the unique double in 1931; Vic Buckingham and the majority of his team that won the FA Cup in 1954; several from late 1950s and early 1960s; quite a few from the 1967–68 and 1978–79 squads under managers Alan Ashman and Ron Atkinson; and a handful from the 1980s and 1990s.

Some, I know, only had short careers with Albion, others much longer, but I feel that those I have featured in this book gave the club excellent service, and I believe most of them achieved something useful with Albion, or would have done if their career had been longer.

Apart from the 100 players listed in this book, I can easily name another 100 straight off (and I'm sure you can too) who have given the club sterling service over the years, several of whom would probably feature in someone else's list of legends.

Choosing photographs is always difficult for any book, and for me, and indeed the publishers, things are not getting easier, inasmuch as over the last 30 years, since the mid-1970s, I have written, co-compiled and assisted with more than 20 books on my beloved Baggies – and that means that an awful lot of pictures have been used in the process.

Therefore, some of the images in the book have had to be repeated – simply because you cannot get a decent second or back-up photograph of the older players. However, this time round, with the help of a lot of friends, I have succeeded, to a certain degree, in getting hold of a few previously 'unseen' photographs, the odd cigarette and trade card and quite a few caricatures. Thanks to you all. I apologise in advance if I have infringed anyone's copyright in respect of certain pictures.

I know, and so do you, that over the years many of the West Midlands' greatest players have been associated with West Bromwich Albion football club and some have even been regarded as the best in their respective countries. I believe that most are included in this book, which I hope you will enjoy as you recall the days when these stars were in their prime and doing the business for the team in navy blue and white stripes.

Tony Matthews, 2010

FOREWORD

By Graham Williams, Albion's 1968 Cup-winning captain

When I arrived at the Hawthorns as a 16-year-old in 1954, I was thrilled to get close to the likes of Ronnie Allen, Ray Barlow, Frank Griffin, Johnny Nicholls and Paddy Ryan, who, a few months earlier, had helped Albion win the FA Cup. But there had been many more star players before I joined the club, there have been many more since and there will be hundreds more in the future.

This fascinating book features 100 of the 1,000 or so players who been associated with the Baggies through the years – and to select 100 is hard, very hard. How do you choose a legend? I don't know. I have my favourites, and so does everyone else.

Obviously, the player who scores the winning goal in a Cup Final, or in a crucial League game or even in a local derby against Wolves or Aston Villa can easily become a legend overnight! But choosing the best 100 players over a long period of time, who served one specific club, is a tough job for anyone.

Football, as we know, is a magnificent and very popular subject for discussion, and supporters are renowned for their knowledge of the game and for their ability to pick a better team – but that is usually AFTER the game has been played. And it is a fact of life that supporters who have watched scores of players, and indeed matches, throughout the last 40–50 years will have their own views about their team's greatest players.

I am far too young to remember the stars of yesteryear, but I did see and play with some brilliant players who graced Vic Buckingham's 'footballing' side that won the Cup in 1954. Jimmy Hagan, too, had a superb bunch of players when he was in charge in the 1960s, as did Alan Ashman when, once again, the FA Cup came to The Hawthorns.

Most of the players under the leadership of Johnny Giles and Ron Atkinson could easily feature in a lot of lists, likewise Ossie Ardiles, and there will of course be a handful from the last decade. But who do you choose? Who do you leave out? You take your pick…it is a matter of personal opinion.

I know who I would select from the last 60 years – and I know full well that these same players would feature in the top 100 of every ardent Albion supporter. But how do you try and choose players who graced the game between, say, 1880 and 1930? That is beyond me. There aren't all that many supporters alive today who can honestly say they saw a specific player feature in an Albion team in the 1920s, or even the 1930s. You can only go on what you read in newspapers, programmes, books and magazines.

It has been an enormous pleasure for me to play with and against some of the game's great players, many of them internationals, and quite a few of them are legends.

As always, Tony has put a lot of time and effort into compiling this book, and I know that questions will be asked as to why he has included a certain player and why didn't he choose him instead, or why leave him out…

It is a matter of opinion – and for me he has chosen well. This book is a fascinating read…enjoy it.

Graham Williams

RONNIE ALLEN

'The Complete Footballer – a terrific goalscorer – he was as sharp as a needle, quick as a flash…
one would hardly be surprised if his middle name was effervescence.'

Born:	15 January 1929, Fenton, Stoke-on-Trent
Died:	9 June 2001, Great Wyrley, Walsall

Albion senior record:

Appearances:	League 415, FA Cup 42, FA Charity Shield 1
Goals:	League 208, FA Cup 23, FA Charity Shield 3
Senior debut:	League, 4 March 1950 v Wolverhampton Wanderers (h) drew 1–1 (scored)
Also played for:	Hanley High School, Staffs County Youths, Northwood Mission, Port Vale, Crystal Palace, West Bromwich Albion Old Stars, England (5 full, 2 B caps), Football League (1 app), FA XI, RAF
Managed:	Wolverhampton Wanderers, Walsall, West Bromwich Albion (2 spells), Athletic Bilbao, Sporting Lisbon, Panathinaikos

It's been said before and it will be said again (many times) that Ronnie Allen was 'the complete footballer'. Though he won only five caps for England, he was certainly one of the best centre-forwards around during the early 1950s, on a par with Stan Mortensen (Blackpool) and Nat Lofthouse (Bolton).

Stanley Matthews described Ronnie as being 'fluid and dextrous', while Tom Finney always said that he was 'Albion's star turn…a player with great awareness and movement. Any centre-half who shadowed him ran a few miles during the course of a game, I can tell you.'

Signed from Port Vale for £20,050 in March 1950 (the extra £50 made him a record buy), Ronnie gave the club 11 great years as a player before joining Crystal Palace in May 1961. His total of 234 goals (208 in the First Division) remained as a club record for 18 years, until Tony Brown beat it in 1979.

Ronnie also set another record which he will always keep – that of scoring in each of the first 20 post-World War Two seasons: 1945–46 to 1964–65 inclusive.

After encountering some difficulty getting into The Hawthorns (no one really knew who he was!) Ronnie scored on his Baggies debut against Wolves before a record League crowd of 60,945. He then top scored six seasons running from 1950–51; was second in 1956–57, 1958–59 and 1959–60 and headed the charts again in 1957–58. When he ended his playing career in 1965 – after four years with Palace – his three-club record was impressive: 309 goals in 702 senior appearances.

Having occupied both wing and two inside-forward positions with Port Vale, Ronnie started on the right flank for Albion. He then filled the other four forward positions before settling down as leader of the attack…this, after director and former player Tommy Glidden had suggested to manager Jack Smith that he should try Ronnie in the centre at a time when goals were in short supply. The switch was made for the 10th match of the 1951–52 season against Middlesbrough. Ronnie scored and quickly became a top-class centre-forward.

At first he played up front and did well, although his stature (5ft 9in tall and 10st 12lb in weight) was against him, especially when faced by a sturdy defender. Then Albion's captain and centre-half Jack Vernon suggested he would be better off dropping deep, away from his marker.

This worked a treat, and when Vic Buckingham became Albion's boss in February 1953 things got even better for Ronnie. Playing brilliantly, he regularly dragged the opposing centre-half out of position, allowing his co-striker Johnny Nicholls to dart into the vacant gap. The record books show that Ronnie and Nicholls (the 'Terrible Twins') became two of the best marksmen Albion has ever had. Between them they netted 136 goals in three seasons – 28 in 1952–53, 66 in 1953–54 and 42 in 1954–55. Ronnie in fact netted twice in the 1954 FA Cup Final win over Preston, his second a penalty which brought the scores level at 2–2. Earlier he had fired home the winner from the spot in the semi-final against his former club Port Vale. Ronnie recalled: 'Johnny Nicholls and I were great mates. We had lots of laughs and jokes together and without doubt he was one of the best goal-poachers I ever played with.'

When Johnny left, Derek Kevan and Bobby Robson moved in alongside Ronnie and Albion continued to be one of the most prolific scoring units in Division One. In fact, in five seasons up to Ronnie's departure in 1961, they bagged 457 goals, including 112 in 1957–58.

In 1952, Ronnie gained the first of his five England caps, playing outside-right against Switzerland in Zurich. Thirty years later, as Albion boss, he returned to that same ground for a UEFA Cup game. His other caps came in 1954 against Scotland (1 goal), Yugoslavia, Wales (1 goal) and the World Champions West Germany. He was also reserve with teammate Joe Kennedy when Hungary beat England 6–3 at Wembley in 1953.

When his playing days ended, Ronnie became a coach with Wolves, whom he later managed (1966–68). Following spells in Spain, Portugal and Saudi Arabia, he bossed Walsall in 1973 before becoming Albion's scouting advisor in 1977. Appointed manager that same year, he was enticed back to Saudi Arabia to run that country's national team and after working in Greece in 1980 he returned for a second spell as Albion boss in 1981, leading them to two Cup semi-finals, both lost.

Ronnie then became general manager at The Hawthorns and remained at the club, as a part-time coach, until just before his death in 2001. He played his last game as a substitute for Albion against Cheltenham in May 1995, aged 66.

Interestingly, Manchester United wanted to buy Ronnie in 1958 after the Munich air disaster, but Albion's chairman at the time, Major H. Wilson Keys, said: 'He's going nowhere.'

As Albion's London area scout, Ronnie spotted Cyrille Regis. He also had a huge part in getting Laurie Cunningham to join Albion.

Besides being a top-class goalscorer, Ronnie was also a fine golfer, winning the Professional Footballers' title in 1959 and 1961 and finishing runner-up in 1963 and 1964.

His son, Russell, an Albion reserve in the 1970s, went on to score 62 goals in 272 League games for Tranmere Rovers and Mansfield Town.

JEFF ASTLE

'A terrific header of the ball – few better in his era.'

Born:	13 May 1942, Eastwood, Nottingham
Died:	19 January 2002, Burton-on-Trent, Staffs

Albion senior record:

Appearances:	League 290+2, FA Cup 23, League Cup 28, Europe 10, Others 8
Goals:	League 137, FA Cup 14, League Cup 19, Europe 1, Others 3
Senior debut:	League, 30 September 1964 v Leicester City (a) lost 4–2
Also played for:	West Notts Schoolboys, Holy Trinity Youth Club (Kimberley), Coventry City (trial), John Player FC, Notts County, Coventry City (trial), John Player FC (Nottingham), Hellenic FC (South Africa), Dunstable Town, Weymouth, Atherstone Town, England (5 full caps), England XI (5 apps), Football League (2 apps)

Jeff Astle was a legend at The Hawthorns. The fans loved him and, appropriately, they nicknamed him 'the King'. A brilliant header of the ball, Jeff's 1970s teammate John Wile described him as being 'a master of his art'. 'I have never seen anyone head the ball like Jeff,' said Wile. 'He was magnificent. He was also pretty useful on the ground and had a superb strike-rate. He was a fantastic all-round player and a great guy.'

Wile also reflected on Jeff's up-beat personality, saying: 'He was a very funny bloke. It was a laugh a minute, which was good for the dressing room. He always made light of the situation and was eager to join in any mickey-taking that was going around. The nice thing about Jeff was that he was a very humble fellow. After he finished playing, he didn't think football owed him a living. He buckled down and made a new life for himself.'

Born in the same street, or so he claimed, as the writer D.H. Lawrence, Jeff played junior football in and around Nottingham prior to joining Notts County as an amateur in June 1958, having been recommended to the club by his headmaster. He then gained match experience with John Player FC before turning professional at Meadow Lane in October 1959. He made excellent progress and in 1962–63 linked up with Tony Hateley in the Magpies' attack, the pair forming a potent scoring partnership. However, when Hateley left for Villa Park, Jeff struggled to adjust to life alongside Terry Bly and in October 1963 handed in a transfer request to manager Eddie Lowe. A move did not transpire for almost a year, but when it did, it proved to be a very good one for both Jeff and West Bromwich Albion.

Having scored 41 goals in 116 appearances during his time at Meadow Lane, Jeff signed for the Baggies in September 1964 for £25,000, brought in by manager Jimmy Hagan. He was given his first outing at Leicester City just 24 hours after joining before scoring twice on his home debut in a 5–1 thrashing of local rivals Wolves on 10 October.

Over the next decade Jeff set The Hawthorns alight with some exciting centre-forward play and superb marksmanship. He went on to net a total of 174 goals in 361 senior appearances for Albion, the most memorable of which came in the 1968 FA Cup Final win over Everton. With the game in extra-time, Jeff collected a ricochet and unleashed a ferocious left-foot shot from 20 yards, which flew past 'keeper Gordon West to hand the underdogs a 1–0 victory. The goal not only secured Jeff's status as an Albion great, but also guaranteed him a place in FA Cup folklore as he joined the band of players who have scored in every round of the competition in the same season.

Two years later, Jeff headed an early goal in the League Cup Final defeat by Manchester City and in doing so became the first player to score in both major domestic Finals at Wembley.

Earlier, Jeff had helped Albion win the League Cup in 1966 and was in the team that lost to QPR in the Final the following season. In those two campaigns he was superb, scoring some cracking goals including two hat-tricks in four days in September 1965 – a feat he would repeat towards the end of the 1967–68 season.

Jeff top scored for Albion four times: in 1964–65 (jointly with Clive Clark on 11), in 1967–68 (when he struck 35 goals, the most for the club since Ronnie Allen in 1951–52), in 1968–69 (when he netted 26 times) and 1969–70 (with a haul of 30). At the end of that campaign he was named in the England squad for the World Cup Finals in Mexico but, as we all know, he missed a great opportunity to equalise against Brazil, although, to set the record straight, it proved meaningless as England still qualified for the quarter-finals, only to lose 3–2 to West Germany, while Brazil went on to lift the trophy for a record third time.

Jeff won a total of five full caps for his country (the first against Wales in May 1969) and he also played for the B team, on four occasions for an England XI (seven goals scored including four against Liga University in 1970), and twice represented the Football League (four goals). He was also voted Midland Footballer of the Year in 1968.

Following a good 1970–71 season in which he notched 16 goals in 48 outings, thereafter Jeff was plagued by injury, a troublesome right knee being the major problem. In fact, over the next three years (from August 1971 until April 1974) he made only 43 appearances and scored 10 goals.

After a deserved testimonial, Jeff reluctantly left The Hawthorns in May 1974, signing for the South African club, Hellenic. He returned to England two months later, teaming up with George Best at Dunstable Town, and after playing for three other non-League clubs, he finally announced his retirement in May 1977.

Having played in an era when a footballer's yearly income would not match the weekly wage of today's stars, Jeff was forced to pursue an alternative career. He successfully ran an industrial cleaning business from his home at Netherseal near Burton-on-Trent, before coming back into the public eye in 1995 with a tongue-in-cheek singing slot on David Baddiel and Frank Skinner's *Fantasy Football League* television show. Later he did his own 'roadshow', which again involved singing, while also continuing his own business, with the sign on his van stating 'misses no corners'.

Jeff was only 59 when he died in Queen's Hospital, Burton-on-Trent, in January 2002. Eleven months later, South Staffordshire coroner Dr Andrew Haigh concluded that Jeff died from an 'industrial injury', a phrase dramatically at odds with the enduring image of him soaring to score and the romantic terms often used to describe his art. In effect he had suffered brain injuries (dementia/footballer's migraine), caused by repeatedly heading a ball during his 20-year career.

Following his sad death, a campaign was launched to fund a set of gates dedicated to Jeff's memory at The Hawthorns. Situated on the Birmingham Road, close to the Woodman Corner, the gates were unveiled by his widow Lorraine on 11 July 2003. This came a few months after Jeff had become the first person to have a Midland Metro tram named after him.

In 2004, Jeff was named as one of Albion's 16 greatest players, in a poll organised as part of the club's 125th anniversary celebrations.

In 1968, the words 'ASTLE IS THE KING' were painted in large white letters on the brickwork of Primrose Bridge, which carries Cradley Road over a canal in Netherton, in the heart of the Black Country. The bridge quickly became known locally as 'the Astle bridge'.

HAROLD BACHE

'Could have been one of the all-time greats — we shall never know.'

Born:	20 April 1889, Churchill near Kidderminster
Died:	15 February 1916, Ypres-Comines Canal Bank near Ypres, Belgium

Albion senior record:

Appearances:	League 12, FA Cup 2
Goals:	League 4, FA Cup 0
Senior debut:	FA Cup, 21 February 1914 v Aston Villa (a) lost 2–1
Also played for:	Cambridge University, Staffordshire Youths, West Bromwich Springfield, The Corinthians, Eastbourne FC, England (7 amateur caps), Football League (1 app)

Although Harold Bache played in only 14 first-class matches for the Albion, scoring four goals, he was, at the time, regarded as one of the finest amateur footballers in the country...and many thought he was destined to become an Albion legend. And this was at the unpaid level!

Already an established amateur international when he agreed to play for Albion, Harold had scored no fewer than seven goals for England in their 20–0 annihilation of France at Ipswich in 1910. At around this time he was on the brink of being called up to the full England team, and he might well have won a full cap for his country had World War One not broken out when it did.

Harold was just two months short of his 24th birthday when he agreed to join Albion as an amateur in February 1914, having played for the famous Corinthians during the early part of that season. Indeed, he had been in terrific form over the previous four years, during which time he also turned out for the East Sussex club, Eastbourne. He had scored well over 50 goals in more than 120 competitive matches and was at the top of his game.

A small, eager-beaver centre-forward, Harold was a highly skilful footballer who could beat an opponent with ease and in a very confined space. Two of his seven goals against France came after mazy dribbles which took him straight through the heart of the French defence. Unfortunately, all too often he was barged off the ball by the big, burly defenders who were summoned to mark him, but this acted as a favour to his team, as most of the time his colleagues capitalised on the open spaces left around him.

Albion had been struggling to score goals during the two months prior to Harold's arrival at The Hawthorns. Indeed, they had mustered less than a goal a game all season and were desperate to get hold of a class player to accompany Alf Bentley in attack. Harold was handed his Baggies debut in a third-round FA Cup tie away to the holders Aston Villa. He played well, but unfortunately Albion lost the game 2–1 before a crowd of 57,293.

More annoyingly, however, it was announced soon afterwards that Harold had been called up to join the Lancashire Fusiliers in readiness to serve his country at war, and as a result he missed the rest of the season. Thankfully, from Albion's point of view, he was available to start the 1914–15 campaign and lined up at inside-left against Newcastle United at St James' Park. Harold played well, helping his side register a 2–1 victory. He played in 11 of the first 14 League matches that season, scoring in solid wins over Bradford away and Notts County and Bolton Wanderers at home. A twisted knee, however, sidelined him for six weeks before he returned to score the deciding goal in the home clash with Middlesbrough in early January. A week later he appeared in an FA Cup defeat at Hull and, sadly for Harold, that was his last ever game of football.

He was whisked away to Belgium 24 hours later. He quickly rose to the rank of Lieutenant, but less than two years into his Army service he was tragically killed during heavy fighting on the northern bank of the Ypres-Comines Canal. Harold, along with several of his colleagues, was trapped under a narrow ridge some 30 to 40 feet high as gun fire rained down into the sodden trench. Most of those in the vicinity lost their lives. Harold was just 26 at the time of his death.

On hearing of Harold's demise, the editor of the *Albion News* – Harry Keys – wrote in his notes: 'Everyone associated with West Bromwich Albion football club was shocked to hear of Harold's death. Although he had only been at The Hawthorns for a relatively short time, he was already a huge favourite with the supporters and would, I am sure, have given the club great service for many years to come. Our condolences go out to his family and friends, of which he had many.'

Besides being a wonderful footballer, Harold was also a very useful cricketer. A left-hand batsman and slow left-arm orthodox spin bowler, he served Worcestershire from 1907 until 1910 and also played for Cambridge University. He made his County debut against Surrey at the end of the 1907 season and went on to play in 20 first-class matches, 17 for Worcestershire. As a middle-order batsman he amassed 270 runs for an average of just 9.00, his highest score being 36 against Middlesex at Lords in 1910. As a bowler he took three wickets for an average of 13.00 each, having his best return of 2–4 also against Middlesex when he dismissed the great Patsy Hendren and Jack Hearne; his other victim was Robert Relf of Sussex in 1909. Harold, who also played competitive lawn tennis and rugby for Cambridge University, was an exceptionally fine runner and gained winners' and runner's-up medals in both the 100 and 200 yards sprints and 400 and 800 yards track events.

RAY BARLOW

'Highly skilful, fast, wholehearted and enthusiastic.'

Born: 17 August 1926, Swindon, Wiltshire

Albion senior record:

Appearances: League 403, FA Cup 46, Wartime 8
Goals: League 31, FA Cup 5, Wartime 3
Senior debuts: Wartime League Cup, 3 February 1945 v Walsall (h) lost 2–0
   League, 28 September 1946 v Newport County (a) won 7–2 (scored)
Also played for: Garrards FC (Swindon), Swindon Town (trial and World War Two guest), Birmingham City, Stourbridge (trial), West Bromwich Albion Old Stars, England (1 full, 2 B caps), Football League (5 apps), FA XI, the Army

The only surviving member of Albion's 1954 FA Cup-winning team, Ray Barlow is also the third-oldest former Baggies player alive today, and will celebrate his 84th birthday this year.

Tall, highly skilled, fast over the ground, wholehearted and enthusiastic, he served Albion for 16 years — from June 1944 until August 1960 — and during that time appeared in almost 450 League and FA Cup games plus a handful of wartime fixtures.

Spotted playing for Wiltshire-based works team Garrards by former Baggies centre-forward Jimmy Cookson, Ray was 17 when he arrived at The Hawthorns for a trial in the summer of 1944. Within five months he was a professional and he made his first-team debut in the Regional League derby against Walsall in February 1945, partnering England international Joe Johnson on the left. This was Ray's only outing that season, but in 1945–46, playing at inside-left, he scored 10 goals in 32 League (South) games, including a hat-trick in a 5–0 victory over Tottenham Hotspur. He also went on his first Albion tour to Belgium and Luxembourg.

During the 1946–47 campaign he made only 10 starts in Division Two before enlisting in the Army for his National Service, becoming a gunner in the Tank Regiment based in Palestine. Returning to England in April 1948, he went straight into Albion's second team and scored in the last Central League game of the season against Chesterfield.

Still donning the number-10 shirt, Ray started 1948–49 in the first XI but, with so much forward talent available at The Hawthorns, he slipped back into the second XI and spent the first half of the campaign as reserve to Jackie Haines and Cyril Williams before finally gaining a regular place in the senior side in January. Occupying the right-half, inside-right and inside-left positions, he helped the Baggies gain promotion, scoring vital goals in home wins over Leeds United (his penalty decided this contest) and Barnsley and in the crucial 3–0 victory at Leicester City which guaranteed First Division football for 1949–50.

After playing in Albion's first top flight game for 11 years v Charlton Athletic on 20 August 1949, Ray was plagued by a mystery illness and was sidelined for over three months. Thankfully, he regained his health and fitness, and also his first-team place, and remained an Albion regular for virtually a decade, right through to September 1959, captaining the side for the last two-and-a-half years, during which time an FA Cup semi-final was lost to Aston Villa and a tour was made behind the Iron Curtain.

Bedding himself in at left-half towards the end of the 1949–50 season, he occasionally deputised at centre-forward and inside-left, and also played a few games at centre-half towards of the end of his Albion days, but it is in the number six shirt that he is best remembered.

Long-striding, he loved to drive forward with the ball and his passing was second to none. He could switch play superbly by directing a measured 40-yard cross-field pass to the feet of his right-winger – first it was Ronnie Allen, then Frank Griffin and later Jimmy Campbell. And he could also deliver the perfect through ball to his goal-seeking forwards. Once Ronnie Allen and Johnny Nicholls had teamed up as Albion's main striking duo, it was Ray who provided the ammunition for those two hot-shots. He did the same for future goal men Bobby Robson and Derek Kevan.

Ray was outstanding in season 1953–54 when Albion came so close to clinching the double. The scorer of six goals in 46 competitive games, it was he whom Tommy Docherty upended in the penalty-area halfway through the second-half when Albion were trailing 2–1. Allen netted from the spot to set up a 3–2 victory over Preston.

In November 1954, Ray belatedly won his only full cap for England, replacing Portsmouth's Jimmy Dickinson against Northern Ireland in Belfast. He did well in a 2–0 win, but surprisingly was never selected again by manager Walter Winterbottom. Earlier capped twice at B team level v France in 1952 and Scotland in 1953, he went on to represent the Football League five times.

On leaving Albion, Ray had a brief spell with Birmingham City and then almost signed for Stourbridge, pulling out after being given an odd pair of socks to wear during pre-season training. After that he played in Albion's Old Stars team and ran a sub-post office and confectionery shop in Stourbridge.

Alan Neale, the regular *Sports Argus* reporter at Albion games in the later 1940s/early 1950s, was continually impressed by Ray's performances, once stating that…'No one contributed to the success of Albion's forwards more than Ray Barlow, whose classic skill opened up goal avenues time and again.'

Albion's 1970s player-manager Johnny Giles always had a soft spot for Ray, saying: 'I saw him play at Dalymount Park in a friendly match for the Football League against the League of Ireland in 1953. He was such a well-balanced footballer, great on the ball. It was an art and a pleasure to see a player like him. I always admired his football skills after that.'

Stan Rickaby, who played with Ray in Albion colours during the early 1950s, said: 'Ray Barlow was the best attacking wing-half I ever saw. He made the ball talk at times and his passing was unbelievable. Such an elegant footballer, he surely deserved more than the one England cap he was awarded.'

Another former Albion player, the late Jimmy Dudley, agreed with Stan, saying: 'Ray was a brilliant wing-half. Able to bring the ball down from an unusually high height with his long legs, he would then pass it inch-perfect to a colleague with his next move. He was terrific.'

Today Ray lives in Pedmore near Stourbridge.

BILLY BASSETT

'One of the greatest outside-rights of all time.'

Born:	27 January 1869, West Bromwich
Died:	9 April 1937, West Bromwich

Albion senior record:

Appearances:	League 261, FA Cup 40, Others 10
Goals:	League 61, FA Cup 11, Others 5
Senior debut:	FA Cup, 15 October 1887 v Wednesbury Old Athletic (h) won 7–1
Also played for:	Oak Villa, West Bromwich Strollers (not Albion), Old Church Club, England (16 full caps), England XI (1 app), Football League (3 apps), Football League XI, FA XI, England international trialist

After starting out as an inside-forward and switching to the wing in 1887–88, Billy Bassett became one of the greatest outside-rights of all time. Neat and dapper, only 5ft 5½in tall and of slight physique, he was exceptionally fast over the ground, possessed terrific close ball control, had fine judgment and was mighty dangerous near goal.

Idolised by supporters all over the country, he believed at first that he was far too small and lightweight to be become a professional footballer and withstand the severe competitiveness of the English game at that time, but he soon put those thoughts behind him and quickly developed into an established superstar, giving the Baggies great service for many years.

The proverbial flying winger, he was without doubt the Stanley Matthews, George Best or Tom Finney of his day, and was also the first player of national renown that West Bromwich had produced. 'A Black Country gem, a real good 'un, easily the best in the game during the late 1880s and 1890s,' said former Albion secretary-manager Fred Everiss.

Billy lived and breathed Albion for over 50 years – first as a player, then coach, shareholder, director and finally chairman. In his heyday as a player he had only one rival in England (and perhaps in the UK). That was Aston Villa's outside-right Charlie Athersmith…and there was great debate between the two sets of supporters as to who was the best!

According to the neutral Midland football supporter, Billy just got the nod as he won 16 England caps to Athersmith's 12. Indeed, Billy played in his first international against Ireland in Belfast in March 1888, just a week after his scintillating performance in the FA Cup Final had helped Albion beat the red-hot favourites Preston North End 2–1. Billy then went on to play against Scotland eight years running, scoring on his last appearance in April 1896. He certainly had the big-match temperament and, in fact, he never had a bad game for his country, quite often proving to be the match-winner – as he was for Albion. In the pre-20th-century League and FA Cup competitions, wingers were regularly marked by half-backs and very few, if any, could master Billy.

When interviewed in 1912, former Scottish international left-back Bob Smellie (Queen's Park), who played against Billy on three occasions, remembered: 'I was given the run-around by Bassett when England won 5–2 at the Richmond Athletic cricket ground in 1893. He made three of the goals, two of them headers by Fred Spiksley. He couldn't half run. I hardly got near him all afternoon.'

On large grounds, such as the Oval and the Crystal Palace, where there was plenty of room, Billy would frequently touch the ball past his opponent and then sprint outside the touchline (several yards off the pitch), leaving his marker totally bemused.

He could cross the ball splendidly on the run and would often cut in from the wing and have a shot at goal, always preferring to use his right foot. He scored some wonderful goals in his time, many for Albion in vital games. He was top marksman in 1888–89 (the first season of League football) and continued to score regularly for the Baggies right through to his retirement at the end of the 1898–99 season, averaging a goal every four games – not at all bad for a winger.

Billy, who was one of the highest paid footballers in the game in the late 1880s, earning £3 a week – and he deserved every penny – was, surprisingly, the first Albion player ever to be sent off. He was dismissed in a friendly at Millwall in April 1894 for using 'unparliamentary language' towards the referee. He said: 'You don't understand the bally game!'

From early 1891 until August 1897, Billy and chunky Scotsman Roddy McLeod formed a brilliant right wing at Albion. On many occasions they gave the opposition a very testing time with their direct approach. In 1892, Billy was the star of the show when Albion beat Aston Villa 3–0 in the FA Cup Final, setting up the first goal for Jasper Geddes and the second for Sammy Nicholls. But three years later, despite a wonderful individual display, he saw Villa gain revenge with a 1–0 victory. And it was against Villa that Billy actually played his 311th and final competitive game for Albion, in a 7–1 League defeat at Villa Park in April 1899.

After this Billy went into the licensed trade in West Bromwich and took an interest in the cinema, as well as coaching the younger players at the club, mainly in the evenings. He also purchased a number of shares and, in August 1905, some 12 months after qualifying to become a Football League linesman, he became a director at The Hawthorns, moving up to chairman three years later. He was still in that position when he died in April 1937 – a few days before Albion were due to play Preston North End in the semi-final of the FA Cup. During his time as chairman Albion never signed a Scottish-born footballer…despite Billy himself being a great friend of the aforementioned McLeod when they were players together.

At Albion's AGM in 1936, Billy, who had hardly missed a board meeting at The Hawthorns in the previous 31 years, was presented with a silver casket and illuminated scroll/address on the occasion of his completion of 50 years' service with the club.

From 1930 to 1937 he had served as a member of the Football League Management Committee, was an international selector in 1936–37 and became a Justice of the Peace in 1935. After his death at the age of 68, an obituary written by the editor of the *Albion News* described Billy as being a 'guide, philosopher and friend of the club' while Fred Howarth, the secretary of the Football League, declared him to be 'the most popular man in the game.'

NB: Billy's son, Norman Bassett, and his brother, Harry, were both associated with Albion – Norman as a director (1937–52) and Harry as a reserve-team player who once partnered Billy on the right wing in a friendly against the Birmingham & District side in April 1892.

BRENDON BATSON, MBE

'An average player at first – became a stylish and immaculate right-back.'

Born: 6 February 1953, St George, Grenada, Windward Islands

Albion senior record:

Appearances: League 172, FA Cup 13, League Cup 21, Europe 12, Others 2
Goals: League 1, FA Cup 1, League Cup 0, Europe 0, Others 0
Senior debut: League, 28 February 1978 v Birmingham City (a) won 2–1
Also played for: Waltham Forest Boys, Arsenal, Cambridge United, Witton Albion, West Bromwich Albion All Stars, England (3 B caps)

Brendon Batson, one of the pioneer Black footballers in England, became part of a trio (Batson, Laurie Cunningham and Cyrille Regis) at The Hawthorns who became known as the 'Three Degrees' by supporters throughout the country. Following his move from Grenada to England, he recalled what happened at his first school football trial. 'I turned up without any boots and had to play in the pair of plimsolls I usually wore for athletics. My teacher came up to me at the end of the session and asked me where I came from. I replied Grenada, at which point he said "Maybe your game is cricket, Brendon." I was disappointed, but I returned for another game the following week, did well and after that things went marvellously. Within a couple of years I was training at Highbury and then, after playing for Arsenal's junior teams, I was upgraded to the reserves and, in July 1969, manager Bertie Mee offered me a professional contract, which I signed without any hesitancy.

'Mr Mee told me "remember who you are, what you are and what you represent." I never forgot those words.'

Competition for places in Arsenal's first team was intense, but Brendon stuck in there and, after gaining an FA Youth Cup-winners' medal in 1971, he became the London club's first-ever Black player to appear in the Football League when he made his debut as a substitute against Newcastle United in March 1972.

Unfortunately Brendon was unable to gain a regular place in the Gunners' senior side and, after just 10 first-class games, he was transferred to Cambridge United for £6,000 in January 1974.

Later that year Ron Atkinson took over as manager at the Abbey Stadium and when he was appointed boss of West Bromwich Albion in February 1978 Brendon became his first signing, moving to The Hawthorns for £30,000.

After an impressive debut in the Midlands derby against Birmingham City, he quickly made his mark in the First Division, doing so at a time when Black footballers were being subjected to extreme racism from fans up and down the country. Brendon never let the racist chants or comments get to him. He concentrated on playing football and he became one of the best attacking right-backs in the top flight. And one feels that if Viv Anderson and Mick Mills hadn't been around, he would surely have gained full England honours. As it was he was selected for three B internationals in 1980 – and that was disappointing.

Brendon was a key figure at The Hawthorns during the late 1970s and early 1980s. He formed a wonderful full-back partnership with Derek Statham and his enterprising runs down the right flank always gave the team an attacking option. Occasionally he was caught out of position – too far upfield – but that was his game. Brendon loved to drive forward when given the opportunity and he had a helping hand in several goals.

On that note, he only managed to find the net twice for the Baggies (in a total of 220 competitive games), yet both his efforts were beauties. His first was scored against Coventry City in a 4–0 third-round FA Cup replay victory at The Hawthorns in January 1979. After a flowing move involving five players, he darted into the penalty area to fire home with a low, right-footed drive. His second goal came against Ipswich Town in a home League game in April 1981. This time he once again found himself unmarked inside the 18-yard box when Derek Statham's cross came over and he made no mistake, helping Albion to a 3–1 win.

Brendon came close to playing in two Wembley Cup Finals, but each time he went away bitterly disappointed. Ineligible when Albion lost to Ipswich Town in the FA Cup semi-final of 1978, he then played in both the League Cup and FA Cup semi-finals of 1981–82 when Albion lost 1–0 on aggregate to Tottenham Hotspur in the former and by the same score against Queen's Park Rangers in the latter. He was also somewhat despondent when Albion went out of the UEFA Cup at the quarter-final stage in 1978–79.

'I thought we had a great chance of winning the trophy that season. We had beaten a couple of useful teams in earlier rounds, including Valencia, but a lack of discipline cost us dear in the second leg of our quarter-final clash with Red Star Belgrade. We lost 1–0 away and were leading 1–0 in the return leg before they poached a late goal to knock us all for six.'

Sadly Brendon's playing career ended somewhat prematurely. He suffered a terrible knee injury against Ipswich Town at Portman Road in October 1982 and never regained full fitness, despite prolonged physiotherapy treatment and a couple of operations. He officially announced his retirement from first-class football in May 1984 (after a deserved testimonial match) and although he played occasionally for Witton Albion during the 1984–85 campaign, as well as turning out quite often for the West Bromwich Albion Old Stars in charity matches, he was always driving through the pain barrier and called it a day for good in 1987.

Teaming up with Gordon Taylor at the Professional Footballers Association (PFA), Brendon quickly became a senior administrator, rising to the position of deputy chief executive at the organization that he helped develop into one of the richest Trade Unions in the world. For his efforts in this field, and of course for what he did as a player, in 2000 Brendon was awarded the MBE for services to football by the Queen.

Two years later, in July 2002, Brendon returned to The Hawthorns as Albion's managing director, a position he held until June 2003. He is now employed as a Football Consultant by the FA, helping increase the number of coaches from ethnic minorities.

Sadly, in September 2009 Brendon's wife, Cecily, died from a brain tumour. He now resides in Manchester and attends most Albion home matches.

JAMES 'JEM' BAYLISS

'A powerful and prolific goalscorer and a very useful wing-half.'

Born:	14 January 1863, Tipton
Died:	19 August 1933, West Bromwich

Albion senior record:

Appearances:	League 56, FA Cup 39
Goals:	League 12, FA Cup 24
Senior debut:	FA Cup, 15 October 1884 v Junction Street School, Derby (a) won 7–1 (2 goals scored)
Also played for:	Great Bridge Unity, Tipton Providence, Wednesbury Old Athletic, Walsall Town (guest), England (1 full cap), England international trialist

When he joined Albion in August 1884, Black Country-born 'Jem' Bayliss was already an established and indeed prolific goalscorer. Powerfully-built, he was your typically old-fashioned go-for-goal centre-forward, who had already notched over 100 goals in four seasons while playing for Wednesbury Old Athletic, having earlier scored freely for his two other local clubs.

The name Jem was derived from the initials of three of his Christian names – James Edward Mathias – and he was one of the finest marksmen of his era, certainly the best in and around West Bromwich.

A great-hearted performer who played with great spirit, determination and confidence from the first to the last minute of every game he participated in, Jem, in the late 1880s, was to Albion what Archie Hunter was to Aston Villa and Hunter was, without doubt, a terrific footballer.

In his first season with Albion (1884–85) Jem scored over 25 goals and struck at least another 25 the following season, including his first hat-trick at competitive level, in a 6–0 win over Old Westminsters in the sixth round of the FA Cup. Albion went on to reach the Final but went down to a strong Blackburn Rovers side after a replay.

In 1886–87, with Jem again leading the attack supremely well and continuing to score plenty of goals, around 40 this time, Albion raced through to their second FA Cup Final. This time Aston Villa provided the opposition and Jem was quietly confident that Albion, the clear underdogs, could pull off a shock result. But sadly, for the second year running, Jem ended up a loser as Villa won a tight contest 2–0.

Blackburn had played in three successive FA Cup Finals up to 1886 and now it was Albion's turn to equal that feat as they reached the Final in 1888 after a wonderful sequence of results. Jem, who by now had been joined in the attack by wing-wizard Billy Bassett, had been outstanding, scoring another hat-trick, this time against his former club Wednesbury Old Athletic in the first round, slotting home the winner against Mitchell St George's in round four, bagging all four goals in the destruction of Stoke in round five and claiming one in the semi-final victory over Derby Junction.

A record crowd of almost 19,000 packed into the Oval cricket ground to see Albion take on the 'Invincibles' of Preston North End in the Final. Battling against the odds, Jem opened the scoring from Bassett's precise cross and then, after John Goodall had equalised, he fed Bassett, who in turn supplied another perfect cross for George Woodhall to knock home the winner. Albion rejoiced and Jem had played his part in a famous victory. The team returned to West Bromwich and drove through the crowded streets in a four-horse brake, decorated with flags in the club's colours. Jem took centre stage as he held the coveted trophy aloft for all to see.

A few months after this triumph, Albion played their first game in the newly-formed Football League. Their opponents were Stoke and Jem lined up in the team, not as a centre-forward but as a left-half, and he once again ran his socks off as Albion won 2–0 to become the first team to top the new League table.

An ever-present in 1888–89, Jem actually played in five different positions during the course of the campaign, lining up as an emergency right-back at Burnley. Back as a forward in 1889–90, when he struck nine goals, he was sidelined with a knee injury for quite a while the following season and made only 11 appearances in total, but he was fit enough to play in his one and only international match for England against Ireland at Molineux when he lined up at right-half alongside his teammates Charlie Perry and Billy Bassett. He assisted in two of the goals in a comprehensive 6–1 victory.

In the summer of 1891 Jem – for his loyal and dedicated service – was elected to the Board of Directors at the club's Annual General Meeting. He remained on the board, unchallenged, until 1905, acting as chairman for the last two years before he was technically replaced in office by his old buddy Billy Bassett. Four years later, in August 1909, Jem was made a life member of the club – and he deserved it.

As a unique player-director Jem added eight more appearances to his overall tally in 1891–92 before announcing his retirement. He had scored 36 goals in 95 League and FA Cup games and, for the record, he had also notched at least another 120 goals in the various local Cup competitions and friendlies which he played in. Shortly after his retirement, a reporter in a local sports paper wrote: 'For most of his first-class career, Jem was a powerful and prolific scoring centre-forward. In 1890–91 he successfully made the transition to wing-half in which position he exhibited splendid qualities in the tackle.'

Regarded as a real gentleman both on and off the field, Jem, on returning from a family holiday in Gibraltar in the summer of 1897, was shown his own obituary notice, which had been published in a local newspaper. While he had been abroad rumours had circulated around his home town of Great Bridge that he had died of typhoid fever. Nothing could have been further from the truth! Jem was fit and well and he simply took everything in his stride, laughed the whole thing away and lived on for another 36 years. In fact, he cut the obituary notice out of the newspaper, framed it and subsequently hung it on his living room wall for posterity.

'Gentleman Jim', or Jem to his pals, attended his last Albion game at The Hawthorns during the team's double-winning season of 1930–31. He was on the staff of Guest, Keen & Nettlefold for many years. He died in a West Bromwich hospital in 1933, three days after his 77th birthday.

HARRY BELL

'Valuable and perceptive full-back — an awkward one to pass.'

Born:	18 April 1862, West Bromwich
Died:	18 January 1948, Cape Town, South Africa

Albion senior record:

Appearances:	FA Cup 15
Goals:	FA Cup 0
Senior debut:	FA Cup, 10 November 1883 v Wednesbury Town (h) lost 2–0
Also played for:	George Salter Works FC

Harry Bell, one of the founder members of West Bromwich Albion (Strollers) football club, was a well-built, strong-tackling full-back with good technique. He was a player with the club for seven seasons, from the autumn of 1878 until he retired through injury in the summer of 1886, just after making his last competitive appearance in the FA Cup Final replay against Blackburn Rovers. Later on in life Harry returned to Albion as assistant trainer (1905–07) and thereafter worked as a gateman on the turnstiles at The Hawthorns before emigrating to South Africa two years after World War One.

Prior to leaving England for Cape Town, Harry described his early days as a footballer in *The Chronicle*, a local West Bromwich newspaper, and his story made very interesting reading. A former pupil at Beeches Road Junior School, Harry went on to attend Overend Wesley Sunday School while taking employment at George Salter Springs Works in West Bromwich. He played for the works cricket team, as did several other young, enthusiastic sportsmen, most of whom also went to the same Sunday school. One day Harry and a handful of his cricketing colleagues met to discuss the possibility of forming a football club so that they could keep fit and active during the winter. A favourable decision was made – and in no time at all there were at least a dozen or so teenagers all keen to try their luck with a larger ball. West Bromwich Strollers were up and running – ready to pit their wits against the other soccer teams in and around the Black Country.

This was in October 1878. A month later the Strollers played their first game, a 12-a-side friendly against a team from Hudson's soap factory. The game ended 0–0. Harry played at right-back and there he remained throughout the rest of his career. He remembered: 'We commenced playing in Dartmouth Park and everyone who joined the club had to pay an entrance fee of one shilling plus two pence per week subscription. We had a whip round to buy the first football and I well recollect how 'Darkie' Timmins, George Bell, a cousin of mine, Billy Bisseker and myself, all walked to Wednesbury to fetch the ball before we started to play.

'In those days all our games were friendlies and there wasn't much interest shown from the public. After two seasons, however, after changing our name from Strollers to Albion and moving to a new ground, Bunn's Field in Walsall Street, our supporters began to rally around us.

'We bought the timber and fenced the ground ourselves and for our first match we charged 2d admission and took about 31 shillings, making the crowd around the 185 mark.

'Wearing white jerseys with a blue sash and maroon stockings, we played open football in those days and we knew how to score goals, once beating Coseley 26–0 in a local Cup tie. We also beat one of the strongest teams around, Aston Villa, in the English (FA) Cup but were then knocked out by the eventual winners of the competition, Blackburn Rovers.

'I recall that after this defeat some of our supporters set about the referee, some of the ladies present giving him a taste of their umbrellas!

'The success of the Albion around this time was largely due to loyalty among the players and the wholehearted and determined way they threw themselves into their tasks, for in those days football was not a business; we played purely for the love of the sport.

'In order to encourage us to do our best, the committee – no manager in those days – allowed the players half a leg of mutton and this we had to fetch from the local butcher's shop, owned by Mr Belcher.'

Harry also talked about receiving money for the first time as a footballer. 'I was paid 10s a match when we [Albion] were playing at our Four Acres ground in 1884–85 – the highest amount I ever received as a footballer. Unfortunately the following season my wages went down considerably and it also proved to be my last as a player with the club.'

Around that time Albion had a very good team and in 1885–86 they reached the FA Cup Final for the first time in their history. Harry recalled: 'I was told that several of our supporters walked the 100 or so miles from the Black Country to London to see the match against Blackburn at the Oval cricket ground. After a 0–0 draw, the replay was staged at Derby – the first time a Final had been staged outside the capital – but this time, though, Albion were defeated 2–0.'

Harry severely damaged his right leg during a second-half goal mêlée in the replay. In the past Harry had suffered two broken collarbones and had recovered to play on. Unfortunately on this occasion he never really regained full fitness and, although retained as a player for another year, he eventually left the club in June 1887, teaming up with Warwick County for a season. Two other Albion players, George Bell and Tom Lavender, joined with him. After that Harry worked in a nearby steel factory until the summer of 1905, when he was asked to return to the club in a paid position by secretary-manager Fred Everiss. Engaged as assistant trainer to newly-appointed head trainer Bill Barber, Harry retained that post for two seasons and then, for 14 years from 1907 until 1921, he worked part-time at The Hawthorns as a match-day gatekeeper while doing manual work in a factory the rest of the week. Then, quite unexpectedly, he packed his bags and emigrated to South Africa, choosing to live in the Cape Town district. He continued to follow the fortunes of his beloved Albion, albeit via the postal service, and he went on to enjoy the rest of his life in a much warmer climate. He was three months short of his 86th birthday when he died in 1948.

MARTYN BENNETT

'A class act of the seventies.'

Born:	4 August 1961, Great Barr, Birmingham

Albion senior record:

Appearances:	League 180, FA Cup 13, League Cup 20
Goals:	League 9, FA Cup 0, League Cup 1
Senior debut:	League, 7 April 1979 v Everton (h) won 1–0
Also played for:	Derby County (trial) Birmingham & Aston Boys, Aldridge & Brownhills Schools, Walsall & District Schools, West Midlands County Schools, Streetly FC, Worcester City (player-manager), Cheltenham Town, England (9 Schoolboy caps)

Martyn Bennett could easily have signed for Derby County before finally agreeing to join Albion as an apprentice in August 1977. Said Martyn: 'Aston Villa had been watching me but nothing materialised, so I went to train with Derby for a couple of weeks. They had a great record for looking after kids, but so too had Albion. And after speaking at length with coaches Brian Whitehouse and Albert McPherson, and manager Ronnie Allen, I chose Albion as my club.'

With John Wile and Ally Robertson firmly established at the heart of Albion's defence, Martyn was nurtured along smoothly for two years, appearing at full-back for the third team in 1977–78 and most of the time at centre-half for the reserves in 1978–79. In April 1979, Brendon Batson pulled out of the home League game against Everton and Martyn was called up by boss Ron Atkinson for his senior debut.

'I was petrified, absolutely petrified. They had Dave Thomas on the wing, a clever England international and I was playing out of position, having by now settled permanently at centre-half. I thought to myself, "I'll have to get him early",' said Martyn. 'I steamed into him, more out of fear than anything else, sent him up in the air and got a few verbals for my challenge. I couldn't say anything back – I was so mentally shattered. I think he went off injured after about 20 minutes and after that the game seemed to pass me by, although we did win 1–0, thanks to an Ally Brown goal.'

Martyn was called into the first team on four occasions in 1979–80 before having a decent run in the side during the 1980–81 campaign when he scored his first senior goal, a powerful header in a 2–0 win at Leicester in the January. He made 20 appearances that term before Atkinson left and Ronnie Allen moved in as manager.

'In my opinion, Ron wasn't strong enough to be a manager' said Martyn. 'He was a nice guy, fair enough, but he had no control really. We went over to Spain to play against his former club, Seville, in a tournament in August 1981 and one night we asked if we could go out on the town. "Be back by nine o'clock," said Ron. "That's too early!" we said. "Ok, 9.30 then". "No," we replied, "We're not doing that boss". "Ok, make it 10," he said. It went on and on, until in the end he just mumbled, "Come in when you like."'

That season Albion struggled in the League yet reached the semi-finals of both domestic Cup competitions. Martyn had been out of the team until February but was brought in to play as an anchorman in midfield in front of Wile and Robertson. He battled well in both semi-finals, but disappointingly Albion lost them both, going out in the League Cup to Tottenham Hotspur 1–0 over two legs and to QPR by the same score in the FA Cup. Martyn recalled: 'If we had scored against Spurs we would have been at Wembley, and as for the QPR game, that was poor. We never got to grips with a hard, bumpy pitch and, on reflection, the boss played the wrong team and introduced the wrong tactics.'

Ron Wylie took over as Albion's manager in the summer of 1982. 'He was straightforward and to the point,' said Martyn, 'but was over-powered by his assistant, Mike Kelly, who virtually ran the team. Some of us didn't like it. But Ron stuck to his guns, and told us that he had appointed Kelly and would stand by him.' In the end Kelly was sacked and soon afterwards Wylie resigned.

Albion's next manager was Johnny Giles, who returned for a second spell in charge. Martyn thought he was 'not up to it' and inside two years Ron Saunders had arrived. 'He could be quite abrupt, stern and obnoxious at times. But he was a good gaffer,' admitted Martyn. 'He got rid of loyal servant and the player's spokesman Ally Robertson…this came from above, I'm sure. Remember Red Rob, the union leader at British Leyland? Well, that was Ally's nickname. He was our leader, always on hand to help the younger players and report to the chairman. Unfortunately he got the tag of "troublemaker" and was pushed out. Naughty.

'I thought Saunders was a good manager. He came to Albion far too late. I wish he'd been appointed earlier…he really had something. I know we went down when he was in charge and he sold Steve Bull and Robbie Dennison, but he had been one of the best managers in the game…it was a pity he was nearing the end of the road.'

Martyn, who for some time had been fighting a back problem, made 39 League appearances in 1984–85, 25 the following season and 15 in 1986–87. 'Those were three poor seasons,' recalled Martyn. 'Players were coming and going like nobody's business. We were horrible in 1985–86 when we were relegated. I had never been involved in so many bad games in such a short period of time. It was embarrassing for the fans, I know.'

The Wile-Robertson partnership came to an end in 1983 and during the next five years Albion, who made two more managerial changes, fielded no fewer than 10 different centre-back duos, Martyn playing alongside Ken McNaught, Robbo, Micky Forsyth, Paul Dyson, Martin Dickinson and Kevin Steggles. 'Sometimes we didn't know who was in and who was out,' said Martyn. 'It was ridiculous at times.'

Martyn failed to get a single game in the first team in 1988–89 due to injury. He made his last senior appearance for Albion in a 7–0 home League win over Barnsley the following season, when relegation was avoided by just three points. At The Hawthorns for 13 years, he made 218 appearances, scored 10 goals, served under seven different managers, plus one caretaker manager and received a testimonial.

In later years Martyn was associated with Cheltenham Town and Worcester City and, after a spell in Ireland, he went into the luxury car business in Birmingham.

SID BOWSER

'Tenacious and hard-working, he divided his considerable talents between two diverse positions.'

Born:	6 April 1891, Handsworth, Birmingham
Died:	10 February 1961, Acocks Green, Birmingham

Albion senior record:

Appearances:	League 341, FA Cup 28, Others 2
Goals:	League 64, FA Cup 8, Others 0
Senior debut:	League, 2 January 1909 v Grimsby Town (h) won 7–2 (2 goals)
Also played for:	Astbury Richmond, Willenhall FC, Birmingham (trial), Belfast Distillery, Walsall, England (1 full cap), Irish League (1 app)

Sid Bowser divided his considerable talents between two diverse positions: centre-half and inside-forward. In both he was resilient, tenacious and hard-working and above all proved a great asset to Albion, especially during his second spell at the club.

When he arrived at The Hawthorns as 16-year-old in the summer of 1908, Sid had been playing in a good standard of football since leaving school four years earlier. Indeed, he had spent two seasons with Willenhall Town, for whom he scored over 25 goals, and had been an unsuccessful trialist with Birmingham in April–May 1907. Albion, though, saw something in him that Blues had obviously missed and he became a star in double-quick time.

After impressing in the second XI and signing a professional contract, Sid made his League debut (in place of the injured Charlie Hewitt) in the home Second Division match against Grimsby Town on 2 January 1909, and, partnering Welsh international Billy Davies on the left wing, he celebrated the occasion by scoring twice in a resounding 7–2 win. In fact, he became Albion's youngest-ever League goalscorer that day – and that record remained his until Geoff Richards beat it when he scored against Luton Town in December 1946.

Big and strong with stamina to match, Sid played in the next three matches before Hewitt returned, and after a longish run in the reserves, during which he gained confidence and experience, he finally established himself as a first-team regular in December 1909, although during the second half of that season he was utilised in all three central forward positions.

He netted six goals in 26 appearances in 1909–10 in a rather poor and inconsistent Albion side that struggled in the League. However, things changed dramatically the following season when the Second Division title was won after a last-match home win over Huddersfield Town. Sid played his part in that triumph, top scoring with 24 goals in total, 22 in the League, including four twos and vital winning strikes against Fulham, Birmingham and Gainsborough Trinity at home and Stockport County, Leicester Fosse and Lincoln City away.

Maintaining his form, Sid played even better in the top flight, helping Albion establish themselves in mid-table by scoring eight goals in 27 games. He also netted four times in seven FA Cup games as the Baggies went all the way to the Final, only to lose to Barnsley after extra-time in a replay. This was a huge disappointment to Sid. He had been outstanding and was confident of collecting a winners' medal, but it was not to be and he had to wait another eight years before his next club achievement.

Following a decent 1912–13 season, in which he scored seven goals in 35 games, Sid surprisingly left The Hawthorns to join the Irish club Belfast Distillery. In those days it was permissible for a player to 'go over the water' without any transfer fee being involved and Sid's departure stunned the club and more so the supporters. In the early 1970s, I was fortunate enough to meet one of Sid's teammates from that era, Bob Pailor, who told me that Sid had been 'upset' by two officials at the club and decided to 'have a break' from English football. He had a friend in Belfast who was associated with the Distillery club and, with all expenses paid and accommodation found, Sid chose to travel to the Emerald Isle.

Albion certainly missed 'Big Sid' and it appeared that he was doing well in Ireland when, in a roundabout way, it was learned that he wanted to return to England. Albion's secretary-manager Fred Everiss immediately travelled north and got on a boat to Belfast. He met up with Sid, the Distillery officials were contacted and, after a brief meeting, a deal was agreed and the prodigal son duly returned home, Albion welcoming him with open arms.

Quickly back into the fray, Sid played two games in the forward line before being switched to centre-half in place of Freddie Buck. He settled into the heart of the defence and finished the season with 14 more appearances under his belt.

In 1914–15, with war clouds gathering, he missed only three matches before going on to serve Notts County and Southport Vulcan as a guest during the hostilities, playing very few times for Albion. However, in March and April 1919, the Midland Victory League was introduced and Sid helped the Baggies win the title.

The following season saw Albion win the Football League championship for the first and so far only time in the club's history – and Sid played a massive role. He was brilliant week after week and became the first Albion defender to score a hat-trick when he bagged three goals, two from the penalty-spot, in a 4–1 home win over Bradford City on 27 September 1919. In all he netted 10 times (eight penalties) and missed just one game when he was on England duty, playing against Ireland in Belfast, this being his only cap, although he did represent the Irish League when playing for Distillery. In a match report of that Bradford game in the West Bromwich Free Press, it stated: 'Bowser has long been a fine player – but this season he is genius.'

Sid continued to produce excellent form for Albion over the next four years, being an ever-present in 1922–23. However, at the age of 33 and showing signs of pain due to an infuriating knee injury, he eventually left The Hawthorns for good, joining Walsall on a free transfer in August 1924. He had scored 72 goals in 371 senior appearances for Albion in a total of 15 years with the club.

Remaining a Saddler until his retirement in May 1927, Sid chose to enter the licensed trade, taking over a pub in Dudley which he ran for over 25 years. He was almost 70 years of age when he died in Birmingham in February 1961.

WALTER BOYES

'A very effective player, quick and clever.'

Born: 5 January 1913, Killamarsh, Derbyshire
Died: 16 September 1960, Hallam, Sheffield

Albion senior record:

Appearances: League 151, FA Cup 14
Goals: League 35, FA Cup 3
Senior debut: League, 14 November 1931 v Aston Villa (h) won 3–0
Also played for: Sheffield Boys, Woodhouse Mills United, Everton, Scunthorpe United; World War Two guest for Aldershot, Brentford, Clapton Orient, Leeds United, Manchester United, Middlesbrough, Millwall, Newcastle United, Preston North End and Sunderland; England (3 full caps, 1 Jubilee international cap), Football League (2 apps)
Managed: Retford Town, Hyde United

There were some exceptionally fine outside-lefts in England during the mid to late 1930s, among them Cliff Bastin, Eric Brook, Eric Houghton, Joe Johnson, Jack Smith and a certain Wally Boyes, who had replaced Stan Wood in West Bromwich Albion's first team. Standing a fraction over 5ft 4in tall and known as 'Titty' Boyes by his colleagues, Walter began life as an attacking left-half and had also played at inside-left before switching to the wing. A chunky-looking player, with good skills, a smart turn of foot and a fine crosser of the ball, especially on the run, he could score goals as well as make them, and had the pleasure of netting for Albion in their 1935 FA Cup Final defeat by Sheffield Wednesday.

He was 18 when he joined Albion as a professional in February 1931 and spent the majority of his first two years at The Hawthorns in the reserves before finally gaining a place in the first XI in January 1934, coming in to partner another well-built player, Teddy Sandford. Described in a local newspaper as being '…potent, brainy and dangerous' and in a match-day programme as a player with '…determination and aggression who loves to burst through the defence and shoot at goal when least expected,' Wally made his Albion debut at inside-left in front of almost 60,000 fans in the local derby against Aston Villa nine months after arriving at the club, and he scored his first Baggies goal four weeks later in a 4–0 home victory over Chelsea.

As keen as mustard, Wally made 17 League appearances that season but, owing to the renewed form of Wood and also that of Welshman Walter Robbins, he failed to make the first team at all in 1932–33. However, in 1933–34 he was back on duty, scoring six times in 19 First Division starts. He followed up with another 22 goals in 48 outings in 1934–35, helping Albion reach Wembley for the second time in four years, as well as playing for England against Holland (his first senior cap). But in 1935–36, two niggling knee injuries caused Wally to miss several matches and as a result he made just 21 appearances, notching three goals, although he did play for his country against Scotland in a Jubilee international and also represented the Football League.

Switched to left-half (after Jimmy Murphy had been injured) Wally was excellent during the first half of the 1936–37 campaign when he played behind the previously established pairing of Sandford and Wood. But when Sandford was moved to centre-half, Boyes again pushed forward and before the season closed he had occupied three different front-line positions and had starred against Arsenal in a sixth-round FA Cup tie, when a record crowd of 64,815 packed into The Hawthorns to see Albion knock out the holders 3–1.

In February 1938, with Albion struggling at the wrong end of the First Division table, Wally was transferred to Everton for a fee of £6,000. During his seven years at The Hawthorns he scored 38 goals in 165 first-class appearances and 24 in almost 100 second XI games, gaining a Central League championship-winners' medal in 1933. Now he was looking ahead to a new career on Merseyside.

An article in the *Liverpool Echo*, published a day or so after Wally had signed for Everton, stated that: '…he [Boyes] is just the player Everton need to win the League title.' Wally's reply was simple: 'I'm looking forward to a new challenge. I missed out on a lot of things with Albion but now I think this club [Everton] is going to win something.'

And win something they did. After finishing 14th in the League in 1937–38, Everton took the First Division title the following season and Wally scored four goals in 38 appearances. He was also capped twice more by England, against Wales and the Rest of Europe, and at that time was regarded as the best outside-left in the country.

During the war Wally played as a guest for several clubs up and down the country and when League football resumed in 1946, he was still on Everton's left wing. But that was soon to change following the arrival of Tommy Eglington. Come May 1949, having scored 15 goals in 73 competitive games for the Merseysiders, Wally left Goodison Park to become player-coach of Notts County, teaming up with England international Tommy Lawton and helping the Magpies win the Third Division (South) title in his first season at Meadow Lane. From 1950 to 1953 he was player-trainer at Scunthorpe United, playing in the Irons' first-ever League game v Shrewsbury Town. Later employed as player-manager of Retford Town and Hyde United, he took over as Swansea Town's trainer in May 1959 and retained that position for a year, retiring through ill-health in June 1960. Wally died shortly afterwards, aged 47.

NB: As a teenager Wally once scored 17 goals for Sheffield Boys in a 31–2 victory over Rotherham Juniors…and from 1952 to 1958 he was a sports master at the Oakwood Collegiate School, Sheffield.

ALLY BROWN

'A very capable striker with a noteworthy capacity for work.'

Born:	12 April 1951, Musselburgh, Scotland

Albion senior record:

Appearances:	League 254+25, FA Cup 26+2, League Cup 27, Europe 10, Others 14+4
Goals:	League 72, FA Cup 6, League Cup 2, Europe 1, Others 4
Senior debut:	League, 11 March 1972 v Crystal Palace (h) drew 1–1 (scored)
Also played for:	Edinburgh & District Schools, Leicester City, Portland Timbers, Crystal Palace, Walsall, Port Vale, Scotland (2 Youth caps and Under-23 trialist)

Virtually a year after netting the all-important promotion-clinching goal for Leicester City against Bristol City at the end of the 1970–71 season, Ally Brown moved to The Hawthorns in March 1972, signed for the unusual fee of £61,111 by manager Don Howe.

He scored on his Baggies debut against Crystal Palace and went on to serve the club for 11 years, averaging a goal every four games and helping Albion regain their First Division status in 1976.

Tall and quick, with good close control, Ally made a dream start to his playing career with the Foxes, scoring in his first League game, representing Scotland at Youth level and having a trial for the Under-23 side.

During his time at Filbert Street he struck 35 goals in 121 appearances and continued to be a threat to defenders as he bedded himself in at The Hawthorns, claiming seven goals in 48 outings up to the end of the 1972–73 relegation season before surprisingly finding himself out of favour and playing a lot of the time in the reserves under Brian Whitehouse.

Ally recalled: 'I was out of it at first team level for two-thirds of the 1973–74 season and for virtually all of 1974–75, returning for four games late on after manager Don Howe had been sacked. The funny thing was, I had been playing well, but Howe preferred Tony Brown, David Shaw and Joe Mayo as his main strike-force.

'I had gone into the gaffer's office twice to ask about my future and each time he insisted that I was in his plans for the future. I wasn't all that happy but I stuck in there and even had a call from

Frank O'Farrell, who was scouting for Celtic. He asked me if I would like to move back to Scotland. I said that I couldn't commit myself at the time, having spent such a short time in the Midlands. I gather that Celtic's manager Jock Stein wasn't impressed with my response. He probably thought I should have thrown everything in there and then and moved to Parkhead. I couldn't do that and I heard nothing more.

'When Johnny Giles took over as Albion's player-manager, straightaway I knew I was going to fit into his plans, although after playing in the first game at Southampton, which we lost 3–0, I was dropped, and it wasn't until late September that I gained a regular place in the forward line. Playing alongside England World Cup hero Geoff Hurst I scored in a 1–1 draw at Carlisle and never really looked back.'

Ally ended up top scorer that season with 13 goals as Albion regained their First Division status with a last-match victory at Oldham. And it was Ally who set up the vital goal for Tony Brown. He remembered: 'Mick Martin crossed the ball from the right. I headed it down to 'Bomber' who volleyed home in front of our massed ranks of supporters. Afterwards we had some great celebrations; champagne in the dressing room, and more at the Four In Hand pub, which was packed with Albion fans. I had a few drinks that night! Giles was the main reason why we went up. He ran the midfield. Yet if Howe had signed him I still believe we would have gone up that season, as we had some very good players.'

Ally benefited from playing a completely different style of football under Giles, admitting 'It took a while for some of us to get used to his tactics. He played the ball sidewards and backwards, emphasising that keeping the ball was crucial. Howe played the long-ball game, which was effective to a certain degree. It was frustrating for us forwards at first, but we got used to it and everything worked out fine in the end.'

Back in the top flight, Ally scored in an opening day 2–2 draw against Giles's old club Leeds United and kept his place in the team until December when Giles changed things up front by partnering David Cross with Ray Treacy. He was called up occasionally after that and finished the campaign with a goal-haul of six. Then Giles left, to be replaced by Ronnie Allen, who in turn gave way to Ron Atkinson.

'Ron was attack-minded,' said Ally. 'He got us going forward and that suited me fine. I was back in the team, scoring goals and playing very well. We reached the FA Cup semi-final but sadly lost to Ipswich Town at Highbury. That was bitterly disappointing, but we were now a stronger, more efficient and far better-equipped team than we were when I first joined the club.'

In 1978–79, with Laurie Cunningham, Cyrille Regis, Tony Brown, Willie Johnston and Ally as the main front-runners, Albion were regarded as one of the best teams in the country, finishing third in the First Division and reaching the quarter-finals of the UEFA Cup.

Jointly with his namesake Tony, Ally was voted 'Midland Footballer of the Year' that season when he topped the scoring charts with 24 goals – the best tally of his career. In 1979–80 he was handed a more withdrawn role and managed six goals, adding 11 more to his total in 1980–81 and, having been loaned out to the NASL club Portland Timbers for four months, he returned to claim only four in 1981–82 when Allen returned for a second spell as manager.

At this juncture Albion's forward line was changing all the time and, after another managerial change, Ron Wylie taking over from Allen, Ally hardly got a look in 1982–83 and was subsequently transferred to Crystal Palace.

Later with Walsall and Port Vale, whom he helped gain promotion from the Third Division along with two other former Albion players, Wayne Ebanks and Alan Webb, Ally announced his retirement in May 1986 due to a troublesome knee injury.

Switching to the licensed trade, Ally ran a pub in Great Barr, Birmingham, before taking over as steward of the Throstle Club in Halfords Lane, almost directly opposite The Hawthorns, a position he held until 2003.

TONY BROWN

*'One of the best goalscoring midfielders in the game during the late 60s and 70s...
he had a combination of speed, skill and opportunism – pure magic.'*

Born: 3 October 1945, Oldham

Albion senior record:

Appearances: League 561+13, FA Cup 53+1, League Cup 46+1, Europe 16+1, FA Charity Shield 1, Others 27

Goals: League 218, FA Cup 27, League Cup 17, Europe 8, FA Charity Shield 0, Others 9

Senior debut: League, 28 September 1963 v Ipswich Town (a) won 2–1 (scored)

Also played for: South Manchester Boys, Manchester Boys, Lancashire County, Jacksonville (New England) Tea Men (loan, 1981 & 1982), Torquay United, Stafford Rangers, West Bromwich Albion Old Stars, England (one full, 2 Youth caps), Young England XI (1 app), Football League (2 apps)

Tony joined Albion as a £6-a-week apprentice-professional in April 1961 and signed as a full-time professional in September 1963 – just 24 hours before making a scoring debut against Ipswich Town at Portman Road.

An exceptional footballer in every sense of the word, during a wonderful career he played on both wings, as an inside-forward, an attacking wing-half and also as leader of the attack. He gave the Baggies 20 years of wonderful service, breaking records galore along the way.

During his time at The Hawthorns, the 'Bomber' scored more goals (313) and appeared in more first-team matches (826) than any other Albion player. At major competitions alone he netted 279 times in 720 games and followed two other great Albion marksmen – W.G. Richardson and Ronnie Allen – by netting over 200 goals in the Football League. Tony was also successful with 51 out of 61 penalty kicks for Albion and he is one of only three players to have made 500 or more senior appearances for the club.

Tony helped Albion win the League Cup in 1966, finish runners-up the following year, lift the FA Cup in 1968 and clinch promotion to the First Division in 1976. After gaining Youth honours as a teenager, he played once for England at senior level against Wales at Wembley in May 1971 (0–0), twice represented the Football League and was voted 'Midland Footballer of the Year' three times, in 1969, 1971 and 1979, the latter jointly with teammate Ally Brown.

Tony suffered with asthma from an early age but thankfully this disappeared as he grew older. A Manchester United supporter, he was a regular on the terraces at Old Trafford and played football whenever he could. In fact, he was asked to sign for United's arch-rivals Manchester City as a 15-year-old, but turned down the offer and joined Albion instead, following a pre-arranged trip to the Midlands by Albion's Manchester-based scout John Shaw.

Recalled Tony: 'I scored a hat-trick in a trial match on a works ground and things simply took off from there. Within a few weeks I was engaged as an apprentice and was told that there were a few rules

I must know…always pass the ball to a player in a blue and white striped shirt, keep it on the ground and always beat the Villa. And I think I conformed to those pretty well.'

Tony's first competitive match for Albion was for the B team against Birmingham City, a fortnight after signing. He settled down quickly and the following season played regularly for the Warwickshire Combination, Midland Intermediate and club Youth sides, scoring plenty of goals, his first coming in a 4–1 win over Wolves in an Intermediate League fixture, which was soon followed by his first hat-trick in a 7–3 win at Port Vale in the same competition.

The goals continued to flow and, after securing his place in the reserves, Tony finally made his League debut as a 17-year-old in place of Eddie Readfern at Ipswich. 'I was shaking all over when our trainer Wilf Dixon told me I was in the team on the Friday afternoon. I hardly slept a wink that night, just thinking about the game,' said Tony. A crowd of almost 14,000 saw Tony score past 'keeper Roy Bailey that afternoon – and 35 years later the Bomber netted twice past Roy's father, Gary, when Albion beat Manchester United 5–3 at Old Trafford.

Tony bagged five goals in 1963–64 and to be truthful he never stopped scoring. Nine followed in the next season and a further 27 were added in 1965–66, including one in every round of the League Cup, which Albion won at the first attempt. He weighed in with 19 goals in 1966–67, including his first treble in Europe (v DOS Utrecht in the Fairs Cup) but was 'as sick as a parrot' when QPR beat Albion in the first League Cup Final at Wembley. 'I shed a few tears that day,' he admitted.

In 1967–68, the Bomber struck another 15, one of them coming in the 2–0 FA Cup semi-final victory over Birmingham which took Albion to Wembley for the second year running.

Over the next six years, playing alongside Jeff Astle, Tony scored 125 times, and had the ill-luck to lose another League Cup Final. After the King departed, he continued to find the net, top scoring in three of the next four campaigns. He helped the Baggies win promotion under manager Johnny Giles in 1976, his stunning right-foot volley on the last day of the season at his native Oldham earning a 1–0 victory which clinched third spot in Division Two.

Tony recalled some years later: 'That match at Boundary Park was so important to Albion. I rate it as one of the best I ever played in, even surpassing the 1968 FA Cup Final, just for the tension and what it meant to the supporters. If it had been just an ordinary League game, nobody would have remembered it!'

Ron Atkinson – who admitted that Tony was a 'manager's dream' – took over as Albion's boss in January 1978 and four months later the Baggies were playing in another FA Cup semi-final, this time against Ipswich Town. The match ended in a 3–1 defeat – a huge disappointment for Tony. But he recovered his composure and continued to score goals, grabbing 25 that season and 14 in 1978–79. However, 1979–80 was to be his last season. Struggling with his fitness, he appeared in only 24 matches, his lowest tally since 1964–65, and netted just four goals, his 279th and last at senior level coming in a 2–1 FA Cup defeat at West Ham.

Leaving The Hawthorns in August 1981, Tony joined Bruce Rioch's Torquay United before assisting Stafford Rangers ahead of his retirement in May 1983. In February 1984, he returned to The Hawthorns as a coach, initially under manager Johnny Giles. Leaving in May 1986, he was out of football for over a year before returning as coach of Birmingham City in June 1987. He stayed at St Andrew's for two seasons with Garry Pendrey as manager…and whenever possible during the 1980s turned out in charity matches for Albion's All Star XI.

In his book *Bomber Brown,* published in 1998, Tony stated that he had no regrets about any of his time at the Albion. 'None whatsoever, even during the dark days of the mid-1970s. The 20 years I was at the club were brilliant; even the bad spells under Don Howe. I was doing something I enjoyed and the fans were absolutely superb. They gave me such a lift.'

Never sent off and only booked three or four times, Tony was one of those good guys of football and he certainly gave West Bromwich Albion and the supporters plenty to cheer about. Now a columnist for the *Albion News,* Tony also acts as a match-summariser for a local radio station, covering matches at The Hawthorns. He lives in Walsall with his wife Irene.

FRED BUCK

'As a forward he was superb; as a defender he was brilliant…always a big favourite with the supporters.'

Born:	12 July 1880, Newcastle-under-Lyme, Staffs
Died:	10 June 1952, Stafford

Albion senior record:

Appearances:	League 287, FA Cup 32
Goals:	League 90, FA Cup 4
Senior debut:	League, 8 December 1900 v Bolton Wanderers (h) won 7–2 (1 goal)
Also played for:	Stafford Wesleyans, Stafford Rangers, Liverpool, Plymouth Argyle, Swansea Town, Football League (2 apps), Southern League (1 app), Army XI

Albion's secretary-manager Fred Everiss thought that Fred Buck was a truly great player, one of the best of his era. In his story, published by the *Sunday Mercury* in 1949, Everiss wrote: 'Fred Buck was one of the best uncapped footballers I have ever seen. At the end of September (1902) Newcastle United came to The Hawthorns. They were top of the League and had not had a goal scored against them. In their ranks was the brilliant Scottish international Bob McColl, while in the Albion forward line was the then "unknown" Fred Buck, taking the place of Tommy Worton.

'That game made Fred Buck. He was the star and Albion won 6–1. That was the day which gave birth to the "Have you seen Buck?" slogan of our supporters. He was one of the best uncapped footballers I have ever seen and that's saying a lot.' Fred scored twice and had a hand in two other goals in that wonderful win over Newcastle.

An article in a Yorkshire newspaper in 1908 described him thus: 'Of short and solid build, he is determined, fast and brave and has great endurance.' And a pen-picture of him, printed in the Oldham Athletic programme the following season, stated that he was 'An entrancing inside-forward for the purist. He plays an orthodox game with quite an exceptional facility, killing the ball and making a perfectly executed pass exquisitely placed just as a text book would lay down. He is superb at dribbling, possesses a hard shot and has tremendous stamina. Despite his height, he competes aggressively against more solid and bigger opponents and plays with great spirit and resourcefulness.'

Born in Staffordshire, Fred played as a centre-forward for the local Wesleyans team before joining Stafford Rangers in July 1987. After switching to the inside-right position, he was spotted by Albion, who engaged him as a full-time professional in November 1900, paying him £4 a year. He made his League debut the following month, scoring in a 7–2 home win over Bolton Wanderers, and in his second season at The Hawthorns he played in two League games as the Baggies won the Second Division championship. Also in 1901–02 he helped the second team clinch the Birmingham & District League and Staffordshire Senior Cup double before gaining a second Staffordshire Senior Cup-winners' medal the following season when he scored both goals in a 2–0 win over Stoke.

A month after that last triumph Fred surprisingly left The Hawthorns to sign for Liverpool for £1,500 (May 1903). He never settled on Merseyside, netting just once in 13 games, and in January 1904 moved almost 300 miles south to sign for Southern League side Plymouth Argyle for £3,500. He did very well with the Pilgrims, scoring 41 goals in 100 appearances and representing the Southern League before returning to The Hawthorns in April 1906 for a fee of £2,500.

Forty hours after moving back to the Midlands, Fred played inside-right in a 4–1 home Second Division win over Burslem Port Vale and the following season he scored 22 goals in 37 games as Albion reached the FA Cup semi-final, only to lose a close encounter with Everton.

In 1907–08, Fred was an ever-present and also the team's top scorer with 18 goals. A year later he netted 14 times, following up with another 16 goals in 1909–10 when he, Charlie Hewitt and Sid Bowser played splendidly together in a decent Albion attack.

Season 1910–11 saw Albion return to the top flight as Second Division champions. Fred, who had taken over as team captain, had an excellent campaign and his 34 appearances brought him 10 goals, including a vital penalty-winner on the very last day of the season against Huddersfield Town in front of a 30,000 plus crowd at The Hawthorns, which clinched the title for the Baggies ahead of Bolton Wanderers.

After starting 1911–12 in the forward line, alongside Stan Allan and Bowser, Fred was switched into the half-back line in mid-December when the veteran George Baddeley was injured. The following month, despite being only 5ft 5in tall, he took over at centre-half from Frank Waterhouse, who was sidelined with a twisted ankle. He retained that pivotal position for most of the remainder of his Albion career, putting in some sterling displays at the heart of the defence. He helped the Baggies reach that season's FA Cup Final, but sadly ended up a disappointed loser when Barnsley pinched the trophy in the very last minute of the replay at Sheffield. To this day Fred is one of the smallest ever centre-halves to play in a major Cup Final.

During the course of the 1911–12 season Fred twice represented the Football League, against the Southern League and the Irish League. He deserved a lot more – a full cap would not have gone amiss. On leaving The Hawthorns for a second time in May 1914, Fred signed for Swansea Town for £1,000 and during World War One he served in the Army in France before announcing his retirement from football in May 1917, two months before his 37th birthday. He had been struggling for a couple of years with a hip injury and decided to call it a day when he returned from active service in France.

Shortly afterwards he returned home to his native Staffordshire to take over the George pub in the county town of Stafford. Remaining in the licensed trade for 24 years, Fred died, three weeks short of his 72nd birthday, in June 1952.

Quite a few of his relatives live in Devon (near Newton Abbot) and Stafford respectively and they have kindly loaned or donated a lot of memorabilia relating to Fred's football career for display in The Hawthorns Museum. The 'old' ball used in that Huddersfield Town game back in 1911, which Fred hammered into the net from the penalty-spot, is also on show in the museum.

VIC BUCKINGHAM

'Under his leadership, Albion played with a lot of style and commitment – and scored goals.'
'He instilled in the players a method and purpose, placing the accent on pure football.'

Born:	23 October 1915, Greenwich, London
Died:	27 January 1995, Worthing, Sussex

Played for: Bromley, Northfleet, Tottenham Hotspur; World War Two guest for Crewe Alexandra, Fulham, Millwall and Portsmouth, England (2 wartime caps), FA XI
Also managed (coached): Bradford Park Avenue, Ajax, Sheffield Wednesday, Fulham, Ethnikos (Greece), Barcelona, FC Sevilla

After captaining his school team and representing London Schools against Glasgow Schools, Vic Buckingham joined Tottenham Hotspur as an amateur in 1931. After a loan spell with Northfleet (to gain experience) he turned professional at White Hart Lane in May 1935 and went on to make over 300 appearances in 14 years for the London club as an efficient full-back or wing-half. He also assisted four League clubs as a World War Two guest, played for his unit and the FA and won two wartime caps for England in 1941, both against Wales, at Cardiff and Nottingham. In fact, his partner in these internationals was Stan Cullis, whose team, Wolverhampton Wanderers, would deny Vic the double 13 years later.

Retiring as a player in May 1949, encouraged by the England manager Walter Winterbottom, Vic coached in Norway, France, at Oxford University, with Spurs (briefly) and Pegasus, leading the latter to Amateur Cup Final glory over Bishop Auckland in front of 100,000 spectators at Wembley in April 1951. He also acted as chief scout for the Middlesex FA before being appointed manager of Bradford Park Avenue in June 1951.

Intelligent, debonair and articulate, always displaying a silk handkerchief in his jacket pocket, Vic guided the Yorkshire club to eighth in the Third Division North in his first season and he spotted a future England international who became an Albion hero – Derek Kevan. Several clubs monitored Vic's progress, including Albion, and in February 1953 Vic was asked to become manager, taking over from Jesse Carver. Albion's chairman Major H. Wilson Keys said: 'We've got just the man we wanted.' Vic himself admitted: 'I was fortunate to get the job. Any one of 20 managers could have got it; I was delighted it was me.'

Vic inherited a very useful team and that season the Baggies finished fourth in Division One, just four points behind the champions Arsenal. Brought up playing 'push and run' football, he successfully introduced this style to The Hawthorns, with some variations. And he had the skilful players to work with – Jimmy Dudley, Ray Barlow, Paddy Ryan and Ronnie Allen, to name just four.

With his former playing colleague Freddie Cox as his assistant, Vic got Albion buzzing in 1953–54, and what a tremendous season it turned out to be. In fact, if injuries hadn't robbed him of two key outfield players, right-back Stan Rickaby and late on winger Frank Griffin, as well as goalkeeper Norman Heath, who was seriously hurt at Sunderland, then Albion would have completed the double.

So concerned was he about Heath's injuries, that Vic said to his secretary: 'Get me a plane – I'm going to fly up to Sunderland to see how he is.' This caused some consternation, but he got his own way and it cost the club £40 for the return trip.

In 1954, Albion won the FA Cup and finished runners-up in the League to Wolves, but Vic claimed: 'We were by far the better team overall and I was disappointed not to have won the championship.'

During his reign at The Hawthorns, Albion fielded at least six teams every weekend and quite often Vic would attend one of the morning matches. 'I would be out looking for a player of the future,' he said, adding 'All good players have to start somewhere. They don't just appear out of thin air and you will, at some stage, spot a talented youngster. I found a few over the years.'

With the aid of his scouting system Vic signed, among others, Davey Burnside, Bobby Cram, Chuck Drury and Alec Jackson and these four between them made a combined total of 766 first-class appearances for Albion alone.

Always eager to watch an Albion side in action, in November 1954 Vic went on the coach to Hereford for a testimonial match. Albion lost 10–5 and so disgusted was Vic that he didn't want to face the players, choosing to return to West Bromwich in Freddie Cox's car. Sadly, on a slippery bend, Cox's car skidded and hit a tree. Both men were badly hurt and taken to hospital and it was a while before they were allowed to resume their normal daily duties.

In August 1955, Vic gave League debuts to Don Howe and Derek Kevan against Everton. Both players became Albion stars and England World Cup players. During his time in charge he also signed future Cup-winning captain Graham Williams, Maurice Setters, winger Derek Hogg, goalkeeper Ray Potter and a certain Bobby Robson who, as we all know, became a soccer legend in his own lifetime.

Under Vic's guidance, Albion finished in the top four of the First Division on four occasions and almost made it to a second FA Cup Final, losing in a replay to Aston Villa in the 1957 semis. The club also toured Russia, becoming the first British professional team to win behind the Iron Curtain, and underwent a tour to Canada and North America in 1959. Unfortunately something happened in Canada and Setters was one of the players involved in an incident with his manager. As a result, Setters was sent home early and when Vic returned with the rest of the party, he shocked the club, players and supporters by announcing his resignation.

He took over as coach of Ajax Amsterdam in May 1959 and while there spotted Johan Cruyff, won the Dutch League title in 1960 and the Cup in 1961.

Two years later he was appointed manager of Sheffield Wednesday and while at Hillsborough saw three of his players, Tony Kay, Bronco Layne and Peter Swan all arrested in a bribery scandal. After a surprise sacking from Hillsborough, in January 1965 he bedded in as manager of Fulham, but three years later, unable to tolerate the flamboyant Rodney Marsh, he left to be replaced by one of his greatest buys for Albion, Bobby Robson.

After a popular spell as manager of Ethnikos in the Greek League, in December 1969 Vic was named boss of Barcelona, who went on to finish 10th in La Liga that season, only eight points behind the champions Atletico Madrid, and in 1971 won the Spanish Cup after beating Valencia in a classic Final. However, Vic was dismissed in March 1972 and replaced by Marianus Michels of Ajax. Later manager of FC Sevilla (Spain), Vic quit football in 1975 and went to live in Worthing, where he died in January 1995, aged 79.

Albion's manager for six years, he brought flair, goals, brilliant football and a general air of optimism to the club. He was a wonderful football man.

DARYL BURGESS

'A distinctively strong defender and loyal club man.'

Born: 24 January 1971, Marston Green, Birmingham

Albion senior record:

Appearances: League 317+15, FA Cup 9, League Cup 19+3, Others 14
Goals: League 10, FA Cup 0, League Cup 3, Others 0
Senior debut: League, 26 August 1989 v Port Vale (a) lost 2–1
Also played for: Chelmsley Wood Boys, Knowle North Star, Solihull & District Boys, Northampton Town, Rochdale, Kidderminster Harriers, West Bromwich Albion Old Stars

Daryl joined the apprentice ranks at The Hawthorns as a 16-year-old in April 1987, turned professional in July 1989 and over the next 12 years went on to appear in 377 competitive games, scoring 13 goals and helping Albion gain promotion in 1993, although he didn't appear in the Play-off Final against Port Vale, Garry Strodder and Paul Raven occupying the two central defensive positions while Nicky Reid played at right-back.

Daryl was badly injured after colliding with the Swansea City goalkeeper Roger Freestone in the first leg of the Play-off semi-final clash at Vetch Field. In the incident City's tall striker, Andy McFarlane, back defending, conceded an own-goal which got Albion back into the match at 2–1.

Recalling what happened, Daryl said: 'I went up for a high ball, fairly I might add, and the next thing I knew, I was lying face down in the penalty area, not knowing whether we had scored or not. I had to ask our physio, Danny Thomas, if it had gone in – the ball that is! "Yes", he replied, "but more importantly, how are you?" "It's the top of my leg," I said. It's killing me."'

It transpired that Daryl had a serious injury and as a result missed the return clash at The Hawthorns and also the Wembley showdown with Port Vale, the club he had made his League debut against four years earlier.

As a 15-year-old Daryl – an ardent Birmingham City supporter, like the rest of his family – reached the English Schools Trophy semi-final with the Solihull District side, but lost to Hull at Villa

Park. That game was watched by Blues scout Norman Bodell, and at around the same time Daryl was attending training sessions at Villa Park, St Andrew's and The Hawthorns on different nights of the week – hoping that one of the clubs just might sign him. Norman was then sacked and immediately joined Albion, where Roy Horobin was scout. Daryl recalled 'Norm insisted Albion should sign me, which they did, to my delight. I will never forget him for that – and when I was on holiday in Majorca a year or so later he was in the same hotel as me, incredible. At first I had to carry out all the general groundstaff duties under the supervision of Dave Matthews, a harsh but fair taskmaster. Ron Saunders was manager at the time, a direct sort of bloke, but he wasn't the best despite what he had achieved earlier. He was quickly replaced by Ron Atkinson.

'World Cup-winner Nobby Stiles was coaching the youth team. I played at right-back, my best position, and after losing to Manchester City in a Youth Cup tie, Big Ron gave me, a mere 16-year-old, and a few others, a real rollicking. Welcome to the world of football.'

After Big Ron had been replaced by Brian Talbot – Albion's third gaffer in three years – Daryl continued to make steady progress and, having been named as an unused substitute for a League Cup tie against Walsall in August 1987, he made his League debut in a 2–1 Second Division defeat at Port Vale two years later.

As time progressed, Daryl witnessed more managerial changes. As Albion struggled on the pitch, Stuart Pearson took over the mantle from Talbot; then Bobby Gould arrived, only for the team to suffer relegation to the Third Division for the first time in the club's history.

Daryl, who hurt his back late on in the 1990–91 season – an injury that would plague him for the rest of his career, along with a tedious ankle problem – battled on, sometimes fighting through the pain barrier, even wearing a weightlifter's belt just to get into the action.

Then, in the summer of 1992, Ossie Ardiles took over as Albion's manager. He brought with him Keith Burkinshaw and between them they got Albion buzzing. 'Ossie was a great guy,' said Daryl. 'He got us playing football, good football, and it was down to him – and Bob Taylor's goals of course – that we won promotion.'

Over the next eight years – when managers came and went like the flu – right up until his departure at the end of the 2000–01 season, following a deserved testimonial, Daryl played at right-back, as a sweeper and also in the centre of the defence. It did not bother him one iota, just as long as he was in the team. Strong in the tackle, he always maintained a high level of performance and it must be said that he never let Albion down, always giving 100 per cent and more out on the pitch.

Sent off four times during his Albion career, Daryl was never a dirty player. He mistimed his tackle occasionally, as do all defenders, but he was generally a wholehearted defender, totally committed to his duties out on the field of play.

He had his best season, in terms of appearances, in 1995–96 when, for the second time, he was voted the club's Player of the Year. He starred in 56 matches that term and, in fact, over a period of two years, from February 1995 to February 1997, he missed only 14 games out of a possible 104, most of them through injury.

Transferred to Northampton Town in the summer of 2001, he spent two years with the Cobblers before moving to Rochdale in August 2003 and then, in July 2005, he returned to the Midlands to sign for Kidderminster Harriers, where he stayed for two seasons.

In a wonderful 21-year playing career (1986–2007), 'Brummie' supporter Daryl amassed a grand total of 507 senior appearances for his three Football League clubs and he also played in 120 reserve and intermediate games for the Baggies plus another 50 for Kidderminster.

In 2007–08 Daryl started Total Football UK with another ex-Albion star, Richard Sneekes, and the former Walsall player Chris Marsh. The company offers coaching courses to youngsters.

Daryl saw it all with Albion – promotion, relegation, good seasons, bad seasons, disastrous seasons. He played under 10 different managers and almost as many caretaker managers, but still kept on running, competing and defending for the club…That's why he's a legend.

LEN CANTELLO

'A totally committed all round midfield player.'

Born:	11 September 1951, Newton Heath, Manchester

Albion senior record:

Appearances:	League 297+4, FA Cup 22, League Cup 21, Europe 7, Others 18
Goals:	League 13, FA Cup 3, League Cup 3, Europe 0, Others 2
Senior debut:	League, 7 December 1968, substitute v Ipswich Town (a) lost 4–1
Also played for:	Dallas Tornados (NASL), Bolton Wanderers, Eastern Athletic (Hong Kong), Burnley (trial), Altrincham, Stafford Rangers (2 spells), Hereford United, Bury, SC Cambuur (Holland), Peterborough United, Northwich Victoria, England (8 Under-23, 4 Youth and 2 Schoolboy caps)
Managed:	Radcliffe Borough

Lancastrian Len Cantello appeared in over 350 competitive games for Albion and certainly qualifies for inclusion in this book. He gave the Baggies 12 years of excellent service, mainly performing in midfield, although at times he did play at full-back and even on the wing, and while serving his apprenticeship he occasionally appeared as a striker. 'I didn't fancy that,' said Len, 'I wanted to be on the ball all the time and I felt that being in the hub area, the midfield, I was always involved in the action.'

A pupil at Albert Memorial School in Manchester, Len represented Manchester & District, Newton Heath and England Schools before joining Albion in July 1967. He turned professional in October 1968, quickly gaining international honours at Youth team level. At the end of that season he played in the FA Youth Cup Final against Sunderland and Len recalled: 'Jimmy Dunn was in charge of our youth team, he was an experienced guy who played in an FA Cup Final for Wolves. He knew his football and got us all "on top of our game." We had a good crowd for the first leg at The Hawthorns, around 17,000. We won the game quite comfortably but then it all went wrong at Roker Park. Pre-warned about complacency…we were awful. Jim Holton and Asa Hartford were both sent off and we were well and truly hammered, 6–0. It was a miserable journey home that night for us all.

'We had some decent players in our team who would, in later years, do well with Albion. Among them, of course, were Hartford, who became my best mate, and Ally Robertson, goalkeeper Gordon Nisbet, who was transformed into an England Under-23 right-back, and Lyndon Hughes, and I can't forget Big Jim (Holton). He was a great guy who went on to play for Manchester United and Scotland and sadly died at an early age.'

Six months before that Youth Cup Final Len had tasted League football for the first time, coming on as a second-half substitute in Albion's 4–1 defeat at Ipswich. He made two further senior appearances that season, at Sunderland and Burnley, before getting more opportunities in 1969–70. Said Len 'When the season started, Danny Hegan and Bobby Hope were Albion's two main midfielder players. I was basically a squad member, having to fight for my place with the rest of the reserves. Having been given half-a-dozen chances by manager Alan Ashman during the first half of the season, by the end of January I was in the first team and heading for Wembley! That's right…I couldn't believe it. Albion had reached the League Cup Final and they would play Manchester City in March. I had only appeared in one earlier round, scoring against Bradford City, but when the boss told me I was in the team for Wembley I almost broke down in tears. We were favourites to win the Cup, having defeated City 3–0 in a League game five weeks earlier, but on a terrible, muddy pitch, we didn't really perform and lost 2–1 after extra-time. Disappointing, yes, but it was an experience I will never forget.'

Over the next three seasons, the second two under a new manager, Don Howe, Len made well over 100 appearances in the first team, donning nine different numbered shirts, and playing in eight England Under-23 internationals. Unfortunately, at the end of the 1972–73 campaign, Albion got relegated and that was a bitter disappointment to a lot of players, including Len, who said: 'We weren't the worst team in the Division. We made a rubbish start and were playing catch up after that. We only had ourselves to blame. Our away record was rubbish; we only won one match on the road. That was diabolical.'

After a couple of moderate seasons in Division Two, Albion made another managerial change, Johnny Giles taking over from Howe. 'He had class,' said Len. 'He could make the ball talk and we soon started to play easy, simple football. He switched the team around and in the end we won promotion, albeit on the very last day at Oldham. That was some afternoon. The ground was packed with Albion fans…we had to win for them…and we did, thanks to Bomber's brilliant volley.'

Len was playing well at this juncture, although he suffered a few injuries over the next two seasons and once again tasted disappointment when Albion lost to Ipswich Town in the 1978 FA Cup semi-final.

'Ron Atkinson was the boss then and he put me on the bench. I came on for John Wile who, as you know, suffered that horrific head injury in a clash with Brian Talbot as he scored the game's opening goal. We might have got something late on after Bomber's penalty, but once Mick Martin had been sent off that was it.'

Len remained at The Hawthorns for one more season, which was a good one, Albion finishing third in Division One, their highest placing for 25 years. They also reached the quarter-finals of the UEFA Cup.

Len, though, had already told everyone (or nearly everyone) that he would leave the club after his testimonial match in May. He kept his word, and for his 'farewell match' a good-sized crowd of over 7,000 turned up to see Cyrille Regis's all-Black XI take on Len's select XI. Unfortunately it wasn't the sort of friendly you expected to see! There were several unsavoury incidents and before the final whistle Len was substituted by Barry Cowdrill…to escape a booking, or even a dismissal! Some of his teammates were quite annoyed by his decision to leave at the time he did.

Len joined Bolton Wanderers for £350,000. Why? He never really said…it was personal. He spent three years at Burnden Park before moving around the country, finally ending up as a scout with Blackpool and taking evening coaching classes at Manchester City's School of Excellence.

JOE CARTER

'Hard and wiry with a fine body-swerve and a good shot.'

Born:	27 July 1899, Aston, Birmingham
Died:	7 January 1977, Handsworth, Birmingham

Albion senior record:

Appearances:	League 414, FA Cup 37
Goals:	League 145, FA Cup 10
Senior debut:	League, 9 December 1922 v Bolton Wanderers (a) lost 3–0
Also played for:	Westbourne Celtic, Sheffield Wednesday (six days), Tranmere Rovers, Walsall, Vono Sports (player-manager), England (3 full caps), Football League (1 app), FA XI (1 app), England international trialist

Joe Carter was an artist in his profession, an inside-forward whose play was both artistic and intellectual. Born deep in rival territory, he was playing for a local Handsworth club, Westbourne Celtic, when West Bromwich Albion recognised that he was a 'man of merit'. Aston Villa were also keen to sign Joe, but Albion's secretary-manager Fred Everiss and club director and former player Dan Nurse got in first and engaged him as a professional at The Hawthorns in April 1921.

Joe never looked back and went on to give the Baggies 15 years of dedicated service, amassing a total of 451 first-class appearances and scoring 155 goals. To this day only nine other players have made more appearances for Albion than Joe, and only five have scored more goals. Besides his first-team record, Joe also scored 34 goals in 57 Central League games for Albion, collecting two championship-winning medals in 1923 and 1924.

He made his League debut some 18 months after joining the club, taking over from the injured Ivor Jones in a 3–0 defeat at Bolton in November 1922. Joe made seven more appearances towards the end of that season, scoring three goals, his first goal in a 4–0 home victory over Sheffield United. In 1923–24 he played in 22 senior games and netted 10 goals, four in one game against Tottenham Hotspur at The Hawthorns.

For the next 12 years, from September 1924 until April 1936, discounting injuries, illness and international call-ups, Joe was a regular in Albion's forward line. Tommy Glidden accompanied him on the right wing for most of that time and they were regarded as one of the best partnerships in League football in the early 1930s. When Albion finished runners-up in the First Division behind Huddersfield Town in 1925, Joe and Tommy played together. Joe was rewarded with three full England caps, lining up twice against Belgium in Antwerp and Brussels (1926 and 1929) and versus Spain in Madrid, also in 1929, when he scored twice in a 4–3 defeat, England's first at the hands of foreign opposition.

Besides scoring plenty of goals, Joe also made quite a few for his fellow forwards, especially Stan Davies, Jimmy Cookson and W.G. Richardson. In 1926–27 he and Davies netted 15 League goals apiece and the following season he bagged the same number while Cookson weighed in with a club record 38, at least one-third of them being created by the classy Joe. When Albion claimed a club record 105 League goals in Division Two in 1929–30, Joe scored 19, his wing-partner Glidden notched 20 and the irrepressible Cookson bagged 33.

When, in 1930–31, Albion achieved the unique double by winning the FA Cup and gaining promotion in the same season, a feat never accomplished before or since, Joe was outstanding. He contributed a total of 11 goals, including vital point-savers at Bury, Swansea and Southampton, and had a hand in one of W.G.'s two goals in the Cup Final victory over Birmingham.

A write-up of Joe in the official programme for that Wembley encounter described him as being: 'The artist in attack, his ball control is exceptionally good and the subtlety of his play most difficult to combat. He excels in holding the ball and drawing opposing defenders before passing.' In an article in the *Evening Despatch* on the eve of the Final, the correspondent wrote: 'Joe Carter is upright, physically strong, hard and wiry with a fine body-swerve and a strong shot.' A pen-picture of him in a late 1920s Chelsea programme said that he was 'A real workhorse, a brainy, thoughtful inside-forward who can dribble, shoot with both feet and head the ball as good as anyone and his creative ability is second to none.'

Billy Bassett, Albion's chairman when Joe was at The Hawthorns, thought that he was worthy of more than the three England caps he gained. He said: 'He had enormous talent. He was, without doubt, an uncommonly fine forward who, in my mind, rarely had a poor game.'

Joe was a very consistent performer and it was only when he began to be affected by injuries that he lost his composure and, to a certain extent, his drive and enthusiasm. Joe and Albion were all set to win the FA Cup again in 1935, but unfortunately, in a home League defeat by Everton just eight weeks before the Final with Sheffield Wednesday, Joe suffered a bad injury to his right knee which later required an operation.

In fact, he didn't play again until the Final when, after a long discussion with the player, his boss Fred Everiss and the club's trainer Fred Reed, it was decided to gamble on him lasting the 90 minutes against the Owls. Joe sadly broke down early on and he struggled on bravely for 80 minutes, along with his skipper Glidden, who was also suffering with a troublesome knee injury. With Albion effectively carrying two players who were far from 100 per cent fit, Wednesday went on to lift the trophy, winning 4–2 with two late goals by Ellis Rimmer, who ironically in later years became a good friend of Joe's.

Surprisingly, in February 1936 Wednesday signed Joe for a fee of £1,500. He spent only six days at Hillsborough, however, returning to The Hawthorns after failing a medical on his dodgy right knee. Three months later, following surgery, Joe finally left Albion, joining Tranmere Rovers for £450. He remained at Prenton Park for six months before moving back to the Midlands to sign for Walsall. In the summer of 1938 he quit League football to take over the position of player-manger of Vono Sports, retiring from all aspects of the game in May 1942.

Thereafter, Joe was the long-serving and popular landlord of the Grove pub in Handsworth. He was 78 when he died of dehydration in January 1977.

CLIVE CLARK

'As fast as a whippet, a terrific goalscoring winger.'

Born:	19 December 1940, Leeds, Yorkshire

Albion senior record:

Appearances:	League 300+1, FA Cup 25+1, League Cup 19, Europe 7
Goals:	League 80, FA Cup 7, League Cup 10, Europe 1
Senior debut:	League, 14 January 1961 v Preston North End (h) won 3–1
Also played for:	Huddersfield Town (trialist), Leeds United, Queen's Park Rangers (two spells), Preston North End, Southport, Telford United, Washington Diplomats, Philadelphia Fury, Skegness Town and England (1 Under-23 cap)

Clive 'Chippy' Clark was one of the fastest wingers – on either the right or left flank – in the entire Football League during the 1960s. A real speed-merchant, he was direct, possessed good ball control, centred with accuracy, packed a decent shot (using mainly his right foot) and was also useful with his head, often sneaking in from the flank to send a brave, courageous diving header towards the target. If you check the record books you will see that he scored quite a few times with his head over the years, at least 10 times for Albion, including superb efforts in home League games against Sunderland in 1964 and Newcastle United in 1967.

After an unsuccessful trial with Huddersfield Town and a couple of ordinary seasons with Leeds United (the team he supported as a lad), Chippy surprisingly moved nearly 300 miles south to sign for Queen's Park Rangers in August 1958. Manager Jack Taylor, a former Wolves full-back, said at the time: 'We've got a good 'un here. This lad can score goals as well as make 'em.' And Chippy did just that – for the remainder of his career.

He made his League debut for Rangers against Bournemouth a month after joining and, over the next two-and-a-half years, netted seven times in 63 appearances for the London club before leaving Loftus Road for The Hawthorns, snapped up by his namesake, Albion boss Gordon Clark, in January 1961 for £20,000. 'This player is the best winger outside the First Division and I'm sure he will prove his worth to this club for many years to come' said Albion's chairman at the time, Major H. Wilson Keys.

The seventh player to be used on the left-wing by Albion that season, 20-year-old Clive made an impressive home debut just 48 hours after signing, setting up one of the goals in a 3–1 home win over Preston North End (his future club). He ended his first half-season with 15 appearances to his name and one goal, the winner against Leicester City at The Hawthorns in March.

Of average build and weight, Clive would take an awful battering from the burly full-backs he opposed over the next few years, but he always came up smiling, often having the last laugh by either scoring a goal or creating one (or two) for his colleagues.

He was a good friend of mine from the time he joined the club – I used to pick him up from his digs on Tantany Estate and drop him off at The Hawthorns most days. Clive would often go for long walks around West Bromwich on his own after a morning's training session, and, in fact, it was quite some time before he learned to drive, saying: 'None of my family had a car and I used to go around on a bike and the bus. It didn't bother me at all…that's how I kept myself fit. I once ran 100 yards in 11 seconds as a 16-year-old and I never lost my speed. It certainly helped me progress as a footballer.'

It certainly did. Clive was fast, direct, had an eye for goal and could turn defence into attack in seconds. Teammate Derek Kevan recalled: 'In a home League game against Fulham at the start of the 1962–63 season, we were under pressure, defending a corner. Our goalie Tony Millington gathered the ball and threw it out to Clarkey on the left. He charged away down the wing and had to wait a few seconds for one of us to get into the penalty area before he could whip over a cross. He was quick, bloody quick. I never came across one as fast as Chippy, not even a greyhound. He gave George Cohen a real old pasting that afternoon and, as I recall, laid on three goals in a 6–1 win. Clive also murdered England's right-back Jimmy Armfield when Albion battered Blackpool 7–1 at The Hawthorns at the end of the 1961–62 season. I know he set up two of my four goals with smashing crosses from the left.'

Besides creating goals aplenty, Clive also scored some beauties himself, several of them of proving decisive in the context of the game. And he 'won' a few penalties for Tony Brown. When Albion won the League Cup in 1965–66, he scored in the second leg of the Final victory against West Ham and the following season netted in every round of the competition, including scoring two goals in the Final, which Albion amazingly lost 3–2 against his former club QPR after being 2–0 up at the break. In fact, in 1966–67 Chippy finished up as leading scorer with 29 goals, the most ever by an Albion winger in one season.

In the successful 1967–68 FA Cup-winning campaign, Clive scored against Colchester in a third-round replay, in the 2–0 fifth-round win at Portsmouth and the winner in the quarter-final second replay against Liverpool, before playing his part in the 1–0 Final victory over Everton – making up for that League Cup defeat 12 months earlier.

He won two major trophies with Albion and also played for England at Under-23 level against Wales in 1961. He was also on the brink of full international honours in the mid-1960s but sadly never won a full cap – John Connelly of Manchester United getting the nod. And when Alf Ramsey took charge and did away with orthodox wingers, Clive's chances disappeared completely. But Jeff Astle believed he should have won a cap: 'He was a brilliant little winger who was frightened of no one. He was as good as any I saw.'

Badly injured on Albion's 1968 close-season tour to East Africa, Clive's last season at The Hawthorns was his worst. 'I couldn't get fit,' he said, 'my knee kept giving way and in the end I had to have an operation.'

After scoring 98 goals in 357 appearances for the Baggies, Clive was transferred back to his former employers, QPR, in June 1969, Allan Glover joining Albion in part-exchange. He later joined Preston North End (managed by Alan Ball's father), for whom he scored 11 goals in 82 games between 1970 and 1973. And, after a spell with Southport, he rounded things off by playing in the NASL and for two non-League clubs before coaching youngsters at Butlin's in Filey. Now in a nursing home in Skegness (after a series of personal tragedies affected his health) Clive still enjoys reunions with his former teammates as a member of Albion's former players' association.

IKE CLARKE

'A real driving force, his enthusiasm for the game was infectious.'

Born:	9 January 1915, Tipton, Staffordshire
Died:	2 April 2002, Canterbury, Kent

Albion senior record:

Appearances:	League 108 FA Cup 9, Wartime 96
Goals:	League 39, FA Cup 4, Wartime 55
Senior debut:	League, 11 September 1937, v Charlton Athletic (a) lost 3–1
Also played for:	Boys Brigade FC (Tipton), Princes End Baptists, Coseley Juniors, Toll End Wesley, for Nottingham Forest and Walsall as guests during the war, Portsmouth, Yeovil Town and FA (5 tour apps)
Managed:	Sittingbourne, Canterbury City and Ashford Town

Several Albion players, among them Ray Barlow, Alun Evans, Cecil Shaw and Dave Walsh, all believed that Ike Clarke would have played for England had World War Two not broken out when it did. Barlow said: 'He could head a ball as good as Tommy Lawton and shoot as powerful as Stan Mortensen,' while Walsh described him as being 'Big and weighty…just the sort of player you want alongside you when taking on big, sturdy opponents. Ike would rough it with the biggest and toughest defenders in the game and always gave a good, honest account of himself.'

A well-proportioned, all-action, robust inside or centre-forward with a strong right-foot shot and good heading ability, Ike scored almost 100 goals in just over 200 appearances for Albion, whom he served for 10 years. Black Country born and bred, Ike played for a number of local junior and intermediate clubs in and around the Tipton area and in one Saturday afternoon Cup game scored nine goals for Toll End Wesley. Surprisingly he was 21 years of age when he joined Albion as an amateur in January 1937. However, he quickly made up for lost time and, having scored a hat-trick in his first game for the club in a

Birmingham League fixture, three months later he was upgraded to the professional ranks by secretary-manager Fred Everiss.

Ike netted once in two Central League games towards the end of 1936–37 before making his senior debut in a 3–1 League defeat at Charlton in September 1937, replacing the injured Harry Jones at inside-right. He was handed 29 appearances during the course of the season, scoring six goals while playing alongside Jones and Albion and England centre-forward W.G. Richardson.

In 1938–39 Ike established himself firmly in Albion's forward line, which also featured two exceptionally fine wingers in Billy Elliott and England international Joe Johnson, as well as Jones and Richardson, plus at times Meynell Burgin and Sammy Heaselgrave. He notched 15 goals in 35 competitive matches in that last full pre-World War Two campaign and then during the hostilities (1939–46) he produced some excellent performances, netting 55 goals in almost 100 outings, twice finishing up as the club's leading scorer in 1944–45 and 1945–46.

Ike also assisted both Nottingham Forest and Walsall as a guest player and had the audacity to score twice for Forest against his employers, Albion, in a 5–3 defeat at The Hawthorns in December 1940. He helped Albion win the Midland Wartime Cup in 1944 when his vital extra-time goal in the second leg of the Final against Nottingham Forest gave the Baggies an aggregate 6–5 victory. In the transitional season of 1945–46, he whipped in a superb four-timer in an 8–1 home win over Chelsea and a hat-trick in a 6–0 home triumph over Newport County. Ike certainly loved playing against Newport! In the away fixture that season he found the net once and then, when League football returned for the 1946–47 campaign, he weighed in with his second four-goal haul in Albion's emphatic 7–2 win at Somerton Park.

At this juncture, Irish international centre-forward Dave Walsh was Ike's new strike partner and between them they netted a total of 48 goals in League and Cup competitions that season, Ike contributing 19. However, things were about to change dramatically at The Hawthorns and for Ike especially. After just 12 League games had been completed at the start of the 1947–48 season, and without a goal to his name – his worst goalless spell for the club – Ike, who at the time was 32 years of age, was transferred to Portsmouth for a fee of £7,000 in November 1947, much to the disappointment of the Baggies supporters and, indeed, to the shock of some of his teammates. His departure came completely out of the blue but, in an official statement issued by the Albion directors afterwards, it was said that 'Portsmouth had made an offer which could not be refused.'

So, having scored on average almost a goal every two games for Albion, Ike began a new life at Fratton Park. He made a terrific start in the royal blue of Portsmouth, scoring a stunning goal six minutes into his debut against Aston Villa. The fans loved his aggressive approach and he certainly proved an excellent buy for the south-coast club. He went on to net a total of 58 goals in 130 appearances and helped Pompey win back to back League titles in 1949 and 1950. Then, after achieving success at club level, in the summer of 1951 he was chosen for the FA tour to Australia, playing in five matches.

Transferred to non-League club Yeovil Town in the summer of 1953, Ike retired two years later to take over as manager-coach of the Kent club Sittingbourne. He then chose to spend the rest of his life in the Garden of England, going on to boss both Canterbury City and Ashford Town before retiring from football in May 1973, aged 58.

Always keen on cricket, he played regularly for his local team in Tipton during the summer months when he was at The Hawthorns and, in the annual fixture between Albion and Aston Villa in 1942, he scored a half-century in 25 minutes and took 4–12 in three overs of medium pace. In 1969 Ike became a member of Kent CCC and in the mid-1970s he joined the committee as a fundraiser, helping to raise well over £20,000 in the space of just four years.

Ike, who lived out his life in Herne Bay, died in a Canterbury hospital in April 2002.

JIMMY COOKSON

'Fast, elusive and deadly anywhere near goal.'

Born:	6 December 1904, Manchester
Died:	12 December 1970, Warminster

Albion senior record:

Appearances:	League 122, FA Cup 9
Goals:	League 103, FA Cup 7
Senior debut:	League, 27 August 1927 v Oldham Athletic (a) lost 3–1 (scored)
Also played for:	South Salford Lads' Club, Clayton FC (Manchester), Manchester City (reserves), Southport (trial), Chesterfield, Plymouth Argyle, Swindon Town, Warminster Town (player-manager) and FA XI

Blond centre-forward Jimmy Cookson was one of the first players to make his name when the offside rule was changed in 1925. Initially with Manchester City (no first-team outings) and a trialist with Southport, he joined Chesterfield at the end of the 1924–25 season. Fast and cunning, sharp and skilful, he then proceeded to score a total of 44 goals in 1925–26, as defenders up and down the country struggled to come to terms with the new offside regulations. In fact, Jimmy was the League's top marksman that season and the following term he added another 41 to his tally to finish with 85 strikes in just 74 Third Division North appearances for Chesterfield before transferring to West Bromwich Albion for a fee of £2,500 in August 1927.

Employing direct methods of attack, Jimmy used his weight fairly and regularly tried a shot at goal, mainly with his right foot and from any reasonable distance. He wasn't all that willing to use his head. In fact, he scored only four goals in this way during his entire career. He was certainly one of the most dangerous forwards around and he made a great impact at The Hawthorns. He scored on his debut (v Oldham Athletic) and went on to net a club record 38 goals in 38 League games in his first season, grabbing a double hat-trick, all six goals, when the Baggies beat Blackpool 6–3 in a home game in mid-September. This feat was also a club record and remains so to this day.

Jack Grimwood, the Blackpool centre-half, was given a torrid time that afternoon and he said after the game: 'I have never faced such a brilliant player as Cookson. He was quite superb, confident in everything he tried, and it paid off. And what a fine shot he has too.'

When he scored for the 15th time for Albion against South Shields on 17 December 1925, Jimmy created yet another League record by reaching the 100-goal mark in the fewest number of matches, just 85. In an interview Jimmy gave in 1930 to B.J. Evans, a leading London sporting journalist, he admitted that he hardly ever trained with the other Albion players. 'I would only do a couple of laps around the track and managed very few field exercises,' said Jimmy. 'I just wanted to get hold of a ball and practice shooting at goal. I loved it and two of my best mates at The Hawthorns, Joe Carter and Stan Wood, would often assist me by feeding the ball into my path or crossing it low from both wings.'

Jimmy was rated by many as the best centre-forward outside the First Division during the period 1927 to 1930. Then, after Albion had signed another quality centre-forward – W.G. Richardson – Jimmy, despite having notched well over 100 goals in three seasons, finishing as leading scorer each time, surprisingly found himself relegated to the reserves. It was a bitter blow and some supporters weren't too happy. But Richardson did the business and helped Albion complete the unique double in 1930–31 by winning the FA Cup and gaining promotion from Division Two in the same season. Jimmy's contribution that term was 11 League goals.

In 1931–32 – having toured Canada with the FA during the summer – Jimmy appeared in only one more First Division match for Albion, in the local derby against Birmingham at St Andrew's, and in August 1933 he reluctantly left The Hawthorns, signing for Plymouth Argyle on a free transfer. He had scored 110 goals in 131 first-team games for Albion and had also netted 95 times in 92 Central League matches, the highlight being a seven-timer in a 10–1 home win over Liverpool reserves in November 1931, helping the Baggies second XI win their division that season as he finished with a total of 43 goals in 33 outings.

He stayed at Home Park for two seasons, during which time he bagged another 38 goals in 48 games for the Pilgrims. In August 1935, Jimmy moved to Swindon Town, remaining at the County Ground until he announced his retirement through injury in May 1938 at the age of 33. In a tremendous League career Jimmy had scored no fewer than 256 goals in 292 appearances for four different clubs over a period of 13 years.

After calling it a day as a professional Jimmy became player-manager of Warmington Town and also entered the licensed trade, taking over the King's Arms on the edge of Salisbury Plain. He only served as a player for Warmington for one season but continued to turn out, when possible, in local charity matches right up until 1952. During his time in Wiltshire Jimmy also acted as a scout. Indeed, it was he who spotted the great Ray Barlow, who signed for Albion in 1944 and went on to appear in 482 first-team games for the Baggies, as well as representing England.

Jimmy had just celebrated his 66th birthday when he died in Warminster in December 1970.

*Jimmy's elder brother, Sammy, played right-back for Stalybridge Celtic, Macclesfield, Manchester City, Bradford Park Avenue and Barnsley. He made 285 appearances during his time at Maine Road (1918–28) and was joined there by Jimmy for season 1923–24.

LAURIE CUNNINGHAM

*'Brilliant winger with electrifying pace, balance and determination allied to silky skills.
If he'd been with Manchester United in the 1970s he would have won 50 caps.'*

Born:	8 March 1956, Archway, London
Died:	15 July 1989, near Madrid, Spain

Albion senior record:

Appearances:	League 81+5, FA Cup 7+3, League Cup 6, Europe 12
Goals:	League 21, FA Cup 3, League Cup 0, Europe 6
Senior debut:	League, 12 March 1977 v Tottenham Hotspur (a) won 2–0
Also played for:	Highgate Wood Boys, Haringey Schools, South East Counties Schools, North London Boys, Arsenal (schoolboy forms), Leyton Orient, Real Madrid (Spain), Manchester United, Sporting de Gijón (Spain), Olympique Marseille (France), Leicester City, Rayo Vallecano (Spain, 2 spells), Real Betis (Spain), RC Charleroi (Belgium), Wimbledon, England (5 Under-21 and 6 full caps)

Laurie Cunningham was the first English player ever signed by Real Madrid. He was also the first Black player to represent England in a major competitive international match and the first to represent his country at senior level. Born in London in 1956, Laurie was a superb young footballer who represented Stroud Green School (Highgate), Highgate Wood Boys, Haringey Schools (for whom he once scored five goals in a Cup game), South East Counties Schools and North London Boys before joining Arsenal as a 15-year-old (along with Glen Roeder). Not offered an apprenticeship at Highbury, he then turned his eye to one of the clubs he had followed as a youngster, Leyton Orient. Roeder joined him at Brisbane Road.

Signed as an apprentice by the then O's manager George Petchey in August 1972, Laurie became a professional at Brisbane Road in July 1974 and almost immediately attracted the attention of the soccer world after starring against

West Ham United in a Texaco Cup tie the following month. His first touch, dribbling ability and sheer pace quickly made him a firm favourite with the fans and he appeared in 20 first-team matches that season, scoring his first goal on the last day of the campaign to earn a 2–1 home win over Southampton. And that goal was, in fact, a MUST as far as Laurie was concerned. He had turned up late for the pre-match team talk and his annoyed manager told him: 'Go out and score a goal or you will be heavily fined.' Laurie went out and netted a beauty – one of 18 he scored for the Londoners in 96 appearances.

On the eve of the transfer deadline in March 1977 – shortly after his 21st birthday – Laurie was sold to West Bromwich Albion for a fee of £110,000, the deal bringing Joe Mayo and Allan Glover to Orient. After being watched by former Baggies centre-forward and then London-based scout Ronnie Allen, Laurie was signed by player-manager Johnny Giles, who handed him his First Division debut against Tottenham Hotspur at White Hart Lane. Laurie played superbly, helping Albion win the game 2–0.

At around this time speculation was rife as to whether Laurie would be the first Black player to win a full England cap. As things turned out, he was second behind Viv Anderson, who was honoured in a friendly against Czechoslovakia in November 1978. Laurie, however, was the first Black footballer to represent his country at Under-21 level, having been capped by Ron Greenwood against Scotland at Bramall Lane, Sheffield in 1977 and he then became the first to represent England in a competitive match when he played in the Home International against Wales at Wembley in May 1979. He would go on to gain six full caps in total.

Teaming up with fellow Black players Brendon Batson and Cyrille Regis to become known as 'the Three Degrees' at The Hawthorns, Laurie went on to score 30 goals in 114 games for Albion, helping them to reach the quarter-finals of the UEFA Cup and the semi-finals of the FA Cup. He was then surprisingly transferred to the Spanish giants Real Madrid for £995,000 in June 1979 and had the pleasure of scoring on his debut for Real in front of 105,000 fans inside the Bernabeu Stadium. Immediately nicknamed 'El Negrito', he bagged 15 goals in his first season in Spain, helping Real complete the La Liga and Cup double. He later played in the 1981 European Cup Final defeat by Liverpool.

Unfortunately Laurie never recaptured the form he had shown with Orient or the Albion, and, although adored by the Real fans, who also labelled him the 'Black Flash', Laurie's playing career started to go downhill when he became a male model, fashion designer and boutique owner. He skipped training on several occasions and this clearly upset the Real Madrid management. Affected by injuries, he was subsequently loaned out, in turn, to Manchester United, Sporting de Gijón of Spain, Olympique Marseille of France and Leicester City in the mid-1980s before eventually leaving the Bernabeu for Rayo Vallecano in August 1986.

Thereafter he had an unsuccessful trial with Real Betis and a spell with the Belgian club RSC Charleroi before returning to the English game with Wimbledon midway through the 1987–88 season. Although he had only a handful of first-team outings for the Dons, he did make a substitute appearance in their famous 1988 FA Cup Final victory over Liverpool. Soon after that, Laurie was transferred back to Rayo Vallecano in Spain, where he remained until his tragic death in a car crash on the outskirts of Madrid on the morning of 15 July 1989. He was only 33 years of age.

Laurie played in a total of 451 games for his clubs and country and scored 86 goals. His League record was also impressive – 67 goals in 348 appearances. In 2004 he was named as one of West Bromwich Albion's greatest-ever players, in a poll organised as part of the club's 125th anniversary celebrations.

JIMMY DUDLEY

'An admirable wing-half who played at full stretch until the last minute...
one of the soundest and hardest workers in the team.'

Born:	24 August 1928, Gartosh, Glasgow
Died:	25 April 2006, West Bromwich

Albion senior record:

Appearances:	League 285, FA Cup 343, FA Charity Shield 1
Goals:	League 9, FA Cup 2, FA Charity Shield 0
Senior debut:	League, 10 December 1949 v Manchester City (a) drew 1–1
Also played for:	Walsall Conduits, Albright Youth Club, Walsall, Stourbridge, Guest Motors, Scotland (1 B cap)

Over a period of 15 years, between 1945 and 1960, there were very few Scottish-born footballers at The Hawthorns. One of them, however, was the fair-haired, unassuming Jimmy Dudley, the man from Glasgow with a Black Country accent, whose older brother, George, had been with the Baggies a decade earlier. Jimmy's parents originated from Tividale near Dudley and moved to Gartosh from the Midlands before their youngest son was born. The birth certificate clearly stated that he had been born north of the border...and was therefore Scottish.

Jimmy began as a goalkeeper before the former Albion, Sunderland and Scotland wing-half 'Sandy' McNab became his idol. It was Jimmy's admiration for his fellow countryman that encouraged him to adopt an outfield position and there was sufficient football in the Dudley family to ensure that he succeeded, for besides George, another brother, Sammy, had been a professional with Preston North End, Bournemouth, the Irish club Coleraine, Clapton Orient, Chelsea and Exeter City between 1927 and 1935, while his cousin, Jimmy 'Iron' Edwards, was Albion's tough-tackling left-half in the 1931 double-winning team.

Success did not come automatically for Jimmy. Educated at Burnt Tree Mixed and Hill Top senior schools, he played locally for Walsall Conduits FC and the Albright Youth Club before joining Albion as a 16-year-old amateur in August 1944, turning professional 12 months later. He then spent two years in the RAF, chiefly based in Germany, and owing to the presence, and form, of players like Jimmy Duggan, Billy Lunn, George Drury, Jackie Haines, Cyril Williams, Ray Barlow and quite a few others, he had to wait more than four years before making his first-class debut.

Recalled Jimmy: 'I was told I was playing in the away game against Manchester City by our centre-forward Dave Walsh, who had seen my name written on the team-sheet in the manager's office. I was expecting to play in the second XI and my inclusion in the first team came as a bit of a surprise. I received confirmation just before training ended on the Friday morning, manager Jack Smith telling me to go out and do my best.'

Taking over at right-half from the injured Joe Kennedy for the League match at Maine Road, Jimmy played well in the 1–1 draw, and went on to make a further 12 appearances that season, nine of them as an inside-forward. He played in 18 competitive matches in 1950–51, including his first encounters in the FA Cup, and he also scored his first Albion goal, in a 2–1 home League defeat by Derby County. Handed 29 outings the following season, Jimmy finally made the right-half position his own in 1952–53 – after Kennedy had been switched to centre-half in place of Jack Vernon, who had returned to Ireland.

Prior to becoming a first-team regular, Jimmy had remained a pleasant and diligent young man, a complete midfielder with a splendid temperament. He was not easily provoked in the heat of the game and as far as I know he was never sent off and only ever booked once…for arguing with the referee during a League game at Bolton.

A model of consistency, Jimmy never missed a first-team game, wearing the number-four shirt week in, week out from 5 April 1952 until 3 March 1956, making a total of 166 appearances on the bounce, a club record which stood for more than 20 years until fellow Scot Ally Robertson bettered it in the late 1970s. Jimmy's teammate Ray Barlow described him as being 'Mr Consistent', while Albion's manager Vic Buckingham said: 'Jimmy was one of the first names on my team-sheet…such a wonderful player.' Another of his colleagues, England international right-back Don Howe, who played behind Jimmy at least 100 times, said 'He was an extraordinary footballer; tireless, a real workaholic who ran and ran and ran. He was the link between defence and attack and he did a wonderful job. I thought he was superb in what he did.'

Jimmy was part of two truly terrific Albion half-back lines – firstly playing alongside Kennedy and Barlow and then lining up with Jimmy Dugdale and Barlow. He was, without doubt, outstanding during the 1953–54 season when Albion came so close to clinching the coveted League and FA Cup double. It was his deep centre, floated over from the right-wing, which crept past Port Vale's goalkeeper Ray King in the Cup semi-final at Villa Park to bring Albion level and set them on their way to a 2–1 victory. Then, in the Final at Wembley with almost 100,000 spectators present – by far the biggest crowd Jimmy ever played in front of – he covered acres of ground, completely mastering Preston North End's creative inside-forward Jimmy Baxter and helping the Baggies to a deserved 3–2 win.

He also represented Scotland in a B international against England in 1954 when two of his opponents were his clubmates from The Hawthorns, Ronnie Allen and Jimmy Dugdale. Unfortunately this was Jimmy's only honour for his country – he deserved a lot more.

After scoring 11 goals in 320 appearances for Albion at senior level, and five in 115 Central League matches, Jimmy left the club for Black Country neighbours Walsall in December 1949, signed by Saddlers boss Bill Moore for a fee of £4,000. At Fellows Park he played at left-half and teamed up with three other former Albion players, namely right-back Harry Haddington, wing-half 'Tim' Rawlings and inside-forward Ken Hodgkisson. Jimmy helped Walsall win the Fourth Division Championship in his first season, scoring important goals at Rochdale, Barrow and Southport, and in 1960–61 he missed only three games as the Saddlers gained promotion to the Second Division.

He went on to play in 176 first-class games for the club before transferring to Stourbridge in August 1964. Soon afterwards he took employment at Guest Motors in West Bromwich. He played for the works football team (until 1967) and stayed with that company until his retirement in 1993. Jimmy, who surprisingly cut himself off from football once he had stopped playing – he returned to The Hawthorns just twice in 40 years – resided in Great Barr, Birmingham, with his wife Evelyn for the rest of his life. He was 77 when he died in Sandwell Hospital, West Bromwich, in April 2006.

JIMMY 'IRON' EDWARDS

'A strong, forceful player, biting in the tackle and vigorous throughout.'

Born: 11 December 1905, Tipton
Died: 10 April 1982, West Bromwich

Albion senior record:

Appearances: League 182, FA Cup 19, FA Charity Shield 1
Goals: League 9, FA Cup 0, FA Charity Shield 0
Senior debut: League, 31 March 1928 v Hull City (a) drew 1–1
Also played for: Horseley Bridge Youth Club, Tipton Park FC, Newport Foundry FC (Tipton), Stourbridge (2 spells), Great Bridge Celtic, Norwich City, Bilston United, Kingswinford, Dudley Town, Football League XI (1 app)

After doing very well in local football as an all-action goalscoring inside-left, Jimmy Edwards joined West Bromwich Albion as a professional in May 1926. He continued to play in the forward line and in his first season at The Hawthorns netted 16 times in 32 reserve-team matches, gaining a Central League Championship-winners' medal in the process.

In 1927–28 he again flourished in the second XI, scoring 12 goals in 32 games, while at the same time he made his first-team debut in a 1–1 draw away to Hull City, replacing the injured Joe Carter at inside-right. Continuing to develop in the reserves, Jimmy added another 10 goals in 27 Central League appearances to his tally before finally getting a decent run in the first team, playing in 11 of the last 12 Second Division matches at the end of the 1928–29 campaign. Taking over from former England international Harry Chambers, he partnered Arthur Fitton on the left wing and helped himself to three goals, his first coming in a 5–0 home romp over Reading, followed by a point-saver at Preston and a smart effort in a 3–2 victory over Millwall.

However, the following season Albion introduced a new left-wing pairing of Frank Cresswell and Stan Wood and this meant that Jimmy slipped back into the reserves, where he produced some more excellent displays – he finished up second top scorer with 20 goals in 30 outings as the Baggies reserves claimed third place in their division. Drafted in for just three senior games between August 1929 and March 1930, Jimmy then replaced the injured Cresswell for the remaining nine fixtures, helping himself to three more goals, including the winner in the home clash against his favourite 'other' team, Reading.

By the age of 24 Jimmy had developed into a rock-solid competitive footballer, resolute and indefatigable, and, after lining up at inside-left in the opening two games of the 1930–31 season, he was switched into the half-back line, alongside Tommy Magee (on the right) and his bosom pal from the Black Country, Bill Richardson, in the centre.

Albion's team at this time was stronger and more efficient than it had been for almost a decade. Jimmy, with his tree-trunk legs, solid hips and broad shoulders, was a key player, serving as the anchorman in the centre of the field with Richardson, the pair being dubbed 'Iron and Steel' by the fans because of their respective statures.

Always in the thick of the action, Jimmy produced some exquisite performances during the course of the season, which ended in celebration as Albion completed the unique double, gaining promotion from the Second Division and winning the FA Cup. In the Final at Wembley, Jimmy handled Birmingham's talented inside-right Johnny Crosbie splendidly, never allowing the Scot a sniff at goal. On a soggy, strength-sapping pitch, Albion's hard man was in his element and at the end of the game received high praise from Blues centre-forward Joe Bradford, who said: 'Albion were the better side and merited their win. Jimmy Edwards was an inspiration out there. He played with great spirit.'

Mavis, who covered the Final for the *Sport Argus*, stated in his report that Jimmy and his co-defenders 'resisted Birmingham's efforts with a courage and resource one could not help but admire.'

Jimmy played in 50 games in 1930–31 and over the next four seasons, during which time he struggled for long periods with a tedious hip injury. He appeared in 114 first-class matches, including the 1935 FA Cup Final defeat by Sheffield Wednesday. In an interview after that game a disappointed Jimmy said, 'We should have won. They scored two late goals and were second best. Unfortunately the usually reliable W.G. (Richardson) missed a couple of chances and if one of those had gone in we would have cantered home.'

In 1931–32 Jimmy was selected to play for the Football League against the Scottish League and such was his form at that time that he was thought a possible candidate for an England cap. In May 1934 he was named as a standby reserve for the tour games against Hungary and Czechoslovakia, after Arsenal's Wilf Copping had pulled out. However, in the end the management committee chose Harry Burrows of Sheffield Wednesday to fill the left-half position, taking Lew Stoker of Birmingham as the extra half-back. Jimmy never figured again.

With Jack Rix and Jack Sankey pressing hard for first-team football, Jimmy was called into action by Albion just 11 times in 1935–36 before making his 202nd and last appearance for Albion in a 6–2 defeat at Manchester City in early September 1936. In fact, Sankey played in the same half-back line as Jimmy on several occasions and, with Bill Richardson in the centre, the trio were referred to as 'salt, pepper and mustard'…Jimmy being the 'hot one'.

Playing out the rest of that season in the reserves, taking his Central League appearances to 184 (63 goals scored), Jimmy often attended afternoon training sessions at The Hawthorns, passing on tips to several younger players and generally giving them a coaching lesson. One player he advised was a young inside-forward named Sammy Heaselgrave, whom he admired a lot. In fact, Jimmy seriously believed he was international class. Unfortunately war broke out and Sammy's career was severely disrupted.

Transferred to Norwich City for £750 in May 1937, Jimmy spent just six months with the Canaries before retiring to the Black Country, where he played out the remainder of his career in non-League football, eventually retiring in the summer of 1944 aged 39. After that he continued to attend Albion home matches and was a guest at the 1954 FA Cup-winning celebration dinner.

*Jimmy's brother, Ernie, played for Albion from 1913 to 1920, while his cousin, Jimmy Dudley, was an FA Cup-winner with the Baggies in 1954.

BILLY ELLIOTT

'A brisk, clever and dangerous outside-right with a great scoring record.'

Born:	6 August 1919, Harrington, Cumberland
Died:	13 July 1966, Canary Islands

Albion senior record:

Appearances:	League 170, FA Cup 12, Wartime 148
Goals:	League 39, FA Cup 1, Wartime 117
Senior debut:	League, 24 December 1938 v Luton Town (a) lost 3–1
Also played for:	Carlisle United, Dudley Town, Wolverhampton Wanderers, Bournemouth, Bilston United (player-manager), England (1 Wartime, 1 Victory cap), FA XI, Western Command, Army

Outside-right Billy Elliott was one of the fastest wingers in League football during the late 1940s. Rejected as a 16-year-old by Wolves manager Major Frank Buckley, he was spotted by an Albion scout playing for Bournemouth in a first-round FA Cup tie against Bristol City in December 1938. Albion's secretary-manager and director Claude Jephcott moved in swiftly, winning the race with Birmingham boss George Liddell for his signature for a fee of £4,000.

Standing 5ft 11in tall and weighing a fraction over 12 stone, Billy was also stockily built and this stood him in good stead when opposed by tough-tackling left-backs. Highly mobile and blessed with terrific pace over 20–30 yards, he finely retained command of the ball, could leave most opponents standing – in some cases he was far too quick for his own teammates – and had considerable shooting power in his right foot.

Billy also had one personal trick. When flying down the wing, he would suddenly check his stride, draw his right foot over the ball, pull back and immediately set off again, leaving his opponent in his wake. This occasionally went wrong, but generally he was pretty good at it and some international defenders were baffled as to how Billy did it.

Former player and director Cliff Edwards, a teammate of Billy's, said in 1975 when he was helping me compile my book, *Albion At War*: 'He used to try this trick all the time during training sessions and I remember Harry Kinsell grabbing his shirt and telling him to stop making him look stupid! Billy was a wonderful footballer and a fine goalscorer who could have easily fitted in at centre-forward. But he loved to have space…and he got plenty of that on the wing. I played behind him several times and he was always telling me to get the ball to him quickly. That was easier said than done, but I tried my best and I believe that during the mid-1940s we had a good understanding with each other. During a home League game against Nottingham Forest towards the end of the 1946–47 season, Billy tormented their full-back (Jack Hutchinson) all afternoon and had a hand in four of Albion's goals. After the game he (Hutchinson) told Billy that he was better than Stanley Matthews.'

An Albion regular for 12 years, from December 1938 until December 1950, Billy scored his first Albion goal in his second game, a 3–2 defeat at Swansea. But as soon as he had bedded himself into The Hawthorns World War Two broke out, completely disrupting competitive football all over the country. Enlisted as a soldier in the South Staffordshire Regiment, Billy was able to play a lot of football and, indeed, during the hostilities he maintained a wonderful record, scoring a record 117 goals in 148 appearances from his right-wing position.

He equalled Harry 'Popeye' Jones's record of scoring in 11 successive games in season 1941–42 when he was Albion's joint leading marksman (with W.G. Richardson) and was out on his own in 1942–43 with 17 goals and again in 1943–44 with a total of 28. The latter included a four-timer against Northampton Town in September and hat-tricks versus Walsall in January and Wolves in March, but he missed Albion's Midland Cup Final win over Nottingham Forest due to injury.

Billy's performances did not go unnoticed, and in April 1944 he played for an England XI against the Combined Services at Stoke, while the following month he starred for England in a wartime international against Wales at Cardiff. Two years later he won a Victory international cap against Scotland at Hampden Park in front of 139,468 spectators and at around the same time he also represented the FA, Western Command and the Army.

Unfortunately Billy never won a full cap – perhaps because he wasn't with a top flight club when in his prime (1946–49) – but he was certainly top man as far as Albion fans were concerned, especially in 1948–49 when promotion was achieved from the Second Division. Billy missed only two games that season, both through injury, and netted seven goals as Albion clawed back an eight-point deficit on Southampton to go up with champions Fulham.

Baggies centre-forward Dave Walsh struck 23 League goals in 1948–49, half of them coming from direct right-wing crosses from Billy. Dave recalled: 'Seeing Billy racing down the wing, I knew he would get in a cross sooner or later. I just had to make sure I could get there in time.'

A firm favourite with the Baggies fans, Billy was playing splendidly against far better teams in the First Division. In fact he had scored seven goals in 21 matches, bagging his first against Arsenal in mid-September, while also scoring in the local derby against Wolves at Molineux to earn his side a point. Then, during the home game with Manchester United on Christmas Eve, he was block-tackled by Johnny Aston and suffered a serious knee injury that sidelined him for the rest of the season. During his absence Albion signed Ronnie Allen and, when Billy returned to action, he regained his normal position, allowing Allen to switch to the left.

However, injury struck Billy again in October in 1950 and this time he was under treatment for five months, returning in April 1951. After just three more outings he suffered an Achilles injury, which effectively ended his career at The Hawthorns. Billy, who helped found Albion's first Supporters' Club in 1951, departed in the July, signing for Bilston United and later taking over as player-manager of the non-League club before retiring in May 1954.

Although by now a fully-qualified FA coach and member of the Players' Union, soon afterwards he entered the licensed trade as landlord of the Farcroft Hotel in Handsworth, before taking over as manager of the Red Cow in Smethwick. Sadly, while on holiday in the Canary Islands in 1966, Billy suffered a heart attack and died at the age of 47.

FRED EVERISS, JP

'This man was "Mr West Bromwich Albion"...a loyal and dedicated servant.'

Born: 27 May 1882, Spon Lane, West Bromwich
Died: 4 March 1951, West Bromwich

Albion record: Office junior, senior clerk, assistant secretary, secretary-manager, director

Fred Everiss was associated with Albion for 55 years. He joined the club as an office junior in September 1896, became a senior clerk in the spring of 1899, acted as assistant secretary for 12 months and eventually became secretary-manager, taking over from Frank Heaven in the summer of 1902 at the age of 20. He continued in this position until May 1948 when he retired to become a director of the club, remaining on the board until his death in 1951.

Fred played a little football at school and was Albion mad. He saw his first match at the club's old Four Acres ground at the age of five and probably attended virtually every Albion home game from 1887 until his last in 1951. Initially he did the odd jobs within the club: filling in team-sheets, submitting reports and making the tea. Then, after a spell as the club's senior clerk – a responsible position in those days, which he relished – he was upgraded to assist the club's secretary-manager Frank Heaven. When Frank left, Fred was an able replacement, and the board had no doubts about a 20-year-old taking charge of a major League club.

Fred later recalled: 'My appointment as secretary enabled me to get a lot closer to some of the famous men in the game. Several times I met William McGregor, the founder of the Football League, and remember asking him how he came to conceive the idea of such a competition. He told me that clubs were always in trouble with their fixtures. Matches were called off on the slightest pretext, often on a Friday, and the financial loss, quite apart from the disappointment caused to supporters, was something which called for serious consideration. I knew all that to be true from our own particular experience. "Pa" McGregor, as he was known, therefore circularised some of the leading clubs for the purpose of discussing the problem, a solution to which, he claimed, was a settled fixture list with home and away games against each other. It proved to be a great success.'

With the assistance of former player Billy Bassett and senior directors, Fred brought great respectability to the club at a time when things were going pretty well out on the pitch, Albion having just regained their top-flight status as Second Division champions and having made a healthy profit of £3,000. 'That money was badly needed,' said Fred. 'We wanted to put our house in better order, but all of a sudden we got a huge kick in the pants.'

There had been some domestic disagreements, which culminated in chairman Harry Keys resigning from the board. It was then announced, at the end of the 1903–04 season, after Albion had once more been relegated, that the club was broke. There was no money in the kitty and some of the players hadn't been paid. Even the Football League President, J. J. Bentley, was concerned and in a letter to the club, stated: 'Mr Everiss, if you need assistance and guidance please feel free to ask.'

In his memoirs some years later Fred admitted: 'Back in 1904–05 it was touch and go whether or not the club would survive. We had to select our 34-year-old trainer Jimmy Millar for one game – and he hadn't played for three years. Also, the old stand on the Handsworth side of the ground, Noah's Ark, burnt down, ironically on Guy Fawkes' night, along with two refreshment bars, 30 yards of wooden fencing and six turnstiles on the Woodman corner. The fire itself caused around £4,000 worth of damage and to replace the stand alone would have cost around £1,600. We simply hadn't got the money. Enquiries into how the fire started remained a mystery but the club did receive £951 insurance money – which went straight to the creditors.'

Thankfully things improved, albeit slowly. Harry Keys returned as chairman and, with a new board behind him, backed Fred to the hilt. Some key players were sold, replaced by a few unknowns and new signings. Local West Bromwich MP Sir Ernest Spencer launched a public appeal and money came in from various sources, Fred keeping a close on eye on everything that went on. He was a meticulous, serious and understanding person – nothing escaped him and he worked overtime helping Albion get back on track.

With a suitably reinforced team, mainly due to Fred's perseverance and willpower, Albion reached the FA Cup semi-finals in 1907, gained promotion in 1911 (with one of the youngest squads in the country), reached the FA Cup Final a year later and, directly after World War One, won the League championship for the first time (1920).

Fred was praised for his efforts and rightly so. Along with his directors he had worked tirelessly and his efforts were now proving worthwhile. Albion were a big club once again, and with Fred continually striving behind the scenes, five years later runners'-up spot was achieved and in 1931, having suffered demotion again, the Baggies claimed the unique double, winning the FA Cup and gaining promotion from Division Two in the same season.

Over the next 20 years, with Fred working hard as always, Albion reached another FA Cup Final (beaten in 1935) and, following yet another relegation campaign, they won the Midland Wartime Cup in 1944 – the last trophy the club won under the guidance of 'Mr Albion' himself, Fred Everiss.

Not only did Fred give Albion sterling service for all those years, in 1927 he was appointed secretary of the Football League Secretaries' and Managers' Association (later taking over as chairman). During World War Two he combined his internal club duties with those of part-time groundsman and ARP night watchman. Sometimes he was on duty for 18 hours a day. He was a workaholic, but he simply loved his job and West Bromwich Albion. In October 1946 he was presented with a silver casket and an illuminated address on the occasion of his 50 years of service with Albion.

Jack Smith succeeded Fred as Albion's secretary-manager, while the club's secretarial duties were taken over by his astute assistant, Eph Smith. For the last three years of his life Fred, who by now was a local JP, was an important member of the Albion board of directors and his knowledge of the game was unsurpassed.

He was a tremendous club man, one of the greatest in Albion's history.

*Fred's son, Alan, went on to serve Albion 11 years longer than his father. He joined the club in 1933 and remained part of The Hawthorns set-up until 1999, working as a clerk, assistant secretary and secretary, then as an influential shareholder, a director and finally a Life Member, from August 1980 until his death in 1999, aged 81.

BOB FINCH

'A reliable and competent full-back, full of grit and determination.'

Born:	31 August 1908, Hednesford, Staffordshire
Died:	15 December 1908, Hednesford

Albion senior record:

Appearances:	League 216, FA Cup 18
Goals:	None
Senior debut:	League, 27 February 1926 v Leicester City (h) won 3–1
Also played for:	Hednesford Prims, Hednesford Town (2 spells), Swansea Town, Tamworth, England international trialist (2 apps)

Bob Finch was a very useful full-back. Upright, well-balanced and strong in the tackle, he had good pace and kicked long and true with his trusty right foot. One write-up in a matchday programme from the mid-1930s described him as being '...quite dependable, he uses the ball to advantage, tackles firmly and is rarely caught out of position, the Albion full-back is a stout defender.'

Dubbed 'Able Finch' by his colleagues (one of his Christian names was Abel), Bob was a redoubtable player who spent 14 years at The Hawthorns, appearing in 234 senior games and never scoring a first-team goal, although he did plant three past his own 'keeper, including a measured lob over 'keeper Harold Pearson during the home League game against Huddersfield Town in October 1936. Albion still won 2–1. He did, however, score twice in 231 second-team games for the Baggies, and in fact only Arthur Fitton, with 261 appearances, has featured in more Central League games for the club than Bob.

Born into a mining community, Bob joined Hednesford Prims in July 1922, switched to local rivals Hednesford Town in the summer of 1923 and joined Albion in April 1925, initially as an amateur, turning professional five months later. To begin with he was first reserve to former England international Joe Smith and Arthur Perry, but Bob made an impressive League debut against Leicester City in February 1926 and had a run of five outings in the side before slipping back into the second XI.

The following season he had to compete for a place in the seniors with first Perry and Dicky Baugh and then, from December onwards, with ex-England player Billy Ashurst and George Shaw, making only a handful of appearances, while at the same time he gained a Central League championship-winners' medal, the first of four he would win at this level, the others following in successive seasons in the mid-1930s when his full-back colleague was Welsh international Hugh Foulkes. Bob skippered Albion's reserve team on several occasions.

Finally gaining a regular place in the first team, just three games into the 1927–28 season, as partner to the aforementioned Shaw, Bob missed only 11 of Albion's next 140 competitive matches and played in two international trials, but he suffered an irritating ankle injury which started niggling him during matches. This resulted in Bert Trentham being introduced to the team at left-back, with Shaw switching to the right. This was unfortunate for Bob, who watched Albion storm on to complete the unique double, winning promotion from Division Two and lifting the FA Cup at Wembley in 1930–31.

Bob didn't even qualify for a League runners'-up medal, as he appeared in only eight games. 'Without doubt, missing the Cup Final against Birmingham was bitterly disappointing. But I was there inside the stadium, cheering the lads on, and I was so pleased for them all when skipper Tommy Glidden passed me on his way to the Royal Box to collect the Cup. It was a great achievement by the team,' said Bob.

Playing second fiddle to both Shaw and Trentham over the next five seasons, Bob appeared in only 28 First Division matches during that time. But being the dedicated club man he was, and despite several clubs enquiring about a possible transfer, including Sheffield Wednesday and Wolves, he remained loyal to Albion. Then, just after the start of the 1936–37 season, completely out of the blue, Shaw was injured against Derby County. Sid Swinden was given the chance to take over, but in the end the job was handed back to 28-year-old Bob.

With Trentham his partner at first, later followed by ex-Wolves player Cecil Shaw, Bob found himself playing in a struggling Albion team, whose League form was well below par. In fact they suffered some heavy defeats, including a 10–3 mauling at Stoke and a 6–2 drubbing at Manchester City, but in the FA Cup competition their form was good. After knocking out Spennymoor United, Darlington and Coventry City in the first three rounds Albion met the holders Arsenal on a snow-covered pitch at The Hawthorns in the quarter-final. A record crowd of almost 65,000 saw the Baggies, playing some brilliant football, beat the Gunners 3–1 and at that point Bob believed he would get the chance to play at Wembley.

He said: 'Despite our poor League form we were playing very well in the Cup and pinned up on the dressing-room wall was a poster, sent in by a young supporter, saying 'ALBION FOR THE CUP.' We were confident that we could win it, but following the death of our much-loved chairman Billy Bassett during the week leading up to the semi-final clash with Preston North End at Highbury, we failed to perform and lost 4–1. I will honestly say many of the players were still getting over the news of the chairman's demise…I was one of them. We simply didn't compete…disappointing, but that's football for you. You have to take the rough with the smooth, get on with the game whatever the circumstances, and take what comes.'

Bob continued playing for Albion for two more seasons, making his last appearance in the League side at Blackpool in April 1938 before moving, perhaps reluctantly, to Swansea Town in May 1939 for a 'small fee'. Then World War Two broke out and almost immediately he left Vetch Field and returned to his former club, Hednesford Town. He assisted Tamworth as a guest during the early days of the hostilities before announcing his retirement as a 'serious' footballer in May 1942. At that juncture, Bob joined the police force as Constable 475 Finch of the Cannock Division of the Staffordshire County Force. He served as a policeman for the next 14 years, handing in his uniform at the age of 48.

Bob continued to live in Hednesford and played golf twice and sometimes three times a week right up until he was almost 80. Thereafter he would play perhaps once a fortnight. When he reached his 92nd birthday, in August 2000, he was the oldest former Albion player alive at that time.

I had arranged to call and see Bob for one final interview just before his son told me of his passing.

DOUG FRASER

'A gritty player though not without style; a hard tackler, good in passing.'

Born: 8 December 1941, Busby, Lanarkshire

Albion senior record:

Appearances: League 255+2, FA Cup 24, League Cup 29, Europe 10, Others 5

Goals: League 8, FA Cup 0, League Cup 4, Europe 0, Others 0

Senior debut: League, 18 September 1963 v Birmingham City (h) won 3–1

Also played for: Rolls Royce FC, Eaglesham Amateurs, Blantyre Celtic, Celtic (trialist), Aberdeen, Nottingham Forest, Walsall (player, then player-manager), Scotland (2 full and 7 unofficial caps)

Before joining Albion for £25,000 in September 1963, Doug Fraser scored twice in 88 appearances for Aberdeen, whom he served for seven years. He made his League debut at centre-forward in a 2–0 win over Ayr United on the last day of the 1959–60 season and in 1960–61 appeared in both wing-half positions and also at outside-right, eventually settling down at left-half, from where he scored his first senior goal in a 10–3 Scottish Cup win over Clyde in January 1962.

Injured for two-thirds of the 1962–63 campaign, Doug regained full fitness and, after three games at the start of 1963–64, moved from Pittodrie to The Hawthorns, taking over from Bobby Cram in Albion's middle line. Teaming up with fellow Scots Campbell Crawford, Ken Foggo and Bobby Hope, Doug had a good first season with the Baggies, making 37 appearances and netting one goal, in a 2–0 League win at Leicester in mid-December. The following season he played in 34 matches and in 1965–66, when he helped Albion win the League Cup, he featured 52 times.

Talking to me at a book signing evening a few years ago, Doug recalled: 'I was pleased to be part of a very efficient football team and players like Jeff Astle, Tony Brown, Hopey, Johnny Kaye, Clive Clark and Graham Williams were some of the best in their positions in the First Division. Besides our League Cup triumph we didn't do too badly in the League and finished pretty high up in the table.

'In the League Cup, though, we were excellent. The home tie with Walsall was tough but we came through in the end, and we also had to be at our best to knock out Leeds United, but after a draw at Highfield Road, we slaughtered Coventry City 6–1 in the replay and I, for the first time in my career, scored two goals in a game. I was to repeat that feat a year later in the same competition against the team we defeated in round five, Aston Villa. We beat a plucky Peterborough United side over two legs in the semi-final before taking on West Ham in the Final. After losing the first game at Upton Park, we turned things around at The Hawthorns with a 4–1 victory, to win the trophy 5–3 on aggregate, and I sincerely believe we played some of the finest football I had been involved that evening, especially in the first half.'

In 1966–67, Albion again reached the League Cup Final, but on this occasion things didn't go their way. Said Doug 'At half-time in the Final against Queen's Park Rangers we were 2–0 up and in control. But then it all went wrong. Manager Jimmy Hagan swapped the team around and moved 'Yorkie' (John Kaye) back into a defensive position in front of young Dennis Clarke. We lost our way and the match as Rangers came back to win 3–2. At the end of the game our dressing room was like a morgue and poor old Chippy Clark was devastated, having scored both our goals for nothing against his former club.'

Albion had a new manager at the start of the 1967–68 season. Alan Ashman, a former chicken farmer, took over from Hagan. And what a terrific start he made to his Hawthorns career, leading Albion to victory over Everton in the FA Cup Final.

Doug remembered: 'That was some game. We were confident before the kick-off that we could win the Cup and make up for our defeat at Wembley the previous season. It was tough going against very good opposition, but we stuck in there, gritted our teeth and in the end Jeff's extra-time goal saw us home.'

Albion almost reached their fourth Final in successive years in 1968–69, but this time lost to Leicester City in the FA Cup semi-final. Doug, now playing at right-back, admitted: 'We failed to get out of the blocks that afternoon at Hillsborough and fell to a sucker punch of a goal right at the end. That defeat was harder to take than losing to QPR in the 1967 League Cup Final.'

Taking over as Albion captain from Graham Williams, Doug had the honour and pleasure of leading out the team at Wembley for the 1970 League Cup Final against Manchester City, but after taking an early lead, they eventually lost 2–1 after extra-time and again Doug was bitterly disappointed, saying: 'The pitch that day was absolutely horrid. It's not an excuse for us not winning the Final, but I just feel that the surface as a whole seriously affected our performance. We liked to play football, keeping the ball on the ground as best we could. But Wembley that March afternoon was a bog and City got the breaks where we didn't and in the end they lifted the trophy.'

Doug remained with Albion until January 1971 when he was transferred to Nottingham Forest for £35,000. He scored 12 goals in 325 appearances for the Baggies, played in four major Cup Finals, tasted European football and won two full caps for Scotland in 1968, against Holland in Amsterdam and Cyprus in Nicosia, having an excellent game against the latter country when he assisted in two of the five goals by which the Scots won. He also played in seven unofficial internationals in 1967 when on tour to Israel, Hong Kong, Australia, New Zealand and Canada with teammates Eddie Colquhoun and Bobby Hope. Doug actually captained his country five times on that month-long tour.

After netting four times in 94 appearances for Forest, Doug moved back to the West Midlands, sold by manager Dave Mackay to Walsall for £8,000 in July 1973. Taking over as manger of the Saddlers in January 1974, he held office until March 1977. He kept his side in a mid-table League position and guided them to the fifth round of the FA Cup in 1975 while making 31 appearances himself.

After leaving football Doug became a prison officer based at Nottingham Gaol. Retiring in the mid-1990s, he now lives in Ilkeston, Derbyshire, and is a member of Albion's former players' association.

A final assessment of Doug comes from his Albion teammate, Tony Brown: 'He was as hard as nails, committed to the cause, but he could play as well. He was a good passer of the ball, a great inspiration, a shouter who kept everybody on their toes.'

ALF 'JASPER' GEDDES

'A "gem" of a winger who scored his fair share of goals.'

Born:	14 April 1871, West Bromwich
Died:	15 October 1927, Bristol

Albion senior record:

Appearances:	League 73, FA Cup 9, Others 11
Goals:	League 25, FA Cup 6, Others 7
Senior debut:	League, 7 November 1891 v Everton (a) lost 4–3
Also played for:	Causeway Green Villa, Clapham Rovers, Millwall Athletic (two spells), Bedminster, Bristol City, Bristol Rovers, Southern League XI (1 app)

Not too many players have scored a hat-trick in an FA Cup semi-final, but back in March 1892, Albion's outside-left Jasper Geddes did just that, in a resounding 6–2 second replay victory over Nottingham Forest in a blizzard at Derby. His first goal came in the 20th minute, his second arrived just past the half-hour mark and his third was netted on the hour. The moustachioed Jasper was described in the press as a 'gem…a whippet-like left-winger,' who could rip a defence open at will. He could score goals as well as make them and in a wonderful career, serving with five major clubs, he netted 106 times in 287 first-class appearances.

A mercurial outside-left, fast and energetic with a powerful shot, he could also be a very temperamental player and was certainly a little greedy at times, but generally he was an excellent footballer who could turn a game on its head with one bout of brilliance.

Following his treble in the Cup semi-final Jasper, who was just 21 years of age at the time, then went out in the Final against Aston Villa and scored as early as the fourth minute to set up a 3–0 victory in front of a record crowd at Crystal Palace. He had only gained a place in Albion's first team in November 1891, after Albion had struggled to find a top-class replacement for Joe Wilson. In fact, since March 1890, no fewer than seven different players had been used by the club on the left flank. Jasper proved to be the best of the lot, and went on to score 38 goals in almost 100 competitive games for the club in two separate spells. He also appeared in 80 'other' first-team matches (friendlies etc) and notched another 20 goals. After returning for his second 'term in office' in April 1895, his three goals kept Albion in the First Division.

A Black Country man, Jasper played for Causeway Green Villa for two seasons before joining Albion as a professional in September 1891. Nurtured through the second-team ranks for a couple of months, he made a decent League debut in a 4–3 defeat at Everton in mid-November and retained his place until the end of the season, scoring 12 goals in 22 games and of course gaining a Cup-winners' medal in the progress.

In 1892–93 Jasper claimed a further nine goals in 30 first-team appearances and the following season struck 12 times in 36 outings, helping Albion reach the Final of the United Counties League Cup, where they took on Derby County. The game ended in a 1–1 draw, Jasper scoring for Albion. However, the replay was carried over until October of the following season, by which time Jasper had left the club, surprisingly being transferred to Millwall Athletic for £400 in September 1894.

A reporter for a local newspaper covering the south-east London club wrote: 'Alf Geddes' signing is a major coup for new Southern League club Millwall Athletic. He is the first professional to come to the East Ferry Road ground and everyone is looking forward to seeing this talented outside-left.'

At the time Millwall were raiding several First Division clubs for star players and Jasper was rated as one of the best wingers in the game. He certainly did the Lions proud, scoring 13 goals in 20 appearances in his first season and gaining a Southern League championship-winners' medal in the process. Then, out of the blue, with only a handful of games remaining at the end of the 1894–95 season, Albion found themselves in deep trouble at the foot of the table, and in a desperate attempt to stave off relegation they contacted Millwall to ask if they could re-sign Jasper to help their cause. An agreement was reached via the telegraphic service and two representatives from Albion travelled to London to sign Jasper.

It was a gamble that paid off…eventually! With three matches left to play – one away and two at home – Albion, along with Liverpool, Derby County and Stoke, were in danger of losing their top-flight status. The Baggies, needing to gain at least four points from these remaining games and score quite a few goals in the process, made a disastrous start, crashing to a 5–0 defeat at Bolton. But then, with two home fixtures left, they came good, or Jasper did! His goal was enough to beat Nottingham Forest in the penultimate game and then, on the final day of the season, he scored twice in a brilliant 6–0 win over Sheffield Wednesday. Going into the crucial last game Albion knew they had to beat the Owls by at least five goals to retain their First Division status. Jasper was in great form, as were his teammates, and Albion recorded their famous 6–0 victory. They stayed up and Liverpool went down instead.

Jasper then returned to Millwall, where he remained for a further four seasons, taking his overall record with the Londoners to 59 goals in 148 appearances. In fact, he missed only 10 of the Lions' first 100 Southern League matches and captained the team to a second Southern League title (1895–96) and two United League Championships (1896–97 and 1898–99). A huge favourite with the supporters, he also represented the Southern League against a London FA XI in 1897 and some felt that if he had still been playing in the First Division, perhaps with Albion, then he might well have won a full England cap.

Jasper subsequently joined another Southern League club, Bedminster, in May 1899 and later assisted both Bristol clubs, City (24 appearances, four goals) and Rovers (seven appearances), before retiring in May 1908. He remained in the Bristol area and worked as a storeroom assistant for many years before his death in 1927 at the age of 66.

JOHNNY GILES

'No one could pass a ball better than Johnny…he could coax it any length, pace and angle.'
'The fans sang "Johnny Giles walks on water"…he did at times – he was a good 'un.'

Born: 6 November 1940, Cabra, Dublin

Albion senior record:
Appearances: League 74+1, FA Cup 4, League Cup 4, Others 5
Goals: League 3, FA Cup 0, League Cup 1, Others 1
Senior debut: League, 20 August 1975 v Chelsea (h) drew 0–0
Also played for: Dublin City, Stella Maris Boys, Leprechauns FC, Home Farm, Manortown
                 United, Manchester United, Leeds United, Shamrock Rovers, Philadelphia Fury,
                 West Bromwich Albion Old Stars, Republic of Ireland (4 Schoolboy, 60 full
                 caps), All Ireland XI (1 app), UK/Ireland XI (1 app)

Also managed: Shamrock Rovers, Vancouver Whitecaps (head coach), Republic of Ireland

Although Johnny Giles spent only two seasons as Albion's player-manager in the mid-1970s, he improved the team no end. He got everyone, even defenders, playing football and the fans loved him. He put a buzz back into the club at a time when things weren't looking all that rosy.

Johnny started out with Dublin City as a 13-year-old. He then starred for Stella Maris Boys (Dublin) and also represented Leprechauns FC before establishing himself with Home Farm in 1955–56. From there he moved to Manchester United, signed as a professional by Matt Busby in November 1957. After some splendid performances in the second and third teams he made his League debut in 1959, as well as securing a place in the Republic of Ireland team before his 19th birthday.

A regular in United's first team for four years, playing alongside Bobby Charlton and Denis Law, a month after collecting an FA Cup-winners' medal Johnny asked for a transfer and subsequently joined Leeds United for £37,500 in August 1963. He helped Don Revie's team win the Second Division title in his first season at Elland Road and in 1965 saw Leeds come mighty close to completing the League and FA Cup double.

Johnny won two medals in 1968 as United triumphed in both the League and Fairs Cup Finals, and two years later he was disappointed when Leeds, seeking to win three major trophies, lost them all. In 1971 he won his second FA Cup-winners' medal, but missed out on a third a year later and he also saw the League title slip away on the final day of the season when Leeds lost to Wolves. Then, in 1973, Sunderland and AC Milan beat Leeds in the Finals of the FA Cup and the European Cup-winners' Cup.

At the start of 1974–75 Johnny, now the senior player at Elland Road, starred in Leeds's record 29-match unbeaten run, which set them on course for their second League title. But then Revie left to take over the England team. Everyone thought that Johnny would be his successor, but the Leeds board appointed Brian Clough instead. It was a controversial choice. Clough never got on with the players and was dismissed with a big pay-off after just 44 days in charge. Surprisingly Johnny still didn't get the job (it went to Jimmy Armfield) and he continued his role as a player, helping Leeds reach their first European Cup Final.

By this time Johnny was no longer an automatic fixture in the side and, after appearing in the European Cup Final defeat by Bayern Munich, he accepted an offer in June 1975 to become Albion's first-ever player-manager, while still playing for Eire. Signed for £48,000, he replaced Don Howe having scored 115 goals in 524 appearances in 12 years at Elland Road. He also equalled Joe Hulme's record of playing in five FA Cup Finals (he actually beat it if you count the 1970 replay).

Unfortunately Johnny saw Albion make a sluggish start to their first season under his supervision, but after the Irishman had signed Paddy Mulligan and Mick Martin, among others, results picked up and promotion was gained from the Second Division with a last-match victory at Oldham.

Johnny recalled: 'We only entered the promotion race around Christmas time. In fact, we didn't get into the top three until the last month of the season. In the end it was a race between us, Sunderland, Bolton and Bristol City for three promotion places. We finished well, winning four and drawing one of our last six matches. Bolton lost a couple including a 2–1 home defeat by York City; Bristol City won only one of their remaining five games, and Sunderland also registered four wins in April to take the championship ahead of Bristol City with Albion third. It was a tense last few weeks, I can tell you that, but it was enjoyable and the supporters were magnificent.'

Winning promotion capped a wonderful first season for Johnny as a League manager and it continued in 1976–77 as Albion finished seventh in the First Division, their best position for 11 years. But then, out of the blue, he resigned. Goal-ace Tony Brown admitted: 'I was shocked when he told us that he was resigning. I couldn't believe it, nor could the rest of the players. He had hinted that he might leave after we had won promotion but chose to stay on and when he eventually handed in his notice, it came as a body-blow to us all.' The announcement was made on 21 April 1977 and a month later, after a 4–0 last-match defeat at Villa Park, Johnny left and returned to Ireland to become manager of Shamrock Rovers, a position he held until 1982. He returned to The Hawthorns for a second spell as manager halfway through 1983–84 and his experience helped stave off relegation. The Baggies started the following season well and were fifth at Christmas before eventually finishing 12th. But after a miserable start to 1985–86, when nine League games were lost on the bounce, Johnny resigned again, leaving his brother-in-law and former Manchester United colleague Nobby Stiles in the hot-seat.

As manager of the Republic of Ireland international side for most of the 1970s, Johnny certainly revived the team's fortunes. They had struggled for a decade. He introduced Liam Brady to the world scene during the 1976 European Championship qualifiers and then saw his country finish only two points short of qualifying for the 1978 World Cup Finals.

Johnny, who had a loan spell with Philadelphia Fury in 1978 after winning the FAI Cup with Shamrock, captained his country nine times on his way to gaining 60 caps. After quitting as Eire's manager in March 1980, he coached Vancouver Whitecaps for three seasons, being named NASL Coach of the Year in 1982.

His football career ended when he left The Hawthorns in 1985, having been in the game for 30 years as a player, manager and coach. Returning to Ireland, he became a journalist and soccer pundit, working on RTÉ's Premier Soccer Saturday as well as covering international and European matches, particularly those involving the Republic of Ireland. Now a leading soccer analyst on the Irish radio station Newstalk 106, Johnny is respected for his forthright opinions on modern-day football.

Johnny's sons Michael (1981–83) and Chris (1993–95) also played for Shamrock Rovers, and Michael was also on Albion's books for a short time. Johnny's father, Dicky, played as a semi-professional for Bohemians in the 1920s.

TOMMY GLIDDEN

'A splendid goalscoring winger, grand captain and a sportsman through and through.'

Born: 20 July 1902, Coxlodge, Newcastle-upon-Tyne
Died: 10 July 1974, West Bromwich

Albion senior record:

Appearances: League 445, FA Cup 33, FA Charity Shield 1
League 135, FA Cup 5, FA Charity Shield 0
Senior debut: League, 25 November 1922 v Everton (a) won 1–0
Also played for: Sunderland & District Boys, Durham Boys, Sunderland (trialist), Bristol City (trialist), Castledown FC, Colliery Old Boys (Newcastle), Bolden Villa, Sunderland West End, England (Schoolboy and international trialist)

As a youngster Tommy Glidden occupied every position in the forward line and, in 1919–20, scored 25 times as leader of the Old Colliery Boys attack, following up with another 20 goals for Bolden Villa in 1920–21. At this point in his career he was being watched by a number of First Division clubs, including three from the north-east of England and, of course, Albion, whose eagle-eyed scout contacted the club. Former player and then director Dan Nurse went to watch Tommy in action. This was in March 1922 and Tommy, who had already scored 24 goals for Bolden Villa that season, impressed the Albion representative, who recommended that he should be 'given a trial at The Hawthorns.' This took place almost immediately and on 6 April 1922 Tommy joined Albion, his wages being £8 a week during the season and £6 a week in the summer.

A newspaper cutting from a page in an old scrapbook of Tommy's, which he showed me in the early 1960s when he was running his tobacconists/confectionery shop in Bull Street, West Bromwich, read: 'Glidden, who has joined West Bromwich Albion, can play at outside-right or inside-right. He will prove difficult to contain, has speed, dribbling ability and middles the ball with skill. Well built, he has already scored plenty of goals around the local circuit and I am sure he will be a success with the Albion and will certainly test a few defences.' Albion's secretary-manager Fred Everiss, in his memoirs, published in the Birmingham *Sunday Mercury* in 1949, said: 'One of his (Tommy's) best assets was his ability to centre on the run while his left foot in-swinging corner-kicks were deadly.'

In 1924, when the FA changed the rules of the game to allow goals to be scored direct from a corner-kick, cinema companies sought permission to take pictures of the new phenomena, and Albion invited representatives from Pathé News to The Hawthorns to film Tommy taking a series of right-wing flag kicks.

He was an expert and found the net nine times out of 10. Baggies goalkeeper at the time, Hubert Pearson, was amazed, saying: 'I hope there aren't too many wingers around who can match our Tommy. I don't fancy dealing with corner kicks if they come towards my goal like his.'

After occupying both wing positions during his first two seasons at The Hawthorns, Tommy eventually settled down on the right flank in 1924–25 and scored twice in 29 League appearances as the Baggies claimed the runners-up spot in the First Division behind Huddersfield Town. The following season he was on the brink of an England call-up after an impressive international trial. No one had really established himself at outside-right, but in the end Tommy missed out to Jimmy Spence of Manchester United. He never got another chance.

Tommy and Joe Carter, who would go on to become one of Albion's greatest-ever right-wing pairings, teamed up together for the first time on a regular basis during the second half of the 1924–25 campaign and, with the odd exception, remained as partners until the mid-1930s.

Albion were relegated at the end of the 1926–27 season, but Tommy vowed to help his teammates regain their top-flight status and after four seasons this was achieved when, under his captaincy, Albion not only gained promotion, but also completed the unique double by winning the FA Cup as well.

Tommy actually started the 1930–31 season at inside-right, but quickly switched back to the wing, from where he scored some vitally important goals while laying on chances galore for his colleagues. Albion's secretary-manager Fred Everiss wrote in his 1949 *Memoirs*: 'In 1930–31, under the captaincy of Glidden, I had got the whole team very promotion-minded.'

Albion certainly played some excellent football during the course of that season. Tommy, who was outstanding at times, scored a total of 16 goals, including a dramatic 55th minute shot-cum-centre winner in the Cup semi-final against Everton at Old Trafford and a crucial equaliser in the last League game of the season against Charlton Athletic, which Albion went on to win 3–2 to clinch second spot in the Division behind Everton.

He also played his part in the Cup Final win over Birmingham, having a hand in W.G. Richardson's opening goal before going up to receive the coveted trophy from HRH The Duke of Gloucester.

An ever-present for the first time in his career in 1931–32, Tommy scored his 100th Albion goal to earn a win at Arsenal on 2 January 1932 and in October 1933 he made his 400th senior appearance for the club (only six players have bettered that figure). Unfortunately a knee injury started to annoy Tommy during the early stages of the 1934–35 season, but he bravely battled on until Christmas when, after a crunching tackle by Stoke defender Charlie Scrimshaw, he was forced to undergo a cartilage operation. This kept him out of action for almost four months and by the time he returned to the team Albion had again reached the FA Cup Final. Arthur Gale had deputised for Tommy on the right-wing and had scored in each of the opening four rounds, but Albion gambled on Tommy's fitness for the Wembley showdown with Sheffield Wednesday. He just about got through the game, but his partner Joe Carter, who had also been injured, broke down early on and was a passenger for most of the second half as the Owls went on to win the trophy.

Eventually forced to retire (through injury) in May 1936 after 14 years service, during which time he averaged a goal every three and a half games (140 in 479 appearances), Tommy remained at The Hawthorns as a coach until September 1939. He subsequently became a shareholder and was voted onto the Board of Directors in 1951, retaining his position until his death from a heart attack in 1974.

TONY GODDEN

'Agile, excellent shot-stopper, brave and courageous, one of Albion's best goalkeepers.'

Born: 2 August 1955, Gillingham, Kent

Albion senior record:

Appearances: League 267, FA Cup 19, League Cup 27, Europe 12, Others 4
Goals: none
Senior debut: League, 12 March 1977 v Tottenham Hotspur (a) won 2–0
Also played for: Gillingham & District Schools, Medway & Kent Schools, Leonard Star FC, Eastcourt United, Gillingham (amateur), Ashford Town, Wolverhampton Wanderers (trial), Preston North End, Happy Valley, Hong Kong (guest), Luton Town, Walsall, Chelsea, Birmingham City, Bury, Sheffield Wednesday, Leicester City, Peterborough United, Wivenhoe Town, Colchester United, Warboys Town and Torquay United
Managed: March Town, Kings Lynn, Bury Town, Wisbech Town and Rushden & Diamonds (caretaker)

During his long and varied career in football, goalkeeper Tony Godden has been associated with more than 30 different clubs at senior, intermediate and non-League levels, serving several as a coach after retiring as a player in 1993. He appeared in well over 450 competitive games for his major Football League clubs, including 329 for Albion, 229 being made consecutively between 7 August 1977 and 31 October 1981. In that total came 180 League appearances, which beat defender Ally Robertson's then existing club record by nine…and Tony's tally remains a Baggies record to this day.

After doing exceedingly well as a schoolboy and producing some splendid performances for Ashford Town in the Kent League (saving five penalties in 1972–73 and three more the following season) Tony had an unsuccessful trial at Molineux before being signed by Albion's new player-manger Johnny Giles in August 1975. He recalled: 'I knew Albion had been watching me, but I must admit it came as a surprise when Johnny asked me if I would like to join the club. He told me that he had received good reports from within and, at 20, I was just the right age to develop my game at The Hawthorns. John Osborne was the senior 'keeper at the time, Bob Ward was in the reserves and Mark Grew was playing for the youth team. So I knew I would have to wait for my chance in the first team. That came out of the blue really. Wardy had deputised for Ossie in two matches halfway through the 1976–77 season and had done well. But when Ossie was injured again in March, I was called up for my debut in the away game at Tottenham.

'Laurie Cunningham had only just joined us and he, too, was given his first outing by the gaffer. There was a fair-sized crowd in the ground, around 28,000, and it was certainly the biggest I had played in front of; the previous best was about 1,000. I was nervous to start with but after 10 minutes or so, I was fine. Ally Rob gave me an early touch of the ball, so too did Paddy Mulligan. I made a couple of decent saves and looked on as David Cross and Bryan Robson scored at the other end to give us a 2–0 win.' Tony made six appearances that season before starting on that record-breaking run against Rangers in the Final of the Tennent-Caledonian Cup at Ibrox Park in August 1977, a game Albion won 2–0.

On reflection, during the five years before Tony arrived at The Hawthorns, Albion's goalkeepers all had their off days. Ossie had a quite a few, and so too did Peter Latchford, who went on to play for Celtic, Graham Smith, ex-Colchester, and Jim Cumbes. Tony, to a certain extent, followed the trend – remember when he was made to look stupid by Kenny Dalglish in a League game at The Hawthorns in 1978? After collecting a long ball, he rolled it along the turf, only for the Liverpool forward to come up behind him, turn, and score the easiest goal of his career.

Tony remembered afterwards: 'I thought Kenny had been hiding on the Brummie Road End. I never saw him. It was so embarrassing. It's an incident I will never forget or be allowed to forget!' That apart, for his awareness, agility, shot-stopping and bravery, Albion's skipper John Wile thought Tony 'was miles better than the rest.'

At times he was outstanding in 1977–78, as Albion reached the FA Cup semi-finals, and followed suit in 1978–79 when the Baggies qualified for the quarter-finals of the UEFA Cup, conceding only 52 goals in 61 games, 35 in the League.

In 1979–80, for the third successive season, Tony made over 50 senior appearances – no other Albion goalkeeper has done that – and at the same time he became something of an expert at saving penalties. His stop in a League Cup tie at Everton was brilliant. His record-breaking run of appearances came to an end nine weeks into the 1981–82 season following a 3–3 draw at Birmingham, a game Albion should have won with Cyrille Regis's hat-trick. A couple of slip-ups by Tony enabled Blues to force a 3–3 draw.

Languishing in the reserves for the next five months, Tony was recalled by manager Ronnie Allen for a vital relegation battle at Molineux on May Day 1982. He certainly earned his money that afternoon, saving an early Wayne Clarke penalty and helping Albion to a 2–1 win, while at the same time virtually condemning Wolves to the Second Division.

Tony shared the goalkeeping duties with Mark Grew and Paul Barron in 1982–83, also having a loan spell with Luton Town. The following season he was mainly in the reserves and assisted Walsall as a loanee, while in 1984–85 he was back in favour, missing only one League game (a 2–0 defeat at Manchester United) before having to battle for a first-team place again in 1985–86 with new signings Paul Bradshaw and then Stuart Naylor.

After a successful loan period with Chelsea, and a well-deserved testimonial, Tony, who by now had become rather disillusioned, was transferred to the London club for £40,000 in August 1986, having made his last Albion appearance on the same ground where he had made his debut nine years earlier, White Hart Lane, only this time the Baggies crashed to a 5–0 defeat. He had also played in 72 reserve matches for the Baggies, gaining a Central League championship-winners' medal in 1983.

Tony remained at Stamford Bridge for a year, the highlight of his time there being two penalty saves in front of the Stretford End against Manchester United in a 1–0 win.

In 1987, Tony returned to the Midlands to sign for Birmingham City and from 1988 onwards he started his travels around the country, once scoring a goal from a drop-kick for Peterborough reserves against Northampton reserves in 1989–90. He eventually discarded his gloves (as an active player) in the summer of 1993 when he became manager of non-League March Town.

Now a part-time goalkeeping coach, Tony lives in Whittersley, Peterborough.

DON GOODMAN

'Fast and lively, full of energy, a goalscorer of the highest order.'

Born: 9 May 1966, Leeds

Albion senior record:

Appearances: League 140+18, FA Cup 7, League Cup 11, Others 5
Goals: League 60, FA Cup 1, League Cup 1, Others 1
Senior debut: League, 28 March 1987 v Oldham Athletic (a) lost 2–1
Also played for: Castilla FC, Collingham FC (Leeds), Sunderland, Wolverhampton Wanderers, San Frecce Antlers (Hiroshima, Japan), Barnsley, Motherwell, Walsall, Exeter City, Doncaster Rovers, Stafford Rangers

Don Goodman retired in May 2004, having served with 10 major clubs, one of them in Japan, in a 20-year professional career. A fine opportunist striker, in all he netted close on 200 goals in 695 competitive matches during a wonderful career, with 160 of his goals coming in 576 League games. He played the majority of his football in England, although surprisingly never in the top flight, although he did have decent spells in the top divisions of both Scotland and Japan.

Don was nine when he started playing Sunday League football for a team called Hunslet Carr. At the age of 11 he joined Whincover Boys and went on to assist Castilla FC and Collingham before joining Bradford City as a professional in August 1984. In his debut season he helped the Bantams win the Division Three championship. However, this triumph was tainted by the Valley Parade fire disaster which occurred on the final day, which saw his ex-girlfriend killed and the former Albion inside-forward from 1951–52, Andy McCall, badly burned.

Don spent almost three seasons with the Bantams, during which time he netted 20 times in 81 appearances. In March 1987, Albion boss Ron Saunders agreed a fee of £50,000 to bring him to The Hawthorns and he went on to give the Baggies supporters plenty to cheer about, registering his highest goal-tally at club level – 63 in 181 outings – spread over four-and-a-half years, having his best scoring campaign in 1989–90 when he notched 21 in the League

including a hat-trick in a 7–0 home win over Barnsley. Unfortunately, his goals haul of eight in the League in 1990–91 could not prevent Albion from slipping into the third tier for the first time in their history.

Don recalled: 'We were all gutted when it was confirmed we hadn't managed to avoid the drop. We had to win our last game against Bristol Rovers at Twerton Park, but only scrambled a 1–1 draw and that was that. Although we scored probably enough goals, we simply drew far too many matches, 18 in all. Seven came in the last eight games of the season, including three at home, one of which was against Port Vale when we missed two penalties. A win in any of those games would have saved us. That's football – you have to take the good with the bad.'

Don played in only 11 Third Division matches for Albion before leaving The Hawthorns in December 1991, signed by Sunderland for £900,000. He remained at Roker Park for three years and did reasonably well, but agonizingly he missed the 1992 FA Cup Final with Liverpool because he had been Cup tied playing for Albion in the first round against Marlow.

'That was another huge disappointment for me,' said Don. 'Every footballer dreams of playing at Wembley, certainly in a Cup Final. I just sat on the sidelines, as miserable as sin and feeling sorry for myself as I watched Liverpool win 2–0. If the truth be known, I never really got over that afternoon...it was another case of what might have been, especially if Sunderland had come in for me a month or so earlier.'

From Sunderland Don moved back to the Black Country to sign for Albion's arch-rivals Wolverhampton Wanderers in December 1994 for £1.1 million – and his hopes of top League football were almost realised when Wolves reached the play-offs twice in the space of three seasons. But again joy turned into sadness for Don when each time defeat was suffered at the semi-final stage.

At Molineux for three-and-a-half years, top scoring in 1995–96 when playing alongside another ex-Albion man, Steve Bull, Don's time there was hampered by a spate of injuries, most notably a fractured skull, and in 1997–98, after his excellent winning goal against Leeds United had taken Wolves into the FA Cup semi-finals for the first time in 17 years, he once more went home disappointed when Arsenal ended Wolves' chances of reaching their first Final since 1960 with a 1–0 victory at Villa Park.

Don was subsequently given a free transfer in May 1998 as part of a player clear-out by Wolves manager Mark McGhee, at which point the likeable striker made the bold choice to go and play his football in the Far East, signing for the Japanese club San Frecce Antlers of Hiroshima. This proved to be a short-term venture, however, and he was quickly back in England, signed on loan by Barnsley before he decided to try his luck in Scotland with Motherwell, with whom he stayed until March 2001 when he was given a free transfer.

Returning once more to the West Midlands, Don joined Walsall on a free transfer but by now, at his own admission, he was not fully match fit and was struggling to score goals, although he did manage to crack home a vital equaliser in the Play-off Final against Reading at Cardiff's Millennium Stadium, which Walsall went on to win, thereby securing promotion back to the Second Division.

In August 2002 Don – now something of a globetrotter – moved to south Devon, joining Exeter City, again on a free transfer. He failed to make much of an impact with the Grecians and left St James' Park early in the New Year, going on loan to the Conference side Doncaster Rovers, whom he helped regain their Football League status before winding down his playing career with a stint at Stafford Rangers.

In December 2003, when sidelined with a tedious knee injury, Don declared that he would be retiring at the end of the season, which he did. At the start of 2004–05 he was appointed fitness coach by Kidderminster Harriers, a position he held only briefly.

Don is now a regular co-commentator for Sky Sports or BBC Radio 5 Live, or indeed, as a guest on the phone-in show *You're On Sky Sports* and occasionally *Central Soccer Night*, a local midweek show in the Midlands ITV region.

HOWARD GREGORY

'A brisk, penetrative and dangerous outside-left.'

Born:	6 April 1893, Aston Manor, Birmingham
Died:	15 August 1954, Handsworth, Birmingham

Albion senior record:

Appearances:	League 162, FA Cup 13, FA Charity Shield 1, Others 5
Goals:	League 39, FA Cup 3, FA Charity Shield 0, Others 3
Senior debut:	League, 22 April 1912 v Everton (a) lost 3–0
Also played for:	Aston Manor, Birchfield Trinity

Known as the 'Express Man' and 'Greg', Albion's speedy red-haired outside-left Howard Gregory was always likely to produce something special. Often he would hold his position on the touchline, but out of the blue, when it was least expected, he would dart into the penalty area and get in a shot on target, scoring some splendid goals.

One of his finest performances in an Albion shirt came in the 7–0 thumping of Arsenal at The Hawthorns in October 1922. He gave the Gunners full-back Frank Bradshaw a torrid time with his speed, directness and skill. The following week, the editor of *The Albion News* wrote in the programme: 'Although caught offside several times early on, Gregory careered away down the left whenever possible. Arsenal's defenders were at sixes and sevens as he sent over scores of dangerous crosses. And the longer the game went on, the more menacing Gregory became. Albion netted five goals in the space of 13 minutes late on and Gregory had a hand in four of them, bagging number six himself when he converted Fred Morris's pass from eight yards.' Howard and Morris teamed up wonderfully well together on Albion's left-wing. In 1919–20, when the First Division championship was won, they were outstanding, netting 49 of the team's 104 League goals between them.

Born deep in Aston Villa territory, Howard was signed by Albion as an 18-year-old in May 1911, having spent three years playing for his local junior club, Aston Manor, for whom he scored over 50 goals.

He took quite a while to settle in at The Hawthorns. But under the watchful eye of trainer Bill Barber and encouraged by senior players like Jesse Pennington, Joe Smith, Sid Bowser and Bobby McNeal, he soon became one of the lads. After playing well for the second team in his first season in the Birmingham & District League, which Albion won, Howard was handed his senior debut at inside-right against Everton at Goodison Park at a time when secretary-manager Fred Everiss was using every reserve-team player available ahead of Albion's FA Cup Final replay with Barnsley.

Howard played in two more League games at the end of that season and in 1912–13 he added a further 15 to his tally, scoring four goals, including a real beauty in the 2–2 home draw with Aston Villa and a cracker in the 2–0 home win over Notts County. Still basically a reserve to Ben Shearman, Howard was called up for first-team duty just five times in 1913–14 and on seven occasions the following season when Louis Bookman was also in contention for a place on the left wing.

Enlisted in the Army, Howard then went off to war, serving with the 16th Royal Warwickshire Regiment. Playing football whenever he could, but only occasionally for Albion, he was a key member of the Baggies team that won the Midland Victory League title in April 1919, scoring three vital goals in the two games against Aston Villa.

Chosen on Albion's left-wing for the resumption of League football in August 1919, Howard quickly made his mark, scoring in the 3–1 opening game win over Oldham Athletic. He became one of the key players after that, producing some splendid displays, and at one point was earmarked as a possible England candidate. Indeed, he was in line to take part in an international trial, but a niggling injury, suffered at Old Trafford, prevented him from playing.

Retaining his place in Albion's front line, Howard had a moderate 1920–21 season as Albion struggled at times in the League. In fact, he badly strained his left knee in the home game with Preston in late March and missed eight matches. He returned for the last game of the campaign at Bradford but tweaked his knee again and as a result missed the start of the new season, eventually returning in mid-September.

With new signing Jack Crisp, ex-Leicester Fosse, now pressing hard for a place on Albion's left-flank, Howard upped his game and, during the first half of the 1922–23 season, he was outstanding, giving some of the game's best defenders a testing time with his pace, skill and endeavour. The Liverpool and England right-back Eph Longworth wrote in his column in the club's programme: 'I've never felt so uncomfortable as I did in trying to contain the Albion winger.'

After a 5–1 win over Tottenham, one newspaper reporter described Howard's display as one of 'dash, freshness and vivacity', adding 'He was into his stride so quickly that his opponent could hardly keep up with him. He was irresistible at times.'

Unfortunately, in mid-March 1923, Howard suffered another leg injury at Chelsea. This time he was out of action for six months, returning in November 1923. Lacking his usual zest and enthusiasm, which had been his forté in previous years, he struggled to produce a really telling performance, but when he did he was terrific, completely bamboozling the Notts County defence when Albion won 5–0 at The Hawthorns in April 1924 and giving Sunderland's full-back Jim Oakley a testing time soon afterwards.

Following the signing of Jack Byers from Blackburn Rovers in January 1924, Howard's position on Albion's left-wing came under pressure. He was not as fit as he wanted to be and as a result lost his place, only playing in two League games in 1924–25. He remained at The Hawthorns for one more season, appearing in a handful of second-team matches, before announcing his retirement in May 1926 at the age of 33, having scored 45 goals in his 181 first-class games for the club.

A year after quitting football, Howard became landlord of the Woodman Inn next door to The Hawthorns, a position he held until 1932. He remained in the licensed trade for the next 21 years, continuing to attend home matches at The Hawthorns whenever possible. A guest at both of Albion's 1931 and 1954 FA Cup celebration dinners, he became ill shortly after attending the latter function and died in August 1954, aged 61.

*Howard's brother played for QPR and Yeovil & Peters in the 1920s.

FRANK GRIFFIN

'A naturally gifted player with pace and skill'.
'A joy to see, fleet and nimble-footed, a natural winger.'

Born:	28 March 1928, Pendlebury near Swinton
Died:	4 June 2007, Shrewsbury

Albion senior record:

Appearances:	League 240, FA Cup 34, FA Charity Shield 1
Goals:	League 47, FA Cup 5, FA Charity Shield 0
Senior debut:	League, 28 April 1951 v Sunderland (a) drew 1–1
Also played for:	St Augustine's Youth Club, Newton Heath, Hull City (trial), Bolton Wanderers, Eccles Town, Shrewsbury Town, Northampton Town, Wellington Town and G.K.N. Sankeys (Wellington).
Managed:	Worthen United

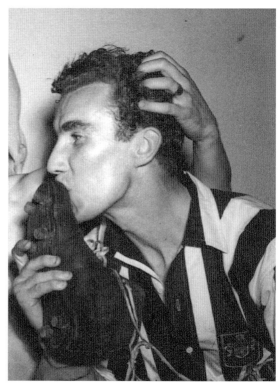

It is a wonder that fleet and nimble-footed right-winger Frank Griffin ever entered the soccer arena, for he was born in Rugby League territory near Swinton on the outskirts of Manchester. In fact, most of his family members were rugby supporters, but although Frank played the oval ball game at Pendlebury Central School, he didn't really like the sport and was often seen outside school hours, happily having a kick-about with his pals with a leather case ball.

Most weekends he would go along with his father or one of his uncles to watch either Bolton Wanderers or one of the two Manchester clubs, City or United, play at home. He never wanted to go and watch a Rugby League game. 'I hated it,' admitted Frank. From the age of eight Frank was into football and at that age he knew what the game was all about. He talked a lot about Ray Westwood, the Bolton centre-forward and Manchester City's outside-left Eric Brook, stating 'I would like to play like Brook when I'm older.'

Frank turned out regularly for St Augustine's Youth Club in Manchester and occasionally for Newton Heath before signing amateur forms for his favourite team, Bolton Wanderers, at the age of 16. Working his way through the A team at Burnden Park, he eventually gained a place in the reserve side, only to break his right ankle during a game at Villa Park. This set him back considerably and it was almost six months before he regained full fitness. His confidence had waned as well and it was hard working his way back once more via the A team. He never quite reached his goal and in May 1944 went back to play for St Augustine's while also signing for Eccles Town.

Spotted by Hull City's scout Harry Chapman, nephew of the great Herbert Chapman, early in season 1944–45, Frank was given a trial at Boothferry Park. He did well, but after serious consideration turned down the offer to sign professional for the Tigers, saying it was 'too far from home.' He ended that season's campaign on a high, helping St Augustine's complete the local League and Cup double, the first honours the club had ever won.

A few years later Harry Chapman came chasing Frank again – this time as manager of Shrewsbury Town. After lengthy talks, Frank finally agreed to sign for the Gay Meadow club, just in time to play for them in their first-ever game in the Football League away at Scunthorpe United on 19 August 1950.

After spending his first season at Gay Meadow mainly in the reserves, being nurtured along by the former Derby County and England player Sammy Crooks, Frank signed as a full-time professional in March 1951 and never looked back. Two years later, in April 1951, he joined Albion for £9,000, signed to replace Billy Elliott on the right wing. 'What a thrill that was. I couldn't believe my luck,' said Frank. 'I was disappointed when I left Bolton, but to join a club like Albion was something special. I knew some of the players at The Hawthorns, having come up against them in Birmingham League games with Shrewsbury. Joe Kennedy, Ray Barlow, Jimmy Sanders and Len Millard were the first who welcomed me to the club and after that everyone rallied round and gave me wonderful support. I remained a close pal of Joe's all the time we were at the club.'

Frank made his First Division debut at Sunderland on the last day of the 1950–51 season and over the next eight years or so remained as Albion's regular outside-right, scoring and making important goals. In 1953–54, he netted seven times in 44 outings when the Baggies came so very close to completing the double. Frank, in fact, had the pleasure, and delight, of scoring the dramatic late winning goal in the FA Cup Final against Preston North End. 'That was something out of this world,' he recalled. 'I was hugging the touchline when Joe (Kennedy) knocked the ball up to Paddy Ryan. He slipped a pass forward and I raced on to slide the ball under the diving body of goalkeeper Thompson. I was swamped by my teammates and even lost my breath. Some of the players had been given oxygen at half-time; I was so excited on the day that I forgot, I could have done with some there and then.'

Albion were on course for a second Cup Final appearance three years later. They reached the semi-finals in style but after twice leading against Aston Villa at Molineux, they were pegged back and then lost the replay at St Andrew's. Frank was annoyed to lose to Villa. 'Ronnie Allen was put out of the game early on by an old pal of ours, Jimmy Dugdale. I know everyone thought it was an accident, but in truth, Jimmy knew what he was doing. We should have won. Derek Kevan struck both posts with one shot and Stan Lynn twice cleared off the line. Still, you can't win 'em all.'

Frank maintained his form into the next season and was playing so well that he was in line for a place in the England team. Manager Walter Winterbottom had contacted Baggies boss Vic Buckingham, informing him that Frank was 'in his plans' for the home international against Scotland in Glasgow and saying he could well be included in the squad for the 1958 World Cup Finals in Sweden.

But then, during a fifth-round FA Cup replay against Sheffield United at The Hawthorns on a cold February evening, Frank fractured his right leg when tackled by Blades defender Joe Shaw. His career was virtually ended there and then. It was a bitter blow for Frank, and although he regained his fitness, he only played three more times for Albion before moving to Northampton Town for £1,500 in June 1959. Later on he assisted Wellington Town and GKN Sankeys before becoming manager of Worthen United in 1962. Four years later he quit football and resided in Shrewsbury until his death on 4 June 2007.

ASA HARTFORD

'Busy little player, always involved, poised and confident – goals were always "on" when he was around.'

Born:	24 October 1950, Clydebank, Scotland

Albion senior record:

Appearances:	League 206+9, FA Cup 19, League Cup 15, Europe 6, Others 20
Goals:	League 18, FA Cup 2, League Cup 2, Europe 3, Others 1
Senior debut:	League, 10 February 1968 v Sheffield United (a) drew 1–1
Also played for:	Drumchapel Amateurs, Manchester City (2 spells), Everton, Nottingham Forest, Fort Lauderdale Sun, Wolverhampton Wanderers (trial), Norwich City, Bolton Wanderers, Stockport County (player-manager), Oldham Athletic, Shrewsbury Town (player-coach), Boston United, Scotland (50 full, 1 Under-21, 5 Under-23 and 3 Youth caps)
Managed:	Shrewsbury Town

In an interview with Peter Keeling in June 2008, Asa Hartford revealed that in November 1971, at the age of 21, he honestly thought his football days were over when he was diagnosed with a hole-in-the-heart problem just before he was to leave West Bromwich Albion for Leeds United in a £170,000 transfer deal. Thankfully, the brilliant midfielder overcame that medical crisis and went on to play 50 times for Scotland as well as amassing 744 League appearances for nine different English clubs.

Asa recalled 'After getting over the shock of knowing I had a heart problem, I vowed to enjoy life as a footballer as best I could. And believe you me I did. I let nothing quench my thirst for the game, no matter what, and I'm still enjoying my football just as much now as I did when I first started playing as a lad at school.

'Obviously when my transfer to Leeds fell through on medical grounds because of the background of the heart problem, from which the cardiologist subsequently gave me my all clear, I had dreamed of being part of a midfield trio of Bremner, Giles and Hartford. At the time Leeds, under Don Revie, were one of the finest teams in Europe and it would have been a great thrill to play for them. But it was not to be.

'However, as time passed by, I was fortunate enough to play alongside many more truly wonderful players, namely Len Cantello and Bobby Hope at the Albion, Manchester City's Colin Bell and Gary Owen, Roy Keane of Nottingham Forest and Lou Macari, Archie Gemmill, Graeme Souness and Don Masson at international level with Scotland. And I am sure that if these were all playing today their names would be highlighted every week! They were good.'

During his nomadic career Asa also played under several managers and he says that Jimmy Hagan, his boss at The Hawthorns when he joined Albion, was a real authoritarian. 'He knew the game and all its nuances inside out. He was one of the best.'

Asa also had tremendous regard for Brian Clough, saying: 'He was simply brilliant, especially in the area which is best to rate a manager's ability – in the dressing room at half-time when you were losing 1–0. Every dot and comma of what was going wrong, what we should do to correct it and regain the upper hand, was dealt with. In my opinion it was one of the tragedies of English football that he never managed England.'

There was also Tony Book at Manchester City and Gordon Lee at Everton and Ken Brown at Norwich. 'I got on with them all,' said Asa. 'They were good managers who loved their football and certainly knew how to treat a player.'

A pupil at Fairfly Primary and Clydebank High Schools, Asa represented Dunbartonshire Boys and played for Drumchapel Amateurs before joining Albion as a 15-year-old apprentice in April 1966, turning professional two years later on his 17th birthday. He made his League debut against Sheffield United at Bramall Lane in February 1968, the first of 275 appearances he made for the Baggies, for whom he also scored 26 goals.

Injuries, illness and international call-ups apart, Asa remained a regular in the first team from September 1968 onwards. He linked up superbly in midfield with Bobby Hope and helped the Baggies reach the quarter-finals of the European Cup-winners' Cup in 1969 and the Final of the League Cup Final a year later.

Asa recalled: 'The League Cup Final against my future club Manchester City was played on one of the worst surfaces I have ever seen. The Wembley pitch was like a quagmire – the annual Horse of the Year Show had been staged there only a few weeks before. We took an early lead and should have sewn the game up, but in the end we lost 2–1 after extra-time. I was disappointed but over the next few years I returned to that stadium many times and enjoyed many happy moments.'

Three years after his proposed move to Elland Road, Asa left The Hawthorns, joining Manchester City for £225,000 in August 1974. He did very well at Maine Road, collecting a League Cup-winners' medal in 1976 before transferring to Nottingham Forest for £450,000 in July 1979. He only managed three games under Brian Clough and before August had ended he was sold to Everton for £500,000. He remained at Goodison Park until May 1984, during which time the Merseysiders reached the League Cup semi-final and twice came close to relegation. After a spell in the NASL with Fort Lauderdale (May–August 1984), Asa returned to England and actually had a trial with Wolves before to moving east to sign for Norwich City. He stayed at Carrow Road for a season, helping the Canaries win the League Cup, and it was his second-half shot which deflected off Gordon Chisholm and past Sunderland 'keeper Chris Turner to decide a tight contest (1–0).

A coaching appointment in Norway followed and, in July 1985, Asa signed for Bolton Wanderers, with whom he collected a Freight Rover Trophy runners'-up medal. Two years later he became player-manager of Stockport County, played briefly for Oldham Athletic in 1989 and in that same year took over as coach at Shrewsbury, stepping up to become manager at Gay Meadow in July 1990, only to be sacked after six months in charge. A spell as player-coach at Boston United followed and after that Asa joined ex-international teammates Kenny Dalglish at Blackburn Rovers and Joe Jordan and Lou Macari at Stoke City in various coaching/managerial roles before taking on an assistant managerial position at Manchester City with Alan Ball in 1995. He stayed at Maine Road as reserve-team coach until May 2005, coached at Blackpool from December 2005 to May 2006 and in June 2007 he was appointed assistant manager of Macclesfield Town. Both he and boss Ian Brightwell were sacked in February 2008. Out of the game for barely two months, Asa returned in April 2008 as coach of the junior and reserves teams at Accrington Stanley.

He was christened Asa after the famous American singing star, Al (Asa) Jolson.

NORMAN HEATH

'Although below average height, he could deal capably and often brilliantly with all manner of shots.'

Born:	31 January 1924, Wolverhampton
Died:	12 November 1983, Great Barr, Birmingham

Albion senior record:

Appearances:	League 121, FA Cup 13, Wartime 35
Goals:	None
Senior debut:	Wartime League (N), 25 September 1943 v Wolverhampton Wanderers (h) won 4–1
	League, 13 December 1947 v Sheffield Wednesday (a) won 2–1
Also played for:	Wolverhampton Boys, Henry Meadows FC (Wolverhampton), Combined Services XI, Army
Managed:	Great Barr Gunners

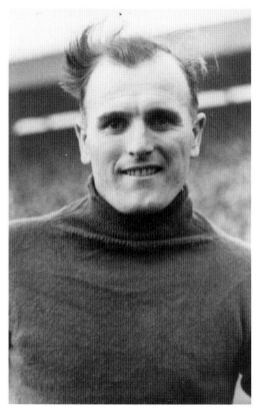

Norman Heath joined Albion as an 18-year-old amateur goalkeeper in May 1942 after being spotted doing well in Wolverhampton Works football. He turned professional 18 months later and gained a place in the Baggies first team during the 1943–44 season when he took over from Jimmy Adams. He made his first debut in the Regional League (North) Black Country derby encounter against arch-rivals Wolves and in all appeared in 29 games that season, helping Albion win the two-legged Midland Wartime Cup Final against Nottingham Forest.

In November of that same year Norman, now aged 20, was recruited into the Army. Serving initially with the King's Shropshire Light Infantry, based at Llandrindod Wells, he was later transferred overseas and served in India, where at Poona he was posted to the 2nd Leicestershire Regiment, rising to the rank of Company Quartermaster Sergeant. He lined up in his platoon and brigade sides and also represented the company and his battalion, as well as playing for the Combined Services XI on several occasions, often lining up against quality internationals.

Owing to his Army commitments, Norman played in only six first-team games for Albion in 1944–45 and never got a game in seasons 1945–46 and 1946–47. Thankfully, after being demobbed from the Army in the autumn of 1947, he returned to full training with Albion only to find three other 'keepers all competing for a place in the first team at The Hawthorns – new signing Jimmy Sanders (from Charlton Athletic), Tom Grimley and Irishman John Tighe.

Biding his time in the reserves, Norman finally gained a place in Albion's senior side halfway through the 1947–48 campaign, and what a fine start he made, saving a penalty on his League debut in a hard-earned 2–1 away win over Sheffield Wednesday. He went on to play in 12 more Second Division games that season but, annoyingly for him, in 1948–49, when Albion gained promotion to the top flight, and again in 1949–50, he had to play second fiddle to the ever-present Sanders.

In fact, Norman starred in well over 100 Central League games before being recalled for a 10-match spell in the first XI halfway through 1950–51. He then proceeded to make 27 appearances the following season, establishing himself as first-choice 'keeper in the process, and he duly held the number one position right through until that ill fated evening on Wearside in March 1954 when severe body injuries cruelly ended his career.

At the time of Norman's mishap, Albion were bang on course to complete the coveted League and Cup double. They were sitting on top of the First Division table, ahead of neighbours Wolves, and had already reached the Final of the FA Cup. But then, during a rearranged League game at Sunderland, Norman suffered serious injuries to his neck, spine and right leg after colliding with home centre-forward Ted Purdon. Rushed to hospital, he was operated on immediately and was later informed by two specialised doctors that he had fractured his neck and was partly paralysed down his back. Worse was to follow. He was told he might never play again.

The news hit the Albion 'keeper hard. However, after several weeks in hospital Norman, with a bright badge of courage on his face, thought otherwise. Discharged and walking with two sticks, with his wife at his side, he said to *News Chronicle* reporter Neil Joseph: 'I will play again the first day I can…if not this season, then next. Soccer's a great game. It's been part of my life ever since I left school and although the risk might be high, I believe I will recover and pull on that green jersey again.'

Sadly that never happened and Norman officially retired in May 1955. For the remainder of his life he was forced to wear a thick collar (to support his neck) and also had callipers affixed to one foot to keep it parallel to the ground. He thus limped rather badly.

Stan Rickaby, Albion's right-back from 1950 up until Norman was injured, thought he was one of the best 'keepers in the country, saying: 'He was a goalkeeper of the highest calibre. Never showy or particularly spectacular, he was simply a class performer who made difficult things look easy. We were permanencies together for several seasons – I think we played at least 100 games in the same team – yet within four days we both became casualties. I was injured in the Cup semi-final win over Port Vale and then Norman was very badly hurt at Sunderland. I was told he could even have died. We were all shocked, I can tell you that. As a result Norman and myself missed the Cup Final against Preston at Wembley – another body-blow to both of us. We each received a winners' medal, but it wasn't the same as actually playing. And Norman was as sick as a parrot, having produced some brilliant displays in the previous rounds. I carried on playing for a few more years, but poor old Norman never regained any sort of fitness and spent the rest of his life practically going around in a wheelchair. It was a tragic end for a very fine goalkeeper.'

In an all too brief career with Albion, Norman certainly produced some outstanding performances, displaying his best form between December 1951 and March 1954 when he missed only eight League games out of a possible 96. He was well-built, extremely agile, a good handler of high balls, courageous and possessed a strong right foot.

He continued to attend various Albion home matches as well as club functions and in April 1956 a testimonial match was staged at The Hawthorns when a star-studded International XI drew 5–5 with the Baggies in front of a crowd of almost 55,500. Norman, who chose to manage a local junior side, Great Barr Gunners, for two seasons in the early 1970s, was only 59 years old when he died in 1983.

BOBBY HOPE

'At his zenith nobody bettered Bobby at passing the ball, either in thought or accuracy.'

Born: 28 September 1943, Bridge of Allan, Stirlingshire

Albion senior record:

Appearances:	League 331+5, FA Cup 19, League Cup 29, Europe 9, Others 10
Goals:	League 31, FA Cup 0, League Cup 7, Europe 1, Other 1
Senior debut:	League, 30 April 1960 v Arsenal (h) won 1–0
Also played for:	Dunbartonshire West Schools, Drumchapel Amateurs, Sunderland (trial), Birmingham City, Philadelphia Fury, Dallas Tornados, Bromsgrove Rovers, West Bromwich Albion Old Stars, Scotland (three Schoolboy, 1 Under-23, 2 full caps and 4 unofficial caps)
Managed:	Burton Albion, Bromsgrove Rovers

Throughout the second half of the 1960s the Albion team centred around one man – Scottish-born midfielder Bobby Hope. Liverpool's manager Bill Shankly once said of him: 'Stop Bobby Hope and you stop Albion.' Over a period of time Albion certainly lost plenty of games, some of them vital, when Bobby was not playing.

After an impressive debut as a 17-year-old in April 1960, Bobby had established himself within a couple of seasons and scored his first goal in Ronnie Allen's final appearance for Albion in a 3–2 win over Bolton Wanderers in February 1961. He missed five League matches in 1964–65, four of them lost, and was absent from Jeff Astle's debut game at Leicester in September 1964.

The following season he also sat out five League games (only one won). He missed the first leg of the 1966 League Cup Final at West Ham which Albion lost 2–1, but was back for the return leg, which was won 4–1. 'That first-half display against the Hammers at The Hawthorns was one of the best, if not the best, I was ever involved in as an Albion player,' said Bobby. 'Going into the game I think West Ham were slight favourites, probably because of their three England boys, Bobby Moore, Geoff Hurst and Martin Peters, but we had the Cup won by the break after scoring four times in the first 35 minutes.'

In November 1966, Bobby had the pleasure of scoring Albion's first-ever goal in a major European competition, in the 1–1 draw against DOS Utrecht in an Inter-Cities Fairs Cup match in

Holland. 'That was a cold night,' shrugged Bobby. 'I was freezing all through the game. We won the second leg 5–2 but then came up against a very good Italian team, Bologna, who beat us 6–1 on aggregate.'

In March 1968, Bobby pulled out of the home League encounter with Everton with a slight injury. Albion were hammered 6–2, but he was back for the FA Cup Final two months later and played his part in a 1–0 victory.

Bobby remembered: 'Everton believed they had the upper hand over us following that big win at The Hawthorns. But they hadn't really. Our manager Alan Ashman told us to close down Alan Ball, Colin Harvey and Howard Kendall, their three midfielders, as quickly as possible and stop them from playing. We achieved that to a certain degree, although they did create a few chances, mainly from attacks down the wings. I was allowed enough space to get things moving for us and in the end I think we deserved our victory.'

The following season Albion reached the quarter-finals of the European Cup-winners' Cup and the semi-finals of the FA Cup, only to lose them both by a single goal. Bobby recalled: 'The first leg of the Cup-winners' Cup game, against the Scottish side Dunfermline Athletic, was tough. We did okay and managed a goalless draw, but I suffered a knee injury and missed the home leg, which took place on a bitterly cold night. Virtually all of our players wore two shirts, gloves and even a pair of ladies' tights. We dictated most of the game but somehow they managed to grab a goal and we were out. It was disappointing.

'Soon afterwards, Leicester City won 1–0 in the FA Cup semi-final at Hillsborough, another game we should have won. I had missed the League game at Burnley two weeks earlier, but played in the next match against Nottingham Forest to prove my fitness. I thought we did enough to win at Hillsborough, but a few minutes from the end Allan Clarke somehow squeezed a low shot past Ossie, our goalkeeper, and we were out: no return trip to Wembley this time round.'

Bobby had, by now, played once for Scotland at Under-23 level (against Wales), twice for the senior side (v Holland, injured and off after just 19 minutes, and Denmark) and eight times on an unofficial 1967 tour (with Doug Fraser and Eddie Colquhoun) to Israel, Hong Kong, Australia, New Zealand and Canada, scoring against the latter. In March 1970 he was back at the Empire Stadium, this time for Albion's League Cup Final clash with Manchester City. The stadium had been the venue for the annual Horse of the Year Show only a few weeks before, and two inches of snow had covered the grass in the meantime. This thawed, leaving a cloggy, muddy surface. 'It was useless…you couldn't play decent football on it at all,' said Bobby, while City's boss Joe Mercer described it as 'a pig of a pitch.'

'Jeff Astle headed us in front very early on and we should have sealed victory. But a lack of concentration allowed City to equalise and the game went into extra-time. A lot of us started to tire and in the end we lost to a scrambled goal from a corner-kick. Another disappointing and frustrating game of football for me, and indeed for the Albion,' said Bobby.

An avid Rangers supporter, Bobby was signed by Albion as an amateur in August 1959, soon after starring for Scotland Schoolboys at Wembley. He turned professional in September 1960 and went on to score 42 goals in 403 first-class appearances for the club before transferring to newly-promoted Birmingham City for the unusual fee of £66,666 in May 1972. He spent four years at St Andrew's, during which time he went over to America to play for Philadelphia Atoms and Dallas Tornados, returning to England to sign for Sheffield Wednesday in September 1976. After two more spells with Dallas Tornados (in 1977 and 1978) Bobby became player-coach of Bromsgrove Rovers, taking over as manager in May 1983. He then bossed Burton Albion for a few months in 1988 before returning to Bromsgrove, where he remained in charge until July 1998 when he was appointed Youth Development Officer at The Hawthorns, later taking over as chief scout.

EZRA HORTON

'He wasn't called "Ironsides" for nothing – this guy was tough, really tough.'

Born:	20 August 1861, West Bromwich
Died:	12 July 1939, West Bromwich

Albion senior record:

Appearances:	League 47, FA Cup 36
Goals:	League 0, FA Cup 1
Senior debut:	FA Cup, 10 November 1883 v Wednesbury Town (h) lost 2–0
Also played for:	George Salter Works, West Bromwich FC, Aston Villa (guest)

Ezra Horton, nicknamed 'Ironsides' because of his hefty, solid frame, was, wrote a journalist in the local *Free Press* 'A very sporting player, a largely defensive right-half, with wonderful positional sense, he was good at heading, strong in kicking and fearsome in the tackle.' One of the early pioneers of the club, Ezra joined Albion in August 1882 and three years later was among those who signed a professional contract, agreeing a weekly wage of five shillings a week, rising to 7s 6d a week after 12 months. He played in several local Cup competitions and friendly matches during his initial season, and celebrated by helping Albion win their first trophy, the Staffordshire Cup, beating Stoke 3–2 in the Final.

In November 1883, Albion contested their first-ever FA Cup tie, entertaining Wednesbury Town at the Four Acres ground on a freezing winter's afternoon. Unfortunately, neither Ezra nor his colleagues played well and they lost 2–0, but better things were around the corner for both player and team. In 1885–86 Albion reached the first of three successive FA Cup Finals, only to lose 2–0 in a replay to the holders Blackburn Rovers. A journalist covering the drawn game for *The Sports and Pastimes* wrote: 'Arthur, the Rovers' goalkeeper, assisted by his backs, proved proof against all the onslaughts of Bayliss, Green and Horton,' adding, 'Horton then hit the leather into the goalkeeper's face with long shot.'

In the replay, Ezra was again in the thick of the action, the reporter for the *Blackburn Standard* saying Horton 'often executed a capital bit of dodging which was much admired,' and that the Albion half-back 'was always striving to equalise, twice causing Arthur to fist the ball away.' Ezra, obviously disappointed with the result, vowed to win the Cup one day, but before Albion did finally lift the coveted trophy they suffered another Final defeat, this time against their arch-rivals Aston Villa, in 1887.

Albion were confident of beating Villa, having knocked out the favourites Preston North End in the semi-final when Ezra produced a sterling performance, but after dictating play for long periods of the first half, Albion conceded a dubious goal soon after the resumption when 'keeper Roberts hesitated, believing the scorer, Hodgetts, was offside, and then let in a second right at the end. After the game a somewhat distraught Ezra, who was never afraid to speak his mind, talked to a reporter from the *Birmingham Daily Times* about Albion's defeat. He said bluntly: 'It was mainly owing to the bad play of the forwards. They were, with the exception of Bayliss and Green, all at sea. I never saw Woodhall play a worse game. He was "fed" admirably by Green, his wing companion, but failed entirely to take advantage of the opportunities offered to him to centre the ball. Paddock and Pearson played randomly on the other wing and shot at goal seemingly without taking a survey of the surroundings. And I must say that Villa's first goal was clearly offside – that's a fact. Both Davis and Hodgetts were in offside positions. Our goalkeeper Roberts rarely makes a mistake. He would have cleared the ball if he thought that the two Villa forwards were on side.'

Villa's Archie Hunter, speaking to the same reporter, said: 'Albion's best players were Horton, the right-half-back, and their goalkeeper Roberts. Horton's sound and judicious play was outstanding; he played a "stunning" game.'

It was third time lucky for Ezra and Albion in 1888 when, at long last, they finally won the FA Cup, defeating the 'Invincibles' of the time, Preston, who in an earlier round had walloped Hyde 26–0. Albion triumphed 2–1, and the match report, in the *Birmingham Daily Post*, stated that early in the game: 'Horton was always harassing Preston's left wing pair of Drummond and Graham…in fact, the probability is that they would both have scored had Horton not been in the position he was.'

In *The Sportsman* it stated: 'Albion's defenders, especially Aldridge and Horton, played grandly. No matter whether the ball was high or low, straight or oblique, they seemed to get in the way of it and they were always close to a Preston player, never allowing him space in which to manoeuvre. Horton's cool and clear judgment often saved his side.'

Albion's first-ever Football League game followed on 8 September 1888 at Stoke and, having played in the club's initial FA Cup tie five years earlier, Ezra became one of only two players to star in the first games of both competitions, the other being Bob Roberts. Albion got off to a flying start, beating the Potters 2–0.

Due to a knee injury, Ezra played in only nine League games that season, but was an ever-present in 1889–90 and, owing to a dislocated elbow and damaged toe, made 16 appearances in 1890–91 before announcing his retirement in June 1891, having appeared in 83 League and Cup games for the club, scoring just one goal, a crisply struck effort in a 7–1 FA Cup win over Wednesbury Old Athletic in October 1887, and around 250 'other' matches. He actually played in all of Albion's first 36 FA Cup games…and that could easily be a national record.

Four years after retiring Ezra qualified a as referee and he also played regularly for the West Bromwich hockey team, having started to knock the small ball around while he was still a footballer. He did very well with stick and ball and became only the second Midlander to represent England at this sport when he appeared against Ireland in 1898.

*Ezra's younger brother Jack Horton, who was born in 1866, joined Albion in November 1882 and, over the next 17 years, appeared in 152 first-class games for the club, lining up in the 1895 FA Cup Final. He also played in Albion's first League match and, in fact, the brothers starred together in some 40 matches.

DON HOWE

'The best right-back in England for two seasons, Don was reliable, sure-footed and tireless.'

Born: 12 October 1935, Springfield, Wolverhampton

Albion senior record:

Appearances: League 342, FA Cup 37
Goals: League 17, FA Cup 2
Senior debut: League, 24 August 1955 v Everton (h) won 2–0
Also played for: St Peter's School (Wolverhampton), Wolverhampton & District Boys, Wolverhampton Wanderers (trial), Arsenal, England (1 B, 6 Under-23 and 23 full caps), England XI (1 app), Football League (6 apps), FA XI (4 apps)
Managed: Arsenal, West Bromwich Albion, Queen's Park Rangers, Coventry City, Galatasaray (Turkey, head coach), England B, Saudi Arabia national team (head coach)

Not too long ago I had the pleasure of chatting with Don Howe and, although we only spent a short time together, the former Albion and England full-back furnished me with some interesting information about his career in football. Don recalled: 'I played as a wing-half at St Peter's School and after our match on a Saturday morning, I went along to Molineux in the afternoon to watch the Wolves. I saw some great full-backs in action, among them Alf Ramsey and Roger Byrne. I admired Ramsey's play and decided that I should try to become a full-back. I was spotted by a scout from West Bromwich Albion and asked to attend The Hawthorns to see manager Jack Smith. Shortly after leaving school, and having had a trial with Wolves, I joined the Baggies as a junior and in my first season played in a variety of positions including right-half, centre-half and full-back. Early in 1953, when Vic Buckingham arrived as manager, I was a regular in the Birmingham Combination side and, after joining the Army, I represented the Western Command with Derek Kevan, who had recently joined from Bradford. We became great buddies, making our League debuts for Albion on the same day against Everton and later playing together for England in the 1958 World Cup Finals.'

Recalling an article he wrote in *Charles Buchan's Football Monthly*, Don continued: 'Every footballer dreams of having a lucky break – one which might transform his career. This happened to me when I was doing my National Service at Oswestry. But my dream was nearly burst by a puncture! When Blackpool's Jimmy Armfield had to drop out of the England Under-23 team to play Scotland at Hillsborough, I was called up at the last minute to fill the vacancy at right-back. An England selector had phoned my CO on the morning of the game (Wednesday 8 February 1956) and asked if I could be released from Army duties to play at Sheffield. I was granted permission, but there was a problem – how could I collect by boots and kit from The Hawthorns and get to Hillsborough on time?

'Up stepped Freddie Cox, Albion's assistant manager at that time. He contacted me and agreed to drive up to Oswestry with my necessities. Everything ran smoothly, my kit arrived and Freddie asked if he could come to the game with me and then drive me back to Oswestry later that night. All was going fine until about 40 miles from Sheffield. Then, travelling at 60–70 miles an hour, we had a puncture. I couldn't offer help in case I twisted something, so Freddie worked on the car alone. Covered in grease and grime, he got the spare wheel on and we completed our journey, arriving at the ground with just half-an-hour to spare – it was a close call. I should have been there an hour before that.'

With only 11 League appearances behind him, this was an unexpected opportunity for Don to play in his first representative match. He didn't let anyone down and performed competently in a 3–1 England victory. Indeed, his display certainly pleased the selectors, who handed him further Under-23 outings against France and Scotland the following season. Then, at the age of 22, on 19 October 1957, Don gained the first of 23 full caps for his country, starring in a 4–0 win over Wales in Cardiff.

Earlier in the year, Don and his teammates had been somewhat deflated when Albion lost to Aston Villa in an FA Cup semi-final replay, but a tour of Russia, his first major trip, quickly made up for that disappointment. Don thought that his excursion behind the Iron Curtain was terrific, saying: 'The supporters in Russia were fanatical. Thousands would turn up just to watch us train and at each of our three games we had full houses. We drew one and won the other two, becoming the first British club side to win in that country.'

By this time (season 1957–58) Don was Albion's first choice right-back and, except for the occasional game at right-half and inside-right, he stayed there until his departure to Arsenal for £40,000, signed by one of his boyhood heroes, Billy Wright, in April 1964, having netted 19 goals in 379 League and Cup games for the Baggies, as well as making 43 second XI appearances.

Don admitted that he enjoyed scoring goals – and one of his best was against the Russian Red Army side in a friendly at The Hawthorns in October 1957. 'That was a night to remember,' said Don. 'It poured with rain yet over 52,000 fans turned out to see us win a real thriller by 6–5.'

After making 74 appearances for the Gunners, Don's career came to an abrupt end when he broke his leg against Blackpool at Highbury in March 1966. He retired the following year and went into coaching, seeing the Gunners complete the double in 1971 before returning to the Midlands to manage Albion from 1971 to 1975. Unfortunately in those four years relegation was suffered, but he did sign Willie Johnston for a record fee of £138,000. Spells in Turkey and at Leeds United followed and, after going back to Highbury, he saw Arsenal reach three successive FA Cup Finals in 1978–79–80.

As the years rolled by, Don subsequently served as coach, assistant manager and manager in Saudi Arabia, with the England B team, at Wimbledon (FA Cup-winners in 1988), Bristol Rovers, QPR, Barnet, Coventry City, Chelsea and Arsenal again, and he also reported on Serie A matches in Italy for Channel 4 as well as acting as a technical advisor.

Awarded an Honorary Fellowship at Wolverhampton University in 2001, Don now resides in Hertfordshire.

LEE HUGHES

'Once the idol of the Brummie Road, "Hughesy" was a born goalscorer.'

Born:	22 May 1976, Smethwick

Albion senior record:

Appearances:	League 172+39, FA Cup 6, League Cup 12+6, Others 2
Goals:	League 89, FA Cup 2, League 6, Other 1
Senior debut:	League, 9 August 1997, substitute v Tranmere Rovers (h) won 2–1
Also played for:	County Boys, Forest Falcons, Stourbridge, Fresher FC, West Bromwich Albion (Schoolboy), Walsall (trial), Oldbury United, Kidderminster Harriers, Wolverhampton Wanderers (trial), Sheffield Wednesday (trial), Coventry City, Featherstone Prison FC, Oldham Athletic, Blackpool, Notts County, England (semi-professional)

After being on schoolboy forms with Albion (under the tutelage of Nobby Stiles) and a trialist with Walsall in 1991 while still attending Bristnall Hall High School, Lee Hughes signed a three-year non-contract with Kidderminster Harriers in October 1991. Anticipating a long spell in the youth and reserve teams, while also working as a roofer in Oldbury, he made steady progress, and after trials with Wolves and Sheffield Wednesday finally broke into the Harriers' first team in 1994 and immediately scored goals. He went on to net 60 (in all competitions) in three seasons, including 30 in the Conference in 1996–97, albeit to no avail, as Kidderminster got pipped for promotion to the Football League by Macclesfield. Rated as one of the best strikers in non-League football, he was also rewarded with England C (semi-professional) honours.

Albion were showing interest (ex-player John Trewick had spotted Lee's undoubted talent) and, in May 1997, manager Ray Harford signed him for £250,000, rising to £380,000, a record for a Conference player at that time. Describing it as 'a dream come true,' Lee quickly made his mark and, after his debut as a substitute against Tranmere Rovers on the opening day of the 1997–98 season, he became the first sub to score twice for Albion with a late brace to earn a 4–3 win at Crewe. He actually came off the bench 20 times before finally getting his first start under Denis Smith in the home game against Stoke City just after Christmas.

Fast, direct and with an eye for goal, Lee became a key player in Albion's front line and rattled in 14 goals that season, followed by 32 in 1998–99 – the most by any player in the top two Divisions. In fact, only seven strikers had, up to that time, netted over 30 goals in a season for Albion – Ronnie Allen (three times), Jeff Astle, Jimmy Cookson (twice), Derek Kevan, Fred Morris, W.G. Richardson (three times) and Bob Taylor.

Another 18 goals were scored in 1999–2000, while his haul of 23 in 2000–01 again proved worthless as Albion lost to Bolton in the Play-offs. In November 2000, Lee became the first Albion player since Jeff Astle in April/May 1968 to score a hat-trick in successive League games, obliging against Gillingham and Preston.

Losing in the Play-offs was a big disappointment to Lee, who desperately wanted Premiership football, and as a result the summer was rife with speculation that he would leave The Hawthorns, but not one Premiership club made an approach. Then, out of the blue, in August 2001, Gordon Strachan, manager of relegated Coventry City, offered £5 million + £1 for the striker. Albion accepted the fee, Coventry paid half of the money up front and Lee left his beloved Baggies.

Despite scoring 15 goals, Lee failed to settle at Highfield Road and in August 2002, by which time Albion were in the Premiership – and to the delight of the fans – Lee returned home. Cash-struck Coventry defaulted on their second payment of £2.5 million, which led to a deal being struck whereby Albion 'wrote off' the balance, effectively re-signing Lee for half of what he had been valued at a year earlier. Unfortunately Lee found it hard going and failed to score in 23 Premiership matches, the worst run of his career. Although Albion got relegated, he stuck in there and his 11 League goals helped them return to the top flight in 2004. His record with the club was now impressive: 98 goals in 237 appearances. But then it all went wrong for the 'Balti Kid' from Smethwick.

Lee had been involved in a car crash near Coventry in November 2003 in which his Mercedes CL500 had collided with a Renault Scenic. A passenger in the Renault, Douglas Graham, was killed, while his wife and the driver, Albert Frisby, were both injured. Lee and his colleague foolishly fled the scene to avoid being breathalysed, but the following day gave themselves up to the police. Lee was subsequently charged with causing death by dangerous driving and leaving the scene of an accident. He was released on bail, thus allowing him to complete Albion's League campaign. In August 2004, Lee was found guilty of the two offences and was sentenced to six years imprisonment. He was also banned from driving for 10 years. Albion immediately terminated his contract.

While in gaol, initially at Ashwell Prison, Rutland and then at Featherstone Prison, Staffordshire, Lee converted to Islam and played for the Featherstone prison team. He scored on his debut but was later sent off, which resulted in a four-month ban. On his release, Lee apologised for what he had done and stated: 'In going some way to facing my responsibilities, I have met the daughter of the man who died, and what was said will always remain a private and personal matter. For different reasons I think we were both glad that the meeting occurred. I made dreadful mistakes and decisions that will live with me for the rest of my life. It also greatly affected my immediate family, including my wife and children, and I will never forgive myself for this.' Lee also said that he would carry out community work centred on the mistakes he had made, hoping that his advice would go some way towards preventing another tragedy.

In July 2009 Lee joined Notts County, and in his first game for the Magpies he scored a hat-trick in a 5-0 win over Bradford City, grabbing another treble soon afterwards against Northampton. Maintaining his form throughout the season, he helped the Meadow Lane club win the League Two Championship, and his brace in the final home game of the season made him the first County player to score 30 League goals since Tommy Lawton in the 1949–50 season. Lee ended 2009–10 with a career record of 222 goals in 491 club appearances.

* While in prison, a distraught Lee helped to organise a charity football match which raised £5,000 for a children's hospice.

ANDY HUNT

'Tall and threatening, Andy was the perfect partner for Bob Taylor.'

Born:	9 June 1970, Thurrock, Essex

Albion senior record:

Appearances:	League 201+11, FA Cup 7, League Cup 12, Others 8+1
Goals:	League 76, FA Cup 2, League Cup 4, Others 3
Senior debut:	League, 28 March 1993, substitute v Bradford City (a) drew 2–2 (scored one goal)
Also played for:	Astill FC (King's Lynn), Norwich City (trial), Kettering Town, Newcastle United, Charlton Athletic, Banana Bank FC (Belize), Belmopan Bandits (Belize)

Andy Hunt became the first player to score for Albion at Wembley for 23 years when he netted the opening goal in the Second Division Play-off Final against Port Vale in May 1993. That was his 11th goal for the club in only his 13th appearance and over the next five years he continued to find the net, eventually taking his tally to 85 in 240 games for the Baggies before switching his allegiance to Charlton Athletic.

Andy began as a centre-half and gave up his job in computer systems to sign professional with Kettering Town. Moving into the forward line, he scored 30 goals in non-League football before joining Newcastle United for £210,000 in January 1991. Maintaining his form, he netted 13 times in 51 outings for the Geordies before March 1993, when Albion's boss Ossie Ardiles, who had been his manager at St James' Park, secured his services on loan as Bob Taylor's strike-partner at a time when the race for promotion was hotting-up.

Albion had been relying too much on 'Super Bob' and, with Simon Garner often injured, Andy was just the sort of player the team wanted to boost the goal tally. After a day's training, Andy scored a dramatic late equaliser on his Baggies debut in the televised game at Bradford City (to end a run of four successive away defeats) and the following week he celebrated his full debut at The Hawthorns, with a second-half hat-trick to stun Brighton, two laid on by the aforementioned Garner.

By scoring three times that afternoon Andy became the first Albion player for 80 years to score a treble on his full debut…since Alf Bentley's four-timer against Burnley in September 1913. He then helped book Albion a place at Wembley with a crucial goal in the second leg of the Play-off semi-final clash with Swansea City before going on to do the business in the Final.

Soon after clinching promotion, Albion signed Andy on a permanent basis for £100,000, but straightaway he had a new boss, Keith Burkinshaw, who had taken over from Ardiles. Tall and lean, with good pace, Andy became a huge favourite with the supporters and, despite missing a quarter of the 1993–94 season, following an injury at Barnsley, he still managed to bag 14 goals, finishing second to Taylor (21) in the scoring charts.

Alan Buckley then became Andy's third manager in double-quick time, and it was he who made Andy into a target man, pushing him right up field. He responded by top scoring with 13 goals in 1994–95 and bagged another 17 the following season when, it must be said, he missed some real sitters as well, including a howler against Bradford City at The Hawthorns when he fired over the bar from less than a yard. Afterwards, in an interview, Andy said: 'I took my eye off the ball and scooped up and over, just like a golf shot – I'm no good at golf anyway.'

As so often in football, things change all the time. With Taylor struggling with a leg injury, Albion decided to bring in the Canadian international Paul Peschisolido to boost their goal-power. He was signed from Stoke City for £600,000 in July 1996 and he and Andy teamed up superbly to form another sharp-shooting Albion partnership. Between them they notched 31 goals, 16 to Andy, 15 to Pesch, while Taylor, who was in and out of the team, also nipped in with 10.

Andy's fourth manager, Ray Harford, was now in charge at The Hawthorns and, with Taylor having been sold to Bolton in the January, and with Peschisolido moving to Fulham, he introduced Lee Hughes to Albion's attack. Andy and his new lieutenant clicked immediately and both players netted 14 goals as the team finished in 10th place in Division One.

At this point, in May 1998, Andy's contract with Albion came to an end and, after failing to agree a new deal with the club, he left under the Bosman ruling and joined Premiership club Charlton Athletic on a free transfer. Andy had asked Albion for £8,000 a week – 'chicken feed compared to what some Premiership players earn' said one supporter – but had it been agreed it would have completely destroyed Albion's wage structure.

Andy's departure was a body-blow to the supporters. He had become a firm favourite with the 'Brummie Road Enders', but when he chose to leave because of the money some weren't too pleased. Apparently he earned £9,000 a week at the Valley, but he wasn't there long, staying just two seasons.

Andy scored seven goals in 1998–99 as the Addicks suffered relegation, but the London club bounced back immediately as First Division Champions, thanks mainly to Andy's 24 goals and the form of future Albion players Dean Kiely and midfielder Mark Kinsella. On the final day of that 1999–2000 season Charlton visited The Hawthorns. They were already up, but Albion needed to win to stay up.

Baggies defender Daryl Burgess remembered that before the game Andy had told him that the last thing he wanted to do was to send Albion down. Albion won the match 2–0 and after the game Andy went into the dressing room and congratulated his former teammates.

Andy was forced to retire from football in the summer of 2000 due to chronic fatigue syndrome. Changing his life completely, he emigrated to Sanignacio, Belize, formerly British Honduras, in Central America, to form his own company, while playing the odd game of football for Banana Bank FC. He returned to Charlton briefly in 2003 to try and earn another contract, playing in three reserve games, but he was not offered a contract and went back to Belize, where he now runs the Belize Jungle Dome and the Green Dragon Adventure Park with his wife, the former MTV presenter Simone Angel. Andy also maintains a blog which details how he became a professional footballer, and his thoughts on different football issues.

ALEC JACKSON

'Could play on both wings or inside…and at times he was brilliant.'

Born: 29 May 1937, Tipton, Staffordshire

Albion senior career:

Appearances:	League 192, FA Cup16
Goals:	League 50, FA Cup 2
Senior debut:	League, 6 November 1954 v Charlton Athletic (a) won 3–1 (scored one goal)
Also played for:	Tipton St John's, W.G. Allen's Works, Birmingham City, Walsall, Nuneaton Borough, Kidderminster Harriers, Warley, Oldbury Town, Warley Borough, Darlaston, Blakenhall, Lower Gornal, Rushall Olympic, Bush Rangers, West Bromwich All Stars, Football League (1 app)

Over the years Tipton, deep in the heart of the industrial Black Country, has produced scores of excellent footballers. Several have been associated with local clubs, some have gone on to play for England, while others have simply been dedicated servants of Midland football, like Alec Jackson, now in his seventies, who starred for the Baggies for 10 years from 1954–64.

Spotted playing for the works team, W.G. Allen's, he was asked to attend The Hawthorns for a trial in May 1954, a week or so after Albion had won the FA Cup. Looked after on the day by Albion's goalscoring hero of the 1930s, W.G. Richardson, with ex-players Teddy Sandford and goalkeeper Harold Pearson also on duty, Alec admitted he was 'nervous' but after he had been walked to the pitch by W.G. he settled down.

Alec recalled: 'W.G. put his arm round my shoulder and said "Go out and do what you're good at. If you want to dribble, then dribble, if you want to shoot, then shoot. Don't be afraid to do your own thing, just be natural."' Alec impressed all and sundry and, after signing amateur forms, was asked back again in July. This time he played in a South Warwickshire League match against Nuneaton reserves, helping Albion's A team win 4–2. A week later he starred in a 4–1 victory over Banbury Spencer before scoring a hat-trick in another 4–1 triumph, this time over Anstey Colliery. Then, after impressing in a 2–0 Central League win over Manchester United reserves, he was upgraded to the professional ranks on 9 September and quickly followed up with a two-goal salvo in a 4–1 success over Burnley's second XI. The editor of the *Albion News* wrote: 'Alec Jackson, bearer of an illustrious football name, is a local boy who signed as an amateur for us in the close season. This 17-year-old is slight in build, but we feel our supporters will enjoy his football in the future.'

After scoring six Central League goals, Alec was handed a surprise First Division debut against Charlton Athletic at the Valley on a cold November afternoon in 1954. 'It came as a complete surprise when our trainer Arthur Fitton took me into the dug-out on the Friday lunchtime after training and told me that I was in the squad for the trip to London,' said Alec. 'Manager Vic Buckingham was in hospital recovering from a car accident and earlier in the day he had liaised with Arthur about the long injury list. At least five first-team players were struggling to be fit, including inside-forwards Johnny Nicholls and Paddy Ryan and winger George Lee, but I never, for one minute, thought that a 17-year-old youngster like me, could be playing for the Cup-holders and lining up with internationals like Ronnie Allen and Stan Rickaby. It was amazing.'

Alec was told that he would be starting the game in the hotel during lunch and, although quite nervous, he was encouraged and nurtured along by the more senior players in the team. Fielding four reserves, Albion went out and beat Charlton 3–1 in front of 36,074 spectators and Alec had the pleasure of scoring on his debut, in the third minute, although he was immediately sidelined with a hip injury, returning after five minutes.

Recalling his goal, Alec said: 'After switching positions with Ronnie Allen, we swapped passes on the edge of the penalty area and as two defenders hesitated, I darted forward to fire the ball low past Sam Bartram in the Charlton goal from about 12 yards. It was as simple as that.'

Called up for the first team only once more that season, Alec was a regular in the second team over the next three years or so, slowly learning the trade while playing alongside some experienced professionals – and he also gained a runners'-up medal when Albion lost in the Final of the 1955 FA Youth Cup to the up-and-coming Busby Babes of Manchester United.

In April 1958 Alec was called up at the last minute for the League game at Tottenham. Winger Roy Horobin had pulled out because of injury, so Alec played inside-left in a shuffled forward line. Unfortunately he suffered a broken right leg following a tackle by full-back John Hills. In those days a player's career often ended with such an injury but Alec, made of tough Black Country flesh and bone, received treatment throughout the summer break and was back in action within four months. He continued to do well in the reserves before finally establishing himself in the first team in 1959–60, mainly occupying the right-wing position that had been vacated by Jimmy Campbell the previous year. Alec netted 12 goals that season and followed up with 12 more in 1960–61, including his first senior hat-trick in a rousing 6–0 home League win over Newcastle.

Now playing his best football ever, Alec was an ever-present in 1961–62 and, as result of his performances, was selected to represent the Football League against the Scottish League at Villa Park in March. Replacing the injured John Connelly, and playing alongside Bobby Charlton, Johnny Haynes and Ron Flowers, he did well in a 4–3 defeat. After the game a modest Alec said: 'I was chosen to make the numbers up really, but it was a honour nevertheless. I enjoyed it.'

Continuing to produce the goods, he took his senior appearance tally with Albion past the 200 mark and scored his 50th goal for the club against Aston Villa before leaving The Hawthorns in the summer of 1964, joining Birmingham City for £12,500. He struck 12 goals in 85 outings for Blues and then, following a spell with Walsall (February 1967 to August 1968), he travelled round the non-League circuit before finally retiring from the game in 1985, aged 47.

A player who serves a club for a decade deserves credit in any book. And Alec Jackson, a keen gardener and wonderful friend of mine for over 40 years, is one of those dedicated footballers who, despite spending some five years in the 'stiffs' at The Hawthorns, for whom he scored 30 goals in 135 appearances, gave Albion and the supporters wonderful service. He was a fine player indeed.

CLAUDE JEPHCOTT

'Injury prevented Claude from playing for England.'

Born:	30 October 1891, Smethwick
Died:	5 October 1950, Penn, Wolverhampton

Albion senior record:

Appearances:	League 174, FA Cup 15, Others 1
Goals:	League 15, FA Cup 0, Others 0
Senior debut:	League, 9 December 1911 v Sunderland (a) lost 3–2
Also played for:	Olive Mount FC, Brierley Hill Alliance (2 spells), Stourbridge, Mount Pleasant, Football League (2 apps), England Select XI (1 app)

A member of a famous West Smethwick sporting and journalistic family, Claude Jephcott had been recruited from Brierley Hill Alliance in the face of strong competition from Aston Villa and Liverpool. A fast-raiding winger with tremendous skill and stinging shot, there is little doubt that he would have played for England had he not suffered a dislocated ankle in a League game at Middlesbrough in September 1921.

An outside-right in the best Bassett traditions, he recovered from that set-back, but the very next season broke his right leg in a First Division encounter at Villa Park, and his all-too-short career was over. Later Claude became an Albion director and subsequently vice-chairman, being a power in the boardroom until his death in 1950.

Besides being a wonderful footballer, Claude was also a fine golfer, with a handicap of 16, and twice came close to winning a major competition before the outbreak of World War One. A keen athlete at school, regularly competing in track events including the 100 and 200-yard sprints, Claude carried his folk memory of a Black Country childhood into his professional preparation. He believed that running was a 'born acquisition and had to be looked after carefully.'

In an article in 1920 he confirmed that he had started running at the age of five. 'I used to run behind carts and race tramcars,' he said. 'I was fascinated by speed and would travel to the ground (The Hawthorns) at least three times a week and do four or five sharp sprints up and down the touchline plus a lap of the pitch at a good pace.' It was hinted in some quarters that if he hadn't been a footballer Claude might well have represented his county, even his country, as an athlete, possibly in the 100 yards.

Surprisingly Claude was never signed as a full-time professional for Albion. He later became a prominent industrialist, yet he loved his football and trained as hard and as often as he could. He was one of the fittest members of the team and advocated 'work and play', combining his football with a real job which he did every day of the week, sometimes on the morning of a Saturday game. He trained when possible, sometimes during his lunch break, occasionally in the evenings and quite a bit on a Sunday, when he seemed to have a lot of spare time – that's if he hadn't done too much in a game the previous day or was feeling a twinge or a pull in some part of his anatomy.

Fred Everiss, Albion's secretary-manager, who signed Claude as a 19-year-old, described him in a newspaper in 1948 as being: 'One of the best wingers in League football during the early 1920s. He was quick, decisive, penetrative and clever. He certainly gave his full-back opponent plenty to think about and very few, if any, ever got to combat his pace and dribbling ability. He was an exceptionally fine player.' This opinion was echoed in a pen-picture of Claude in an Aston Villa programme. It revealed: 'He possesses surging vitality in both strength and enthusiasm. And will give any defender something to think about.'

After doing well with Olive Mount as a 15-year-old, Brierley Hill Alliance (two spells), Stourbridge and Mount Pleasant, Claude joined Albion from the Alliance club for £100 in April 1911 and immediately represented England in a Junior international. After doing well in the second team, he made his League debut at Sunderland in early December of that year, taking over from Billy Wollaston at a time when the outside-right position was causing some concern. In fact, over the previous two-and-a-half seasons, no fewer than eight different players had occupied that position.

Claude settled in well and, with Harry Wright as his partner and hard-working wing-half George Betteley and full-back Joe Smith behind him, Albion were very strong down their right flank. They reached the FA Cup Final that season (1911–12), meeting Barnsley in the Final. However, after a goalless draw at Crystal Palace, the Yorkshire club won the Sheffield replay with a last-minute goal in extra-time to deny Claude and his colleagues a victory they just about deserved.

An ever-present in 1912–13, Claude was absent just once the following season, but missed half of the games in 1914–15 with knee and hip injuries, which disrupted his running. Nevertheless, he bounced back to form, represented the Football League and also played for an England XI in an international trial.

World War One then interrupted football for four years, during which time Claude continued to work with his business while keeping himself in trim by training regularly and playing golf. Fighting fit and raring to go when League action recommenced in August 1919, Claude unfortunately missed the opening five games with a muscle strain but returned in late September with a new partner at inside-right in Tommy Magee as well as a new right-half behind him, Sammy Richardson.

With the team playing superbly well, Claude suffered a dead leg at Manchester City in December which sidelined him for two months, but when he returned he was the star of the attack as Albion stormed on to take their first, and so far only, League title. Claude scored five goals in 21 League games that term, two of them coming in the 4–1 home win over Preston, which prompted one reporter to write: 'His amazing speed and unerring judgment made it one of the greatest games of his life.' Claude also created at least a dozen more chances for his colleagues. He was 'brilliant' in the 4–2 win at Villa Park, setting up a tap-in goal for Fred Morris, the *Albion News* describing his performance thus: 'Jephcott scintillated in the second half. He is supposed to have a hardened muscle in one of his thighs, but the drawback was not apparent…as he wheeled about and ran in and out and finally delivered choice centres.' Claude also had a hand in three of the four goals which beat Middlesbrough on a saturated Hawthorns pitch. 'He could do no wrong' said one reporter. 'His pace on the slippery surface left his opponents in a daze.' Owing to his splendid form throughout this season, Claude earned himself another outing for the Football League representative side.

After producing some good, positive performances throughout 1920–21, Claude was then shaken by the first of two devastating leg injuries. And although he regained full fitness after his dislocated ankle, he failed to recover from his fracture at Villa Park and announced his retirement as a player in May 1923. Eleven years later, after becoming a shareholder, he was voted on to the club's Board of Directors, retaining his position until his death at the relatively young age of 59.

WILLIE JOHNSTON

'In the 1970s nobody was faster over 30–40 yards than Willie.'

Born:	19 December 1946, Maryhill, Glasgow

Albion senior record:

Appearances:	League 203+4, FA Cup 24+2, League Cup 15, Others 12+1
Goals:	League 18, FA Cup 6, League Cup 2, Others 2
Senior debut:	League, 9 December 1972 v Arsenal (h)
Also played for:	Bowhill Strollers, Manchester United (trial), Lochore Welfare, Glasgow Rangers, Vancouver Whitecaps, Birmingham City, South China, Heart of Midlothian, East Fife and Scotland (4 Youth, two Under-23 and 22 full caps), Scottish League (2 apps)

Willie Johnston was a loveable rogue who got himself sent off no fewer than 22 times during his career, mostly for retaliation. He recalled: 'In the late 1960s and during the '70s, it was a case of dog eat dog. I used to get kicked from pillar to post and the referee didn't bat an eyelid. I just felt that I never got protected against robust and foul tackling. At times I was sick to the teeth at the treatment I received at some grounds and it got my back up. I know I was fast and clever and therefore I would often tease and torment defenders before going past them. I was told that the best way to get a player's back up was to beat them by skill, even producing a nutmeg or two by passing the ball through your opponent's legs. Defenders hated that and would really get wound up. I liked to play to the crowd, but it was hard to take when certain players, Paul Reaney of Leeds United among them, continually got away with murder. As a result I simply lost my temper and retaliated…prompting the ref to walk up to me and say "Johnston, you're off." That was it. They didn't even need to show the red card.

'Okay, I did have a few fights. I recall as an Albion player sprawling on the turf with Everton's Archie Styles in a Cup game at The Hawthorns, having a punch up with Ray Treacy at Swindon and fighting with John Emanuel of Bristol City. And I also remember being dismissed for aiming a kick at the referee in a League Cup tie against Brighton. I was totally frustrated that evening. I simply lost it.'

A Partick Thistle supporter as a lad (his grandfather used to take him to see home games at Firhill Park) Willie, nicknamed 'Bud' by his colleagues, had an unsuccessful trial with Manchester United before joining Glasgow Rangers in June 1964 for £6 a week. He was still two months shy of his 18th birthday when he helped the Gers lift the League Cup in his debut season. However, his finest hour with the Ibrox Park club came in the Nou Camp Stadium, Barcelona, in May 1972, when he scored twice in a 3–2 European Cup-winners' Cup Final victory over Dinamo Moscow.

'That was a brilliant night,' recalled Willie. 'We played exceptionally well and even the match referee from Spain congratulated me for not retaliating when I was fouled at least three times by Basalev, the Dinamo right-back. That win more than made up for losing to Bayern Munich in the 1967 Final.'

In November 1971, Willie, after coming on as a substitute, scored a hat-trick for Rangers in a 4–1 League win over St Johnstone. In fact, it was a hat-trick of spot-kicks. He netted with two clean strikes but had his third effort saved, only to fire in the rebound.

Thirteen months after that feat, Willie became a record signing by Albion when manager Don Howe paid £138,000 for his signature in December 1972. However, having been suspended by the Scottish FA for 67 days for a catalogue of disciplinary offences, Willie was not quite match-fit and although he made his Baggies debut against Liverpool 48 hours after signing, it wasn't until after Christmas that he finally got going in a navy blue and white striped shirt. Unfortunately his presence on the left wing couldn't save Albion from relegation that season and it was something Willie had not contemplated – playing in the Second Division. But he stuck in there and produced some superb performances, home and away, before helping the Baggies regain their top-flight status in 1976.

The following season he had the pleasure of helping Scotland beat England 2–1 at Wembley in the Home International Championship when the delirious Scottish fans invaded the pitch, ripped up turf and tore down the goalposts.

However, getting sent home from Argentina in the World Cup of 1978, after he failed a drugs test (after taking Reactivan tablets), was a shattering blow to Willie. The incident seriously affected his family as his wife and kids took an awful lot of stick from all angles. 'I was hung out to dry by the Scottish FA,' said Willie. 'I would have liked them to appeal against it and arrange for me to have a second test, but they didn't bother and they told me to pack my bags and leave. I just wanted to play at a World Cup – it was my ambition. I appeared in one game and got sent home. I am not going to elaborate on the matter. It was hard to take and I accepted the decision…eventually.' In all, Willie represented his country on 22 occasions, 13 as an Albion player. His last cap was awarded against Peru in the infamous 3–1 defeat in the 1978 World Cup Finals.

With Laurie Cunningham often preferred on the wing by manager Ron Atkinson, Willie remained an Albion player until March 1979 when he was signed by his former boss Johnny Giles for Vancouver Whitecaps for £100,000. Seven months later, having helped the Whitecaps win the NASL title, he came back to Britain for a loan spell with Birmingham City and, after helping Blues gain promotion to the First Division, he returned to an ailing Rangers in August 1980. From May to September 1982 he had a second spell with Vancouver Whitecaps and thereafter, until his retirement as a player in May 1985, Willie played for Heart of Midlothian and South China (Hong Kong), rejoined Hearts as player-coach and did a similar job with East Fife. His career realised a total of 162 goals in 720 club and international appearances – a fine record for a fine winger.

In March 1986 he was appointed full-time coach at Raith Rovers and, after entering the licensed trade, he remained associated with football by taking a coaching position with Falkirk for season 1987–88. Willie is now an established pub landlord, running the Port O'Brae Inn on High Street, Kirkcaldy, Fife. The likeable Scot has had two books published about his football career – *Willie On The Wing* and *Sent Off At Gunpoint*.

HARRY 'POPEYE' JONES

'Strong, thrustful, brave — biff, bang, wallop — that was "Popeye".'

Born:	26 October 1911, Haydock, Lancashire
Died:	22 February 1957, Preston

Albion senior record:

Appearances:	League 120, FA Cup 9, Wartime 40
Goals:	League 54, FA Cup 3, Wartime 47
Senior debut:	League, 1 January 1935 v Sheffield Wednesday (a) lost 2–1
Also played for:	Haydock Athletic, Preston North End, Blackburn Rovers (World War Two guest), Everton (World War Two guest), London Army Command, London District Army XI

Many people believed that if World War Two hadn't broken out when it did, then Harry 'Popeye' Jones would have been one of the most prolific marksmen in the country. A jovial, loquacious character, able to play in any of the five forward-line positions, 'Popeye', although not particularly strong or even well-built, was nevertheless an aggressive, fearless, mobile, courageous, all-action player, adored by the fans but hated by his opponents, including goalkeepers.

He regularly barged straight into a 'keeper at a set piece, occasionally sending him crashing to the ground in a heap or seeing him tangled up in the netting, with or without the ball. In the home League game against Black Country rivals Wolves in December 1937, Harry shoulder-charged visiting 'keeper Bob Scott, a giant at 6ft 4in tall and 14st in weight, directly into the back of the net, and it was a couple of minutes before Scott could disentangle himself from the rigging. The same thing happened against Birmingham in April 1938, when Harry sent England's number one 'keeper Harry Hibbs flying backwards with another solid shoulder charge.

In an article in the *Liverpool Echo* during the late 1930s, rock-solid Everton defender Charlie Gee wrote: 'Harry is one of the toughest centre-forwards I have ever faced. He's on the go all the time, continually shoving and pushing you, and he certainly puts the fear of God into a few decent goalkeepers.'

After doing exceedingly well with Haydock Athletic, for whom he scored over 70 goals in three seasons in the highly-competitive Haydock & District and Lancashire Amateur Leagues, Harry joined

Preston North End in July 1928, turning professional on his 18th birthday. He spent five years at Deepdale, yet in that time managed only one League appearance, scoring in a 4–2 home win over Charlton Athletic in January 1933, his goal being created by former Albion left-winger and future trainer Arthur Fitton.

In the summer of 1932, Harry was awarded the Royal Humane Society Medal after he dived, fully clothed, into a Preston canal to save a child from drowning.

In May 1933, Harry was transferred to Albion for the seemingly small fee of just £500 – after secretary-manager Fred Everiss, trainer Fred Reed and director Lou Nurse had travelled north to watch him play in two end-of-season Central League games. 'He is only 21 years of age and we believe he will develop into a first-class goalscorer and hopefully take over from W.G. Richardson,' said Reed, who added: 'We all know he's a good player and I am pleased he chose Albion ahead of three other interested clubs. He was going nowhere with Preston and he said that he wanted regular first-team football. We told him that he would have to work hard at his game and fight for his place. "I'll do that, no problem," he replied.'

Harry started off his career at The Hawthorns in brilliant style, scoring 18 goals in 26 outings, helping Albion's second XI win the Central League championship in his first season. And he also broke into the first team, making his debut on New Year's Day at Hillsborough when he replaced the injured Teddy Sandford at inside-left. Later on he claimed his first senior goal in a 2–2 draw with Chelsea.

He spent most of the 1935–36 campaign in the reserves, notching another eight goals in 19 starts, while also grabbing four goals in eight First Division League matches, including the winner against the subsequent FA Cup-winners of that season, Arsenal. Improving all the time, Harry eventually claimed a regular place in Albion's first team in September 1936 and went on to finish up as second top scorer that season with 18 goals, two coming in a thrilling 6–4 home League win over Sunderland in which he gave centre-half Jim Clark a real tough time. He also played his part in a brilliant sixth-round FA Cup win over the holders Arsenal in front of a record Hawthorns crowd of 64,815. Unfortunately, with the twin towers of Wembley in Albion's sights, Preston North End won the semi-final clash 4–1 at Highbury.

Despite Harry's 11 League goals in 1937–38, Albion suffered relegation and then, in the last season before the outbreak of World War Two, he headed the scoring charts with 20, claiming his first hat-trick for the club in a 4–3 home win over Tottenham Hotspur. During the initial wartime season of 1939–40 Harry was quite brilliant. He bagged a total of six hat-tricks in his haul of 50 goals, 42 of which were scored in only 31 regional League and Cup and the three aborted Division Two fixtures. Between 28 October and 30 December 1939 he simply couldn't stop scoring, setting a new club record by netting in 11 consecutive matches. Only winger Billy Elliott has equalled that feat.

Harry, who served as a soldier in the Army and played several times for the London Command and the London District Army XIs, actually kept goal as a guest player for Everton in a Football League North game at Burnley in February 1942, performing quite well in a 1–0 defeat. He also appeared as a centre-forward in emergencies and overall made 46 appearances and scored 18 goals for the Merseysiders, while playing in seven games and netting one goal as a guest for Blackburn Rovers in 1940–41.

Nicknamed 'Popeye' because of his facial features, which resembled the cartoon character, Harry remained a registered player with Albion right through to August 1943 when a serious knee injury, coupled with illness, forced him into early retirement at the age of 31. After the war he was engaged as a scout by Albion, scanning the local parks in and around Lancashire for two years (1946 and 1947). Later employed as a part-time labourer by a Preston engineering company, Harry was only 45 when he died from a heart attack in 1957. Several members of his family currently live in Haydock.

JOHN KAYE

'Yorkie was a top-drawer defender, strong, powerful, reliable, steady.'

Born: 3 March 1940, Goole

Albion senior record:

Appearances: League 281+3, FA Cup 25, League Cup 31, Europe 10, Charity Shield 1, Others 10

Goals: League 45, FA Cup 2, League Cup 6, Europe 1

Senior debut: League, 24 August 1963 v Leicester City (h) drew 1–1

Also played for: Goole Town Boys, Goole United, Goole Dockers FC, Goole Town, Scunthorpe United, Hull City, Football League (2 apps, 2 goals)

Managed: Hull City, Goole Town, Brigg Town

John 'Yorky' Kaye loved scoring goals as a schoolboy, and in 1954 bagged a double hat-trick in a Cup game for Goole United. Continuing to find the net, he was an amateur with Hull City in 1956 and spent three seasons scoring goals for Goole Town before joining Scunthorpe United as a professional in September 1960. He did very well in the Second Division, scoring 25 goals in 77 League appearances for the Iron, but he always hinted he would like to play in the top flight. His dream came true in May 1963, when Albion's manager Jimmy Hagan contacted his counterpart at the Old Showground, Dick Duckworth. After a brief discussion it was agreed that John should be transferred to The Hawthorns for a club record fee of £25,000.

John recalled: 'I was summoned to the manager's office after a training session. Mr Duckworth asked me to sit down and then told me that West Brom wanted me. "Do you want to go?" he asked. I was surprised and, after gathering my thoughts, I

answered yes, okay, what's the deal? "We'll sort that out and I'll get back to you tomorrow."'

An agreement was drawn up, John met Jimmy Hagan and in no time at all Yorky was at The Hawthorns, teaming up with another newcomer, Terry Simpson. Both players made their Albion debuts against Leicester City on the opening day of the 1963–64 season, John lining up at centre-forward with Ronnie Fenton and Bobby Hope alongside and Ken Foggo and Clive Clark on the wings. John recalled: 'We weren't the biggest forward-line line in the League, in fact, the whole team wasn't over-large, but we were very competitive and became even stronger when Doug Fraser joined us in the September.'

John scored 12 goals in his first season with Albion but, owing to injury problems, bagged only five in 1964–65, by which time Jeff Astle had arrived on the scene. Forming a brilliant partnership up front, they helped Albion win the League Cup at the first attempt in 1965–66 and scored 47 goals between them, Astle edging top spot, 24–23.

At the time it wasn't compulsory to enter the League Cup, which began in 1960, but Albion made the most of their chance and went on and on, eventually beating West Ham 5–3 on aggregate in the last of the two-legged Finals. After losing the opening game at Upton Park 2–1, John quickly brought the scores level with a beauty in the return leg and then played his part as the Baggies overpowered the Hammers – Moore, Peters and Hurst included – to capture their first trophy in 12 years.

Also this season, John picked up the 'Midland Footballer of the Year' prize, an award he would receive again in 1970; twice represented the Football League, scoring twice against the Irish League; and was named in Alf Ramsey's 40-strong squad for the World Cup, although he didn't make the final 22.

During the 1966–67 season, John became a deep-lying centre-forward and did pretty well, helping Albion reach the League Cup Final again, but this time, in front of a near full-house at Wembley, the Baggies were beaten 3–2 by the Third Division champions-elect QPR. 'That was an awful day,' said John. 'We had 'em on the rack at half-time. We were 2–0 up, in control and playing well. But then the manager decided to make changes in the team. Everything went to pot; they hit us hard and in the end won with a dubious goal. Our 'keeper Dick Sheppard was kicked on the head by their defender Hunt. It was foul, no doubt about it. But the referee waved play on and, with our defence in disarray, Lazarus swept the ball home. We were shell-shocked. There were only a few minutes remaining; we couldn't raise our game. It was very disappointing. I do know that a couple of months later our manager Hagan was sacked.' Things were completely different in 1967–68 when, this time round, Albion won at Wembley, beating Everton 1–0 in the FA Cup Final.

In mid-April, manager Alan Ashman had successfully switched John to left-half following an injury to Eddie Colquhoun in the drawn sixth-round FA Cup replay at Liverpool. He fitted in superbly and produced some outstanding performances as Albion powered through to the Final, eventually beating Liverpool at the third attempt, accounting for Birmingham City in the semi-final and then knocking over Everton. 'Although I had to leave the pitch through injury at the end of normal time in the Final, that win more than made up for that League Cup defeat the previous year,' said John, who would suffer two more huge disappointments before he left The Hawthorns. In 1969, Albion lost in the FA Cup semi-final to Leicester City and the following season they were beaten 2–1 by Manchester City in the League Cup Final.

In his eight years at The Hawthorns John made hundreds of friends and no enemies, apart from those opposing him on the pitch. He played through the pain barrier many times and, in the second replay with Liverpool at Maine Road in 1968, he battled bravely throughout the second half with his head swathed in bandages. That courageous display will always be remembered by the army of Baggies fans who cheered their team to victory that night. Another game in which John played on with a bandaged head was against Wolves at The Hawthorns in 1964, Jeff Astle's home debut. Both he and Jeff scored twice that afternoon in a resounding 5–1 win.

Wherever he played, right-back, centre-half, sweeper, inside-right or centre-forward, John Kaye was totally committed. He amassed 361 appearances and scored 54 goals for Albion, whom he left for pastures new in November 1971, joining Hull City for £28,000.

He remained at Boothferry Park as player, coach and manager until 1977 when he returned to his former club, Scunthorpe United, as assistant manager/coach. Later in charge of Goole Town and Brigg Town, he quit football in 1992 and entered the hotel business, later working on oil rigs. He now resides in Kirkella, Hull, making the odd visit to The Hawthorns for a get-together with his former colleagues.

JOE KENNEDY

'Joe always said "when in doubt, kick it out...be safe rather than sorry."'

Born:	15 November 1925, Cleator Moor near Whitehaven
Died:	12 September 1986, West Bromwich

Albion senior record:

Appearances:	League 364, FA Cup 32, Charity Shield 1
Goals:	League 3, FA Cup 1, Charity Shield 0
Senior debut:	League, 9 April 1949 v Luton Town (a) won 1–0
Also played for:	St Patrick's School (Whitehaven), Whitehaven & District Boys, Cleator Moor Celtic, Workington Town, Brentford (trial), Millwall (trial), Gravesend, Freelands FC, Altrincham, Chester, Stourbridge (player-manager), Brockhouse Works, England (3 B caps), FA XI (1 app)

Very rarely did an opposing centre-forward get the better of Joe Kennedy. The Albion centre-half, who also played right-half, inside-right and even as an emergency right-back in the 1954 FA Cup Final, was at times quite brilliant. Many thought (players, supporters and a few managers) that he should have played for England, but unfortunately injuries prevented this from happening, although he was named as reserve on several occasions. It was a pity really that Harry Johnston (Blackpool) and Billy Wright (Wolves) were around at the same time. He did, however, captain the England B team on three occasions and played for an FA XI.

Week after week, match after match, Joe produced some wonderful displays for Albion. His Baggies teammate Ronnie Allen confirmed that Joe was the best centre-half he ever saw play. And another Albion 'star', Ray Barlow, thought Joe was a great player. 'I never saw anyone head a ball as hard as Joe. He used to climb up so high and then just seem to hang there.'

Joe's manager at The Hawthorns in the 1950s was Vic Buckingham and he described him as being 'A supremely self-confident player who attained a high level of consistency and seldom had an

off day despite a spate of knee injuries.' Many newspaper reporters up and down the country also thought Joe was a brilliant centre-half. Tom Blunt (*Birmingham Gazette*), reporting in January 1952 (after Albion's 4–0 FA Cup win over Bolton), said: 'Kennedy stood out as the past-master, keen and incisive in the tackle and immaculate in his service to his forwards. He had Nat Lofthouse in his pocket all afternoon.' In November 1953, Alan Neale wrote in the *Sunday Mercury*, following a 6–1 home League win over Cardiff City: 'Kennedy's headwork, mobility and dominance stood out above the rest of the defenders. He even found time to run 40 yards with the ball, such was his confidence.' Then Jack Clifford of *The People* stated, in December 1955 after Albion's 4–0 home League victory over Portsmouth: 'He (Kennedy) showed a polished style. He was judicious with his tackling, cool under pressure and placed his clearances with unfailing accuracy.' A year later, in November 1956, following Albion's 3–0 home defeat of Everton, Bill Holden in the *Daily Mirror* wrote: 'I haven't seen a better centre-half this season. Kennedy was brilliant.'

The tributes continued to appear. Cyril Chapman wrote in the *Sports Argus* in October 1957, after Albion's 9–2 home win over Manchester City: 'Although Albion's attack dominated this game, centre-half Kennedy was easily the best defender on the field, a first class strategist and notably constructive.' In December 1957, Dick Knight, reporting in the *Birmingham Post & Mail* on Albion's resounding 5–1 win over Burnley, said: 'Kennedy was calm and reliable in defence, especially in headwork and he always came out best in 50–50 situations.'

Peter Morris, a Midlands-based freelance journalist, was full of praise for Joe after he starred in Albion's 4–1 win over Leeds United at Elland Road in February 1960: 'Kennedy, for me, was outstanding. He won all the aerial battles and found time to feed his colleagues with measured passes.' And finally, Charles Harrold from the *Birmingham Post & Mail* wrote in April 1960, after Birmingham City had been thrashed 7–1 at St Andrew's: 'Albion's centre-half Kennedy was outstanding. He won every ball in the air and his passing was of a very high quality. Never flustered, he had a superb game.'

Joe was 23 years of age when he joined Albion in December 1948 for what was to prove a bargain fee of just £750. Despite having spent his early days in non-League football, he soon made his mark with the Baggies, helping them clinch promotion from Division Two in his first season and scoring once in eight games while occupying the right-half and inside-right positions. He made 34 League appearances the following season, 35 in 1950–51 and another 36 in 1951–52 when he took over from Jack Vernon at centre-half. Unfortunately Joe suffered a serious knee injury against Manchester City in February 1953 and was replaced by Jimmy Dugdale. He returned for a 10-match spell halfway through the 1953–54 campaign when Albion were battling it out with Wolves for the First Division title, but was then sidelined again. Taking time to recover and seeing Albion making progress in the FA Cup, Joe gained match fitness in the reserves and then, right at the death, he was asked to play at right-back in the Final against Preston. He did well and helped set up the winning goal for Frank Griffin.

Following Dugdale's departure to Aston Villa in 1956, Joe made the centre-half spot his own and was part of what many say has been one of Albion's best half-back lines ever, with Jimmy Dudley on his right and Ray Barlow on his left.

Joe remained there until the end of 1957–58 when Barlow moved across from the left to take over as pivot. Joe played 21 games in the second XI in 1958–59 before reclaiming the number five shirt for season 1959–60. He stayed on for one more year, taking his tally of senior appearances to almost 400 (plus 68 for the reserves) before joining Chester on a free transfer in June 1961. He spent one season at Sealand Road and, after a spell as player-manager of Stourbridge, retired from competitive football. He sadly died at his place of work, Brockhouses in West Bromwich.

DEREK KEVAN

'A big, rugged, hard-shooting centre-forward who made his presence felt.'

Born: 6 March 1935, Ripon, Yorkshire

Albion senior career:

Appearances: League 262, FA Cup 29
Goals: League 157, FA Cup 16
Senior debut: League, 24 August 1955 v Everton (h) won 2–0 (2 goals)
Also played for: Ripon City, Sheffield United (trial), Bradford Park Avenue, Chelsea, Manchester City, Crystal Palace, Peterborough United, Luton Town, Stockport County, Macclesfield Town, Boston United, Stourbridge, Ansells FC, West Bromwich Albion Old Stars (player and manager), England (14 full and 4 Under-23 caps), Football League (1 app), England XI (1 app)

Although everyone, including the most dedicated Albion supporters, knew he lacked finesse, Derek Kevan made up for it with pure strength and commitment, often bulldozing his way through both First Division and international defences. Referred to as 'the Tank', he certainly thrilled the Baggies fans with his all-action style and his goalscoring ability.

Derek was the first signing made by the former Tottenham Hotspur full-back Vic Buckingham after he had taken over from Jesse Carver as manager at The Hawthorns in February 1953. Secured for what was to prove a bargain fee of just £2,000, Derek completed his National Service in the Army before bedding himself in at The Hawthorns. He recalled: 'I was based initially at Yeovil and then at Preston and played a few games for my battalion. When on leave I also turned out occasionally for Albion's second and third teams. During this time I first met up with Don Howe and Duncan Edwards.'

Derek, who was being coached by the former Baggies goalscoring hero from the 1930s, W.G. Richardson, eventually made his League debut (with Howe) in Albion's 2–0 home win over Everton in August 1955. Replacing the injured Ronnie Allen, he impressed that evening by scoring twice, but it wasn't until just after the start of the 1956–57 season that he finally established himself in the first team. Once in, he stayed to become a legend at The Hawthorns.

Standing well over six feet tall and weighing 13 stones, Derek was as strong as an ox and, despite his bulk, was pretty quick off the mark. He was predominantly right-footed and was exceptionally good in the air. His tank-like thunderings down the middle of the pitch gave opposing goalkeepers (and centre-halves) nightmares more than once.

During the early part of his Albion career Derek had Bobby Robson and Allen alongside him in attack, while Jimmy Dudley and Ray Barlow supplied the passes from wing-half. Then, after Robson had switched to wing-half, a young Bobby Hope came in to thread the ball through to him from centre-field. Derek thrived on the ball placed ahead of him and, given enough space, he was onto it like a flash, often trying a shot at goal whenever possible. He didn't bother about passing to a colleague – his aim was to score for his club, and he did that regularly.

Derek's boss at The Hawthorns, Buckingham, agreed that his control was really no more than adequate at best and he tended to be a shade slow on the turn. But his presence out on the pitch always made defenders think twice, especially when the ball was pumped into the air.

Derek and his teammates were devastated when Albion lost to Aston Villa in the semi-final of the FA Cup in March 1957. He remembered: 'We led twice in the first game at Molineux but were pegged back to 2–2 late on. And then, right at the end, I should have won the tie but missed when clean through with only the 'keeper to beat. Allen was injured in the replay and we lost 1–0.'

Derek scored 20 goals that season, added 23 more in 1957–58, netted 28 the following term, weighed in with 29 in 1959–60 (including a wonderful five-timer in a 6–2 home League win over Everton), notched 18 in 1960–61 and then claimed a total of 34 in 1961–62, finishing joint top scorer in the First Division with Ipswich's Ray Crawford with 33, the highest post-World War Two League haul by an Albion player to this day.

One of the most controversial players to play for his country, and one of the most unfairly abused, Derek's bustling tactics were not viewed with unalloyed approval by some critics, but no one could deny that he made his presence felt on the international circuit. He scored eight goals in 14 appearances, starting off with a great header on his debut against Scotland at Wembley in April 1957 and, after being selected ahead of Brian Clough, netted twice in the 1958 World Cup Finals in Sweden, his first past the great Russia goalkeeper Lev Yashin, his second against Austria. Derek also gained Under-23 honours and netted a hat-trick for the Football League against the Scottish League in 1958.

In March 1963 Derek was stunned when he was told that Albion were transferring him to Chelsea. He had already bagged 16 goals in 28 appearances that season, including hat-tricks against Fulham and Ipswich and a four-timer against Bolton when, out of the blue, he was sensationally (and that's not exaggerating) sold to the London club for £50,000.

Derek said that he never wanted to leave Albion. He had made so many friends and had enjoyed almost 10 years with the club. Indeed, it came as a huge shock when he left. His manager at the time was Archie Macaulay, who had never really appreciated his work-rate and several times Derek had confronted him about this. Then, following a board meeting in March 1963, Derek was told by chairman H. Wilson Keys that Albion had accepted an offer from Chelsea and were selling him. Obviously upset, he later spoke to Macaulay and said 'Thanks very much. I gather you don't want me then?' And off he went to Stamford Bridge, bitterly annoyed. He had scored 173 goals for Albion in 291 games – a superb record. And to make things worse, some Albion players were still in shock as they lost their next match 7–0 to Wolves at Molineux, with Derek looking on from the stands.

Derek remembered: 'When I arrived at Chelsea I immediately fell out with manager Tommy Docherty. I told him to his face that I was not going to play for him and after seven games I was sold to Manchester City.' Derek did well at Maine Road, his 30 goals in 1963–64 helping City gain promotion to the top flight. Relatively unsuccessful spells at Selhurst Park, Peterborough and Luton followed before he finally gained a medal when Stockport won the Fourth Division title in 1967. After winding down his career in non-League football, Derek worked in a pub and was a delivery driver before returning to The Hawthorns in 1983 to work as a Lottery agent, as well as playing for the Albion All Stars charity team, whom he later managed. He now lives with his wife Connie in Castle Bromwich.

HARRY KEYS

'A grand club man...well-respected and looked up to by many.'

Born: 11 March 1861, Douglas, Isle of Wight
Died: 22 August 1929, West Bromwich

Albion career: Director (1896–1903; 1905–08; 1919–20), chairman (1899–1903; 1905–08)

Harry Keys was only three years of age when he came to West Bromwich with his family in the summer of 1864. A pupil at Beeches Road School, he completed his education at Bridge Trust Grammar School, Handsworth, and took a keen interest in most sports, with football and cycling top of his list. During the late 1880s he competed in, and won, several races in both the bicycle and tricycle events, and in 1891, in atrocious weather, he manfully pedalled round the 100-mile route of the Birchfield Wheeling Club in a record time of 6 hours and 36 minutes. Twelve months later he reduced his time by almost an hour. It is said that in his prime Harry was one of the finest race cyclists in the country.

Throughout his life Harry made every effort to encourage sport and as a celebrity he was asked to present many trophies to the winners of competitions in the local area. He was chairman of the Sports Committee linked to the West Bromwich Albion Football Club and helped arrange the annual sports tournament to assist the club financially during the late 1890s, often raising at least £200 for their benefit. Later associated with the West Bromwich Charity Sports Organisation, he filled an important role as Director of Sport from 1905 to 1910.

Harry's interest in football started in his school days and as a teenager he played as a forward for the Sandwell Road club, which at the time (1882–83) was one of the strongest in West Bromwich. It is thought that Harry was 24 when he attended his first Albion match – and he quickly became an avid supporter, never missing a home game. In 1896 he joined the club's Board of Directors and, being a man of strong personality, he quickly assumed command in the boardroom. In 1899, with the club in serious financial trouble, he took over as chairman, a position he retained until 1903. He then had two years 'off' but returned for a second spell in 1905 (to 1908) and for a third time in 1919–20 when he celebrated Albion winning the League championship.

The work he did for the club, and the manner in which he handled the money crisis, earned him the admiration of every sports person in the Midlands – amply demonstrated by the praiseworthy references which appeared in the local press.

Harry was one of the few people to realise that to meet the ever-increasing demand for higher wages and expenses, and if the club was to retain its place in the First Division, it was imperative that a new ground was found. Supported by his close friend and co-director Tom Harris Spencer (later a Sir), the search began to find a piece of land suitable for a new ground. It didn't take long, and by September 1900 The Hawthorns was officially opened with a League game against Derby County when over 20,000 spectators witnessed a 1–1 draw.

With club funds alarmingly low, it was something of a miracle that Harry dared to accept the further responsibility of The Hawthorns ground and the following extract from the *Athletic News* of 4 June 1900 aptly describes the situation: 'Now and again popular support has been wanting at West Bromwich, for the Albion have developed to an extraordinary degree, a habit of going to extreme, but it is to be said to the credit – to the everlasting credit – of Mr Keys, that his sympathies and support have never been known to waver and it must be known that in the important and delicate negotiations necessary in opening up a new ground, the club is able to command the assistance of such a thoroughly sound businessman.'

It is believed that Harry – referred to in some quarters as 'John Bull' – was a man of divided opinions, but he was always impartial and under the surface was very soft at heart. Nevertheless, he could, and often did, deliver a stern rebuke and always did it in a manner which gained for him the respect of everyone who came under his jurisdiction.

Generous to a fault and always loyal to his colleagues, his character soon singled him out for office in higher echelons and in 1905 he was elected to the Football League Management Committee, a position he held until his death. One of his most treasured possessions was a Long Service Medal, presented to him after 21 years of dedicated service. Harry was also a member of the Football Association and the International Selection Committee; President of the Staffordshire Football Association and a Vice-President of the Birmingham and District Football League.

He took great interest in all men serving in the forces during World War One and corresponded regularly with the Albion players and club officials on active service. Unfortunately the war claimed the lives of many of Harry's close friends and acquaintances and few people outside his own family realised what a severe blow he suffered when his youngest son, signalman Fred, aged only 19, went down with his ship after being torpedoed in the North Sea on Trafalgar Day in October 1917. As always in adversity, Harry kept a stiff upper lip and met the world with a smile.

He was a popular and greatly respected figure in West Bromwich and was rarely seen without his white spats and his traditional buttonhole. In 1925 he suffered a heart attack. At the time he was advised by his specialist to refrain from taking long journeys or getting involved in any excitement. This didn't go down too well, as he was a regular at The Hawthorns and as keen on the Baggies as anyone.

Harry, however, was his own man, and against medical advice he continued to make trips to Scotland, Wales and Ireland and to the Continent. He often went to London for football meetings. It was only his iron will that enabled him to make these journeys. Harry was determined to 'wear out rather than rust out.' He simply loved his football and would travel anywhere to be involved.

In addition to his qualifications, Harry Keys was also a brilliant artist and many of his friends were presented with paintings and sketches. A lover of animals, he specialised in pen and ink drawings of the heads of prize-winning dogs and thoroughbred horses, but he also produced many delightful pictures of other subjects, yet never chose to depict a footballer.

Harry, who was the first person to open a cycling school in West Bromwich and the first to teach ladies how to ride, died aged 58 in 1929. When he was buried in All Saints' Churchyard, West Bromwich, over 300 mourners from all over the country came to pay their last respects to one of the finest and most whole-hearted sportsmen West Bromwich has ever produced.

Harry's son, Major H. Wilson Keys, was associated with Albion as a director, chairman and President for 44 years (1930–74) and his brothers, W. Hall Keys and Clement Keys, were also closely linked with the club.

GEORGE LEE

'A strong, pacy winger who crossed the ball with unerring accuracy – and he could also shoot.'
'To opposing right-backs he was a menace as he hared away, showing them a clean pair of heels – and his left foot contained dynamite.'

Born: 4 June 1919, York
Died: 1 April 1991, Norwich

Albion senior career:

Appearances: League 271, FA Cup 23, Charity Shield 1
Goals: League 59, FA Cup 6, Charity Shield 0
Senior debut: League, 20 August 1949 v Charlton Athletic (h) (won 1–0)
Also played for: Knavesmere School (York), York City Schools, Yorkshire County Boys, Acomb
                    FC, Tottenham Hotspur (trial), Scarborough, York City, Bradford Park Avenue
                    (World War Two guest), Lincoln City (World War Two guest), Chester (World
                    War Two guest), Nottingham Forest, BAOR Select XI, Lockheed Leamington,
                    Vauxhall Motors
Managed: Norwich City reserves

Outside-left George Lee was a member of the Albion playing staff for nine years and a first-team regular for eight. During his time at The Hawthorns he scored 65 goals in 295 competitive games, helping the Baggies win the FA Cup and finish runners-up in the First Division in 1953–54. He also netted nine times in 36 second XI games.

Nicknamed 'Ada' from an early age, George was a major signing by the club in July 1949, costing £12,000 from Nottingham Forest. The outside-left position had been causing the Albion management some serious concern. Indeed, no fewer than nine different players had donned the number 11 shirt the previous season, including full-back Harry Kinsell, and George's arrival was certainly welcomed by the directors, supporters and players alike.

Unusually powerful for an out-and-out winger, raven-haired George loved hugging the touchline. He had a high-stepping action, was blessed with terrific pace and could unleash a crackerjack of a shot with his powerful

left foot (he hardly used his right). He could also cross the ball on the run with unerring accuracy and was at his most dangerous when cutting inside his full-back and shooting at goal (from varying distances). He was a potential match-winner without a doubt.

One newspaper reporter wrote (after Albion had whipped Newcastle United 7–3 in a League game at St James's Park in 1953): 'Lee, Albion's outside-left, gave the Newcastle right-back (Bobby Cowell) a torrid time. He showed great determination every time he had the ball. He used his pace and strength to good effect and his deliveries from out wide caused panic in the home defence time and again.'

During Vic Buckingham's early years as manager at The Hawthorns (he took over the reins in February 1953) George was encouraged, when the opportunity arose, to drive the ball low and hard across the face of the goal, simply because Albion's main strike-force at the time of Ronnie Allen and Johnny Nicholls and even reserves Wilf Carter and Ken Hodgkisson, were not tall men. And this ploy paid dividends as George's centres often caught 'air-minded' defenders off their guard.

Reading through old match reports, I can honestly say that George's crosses, passes, deliberate corner-kicks and fouls on him inside and outside the penalty-area in 1953–54, brought Albion at least 25 goals. One of his measured flag-kicks was volleyed home superbly by Allen when Newcastle were defeated 3–2 in a rip-roaring fifth round of the FA Cup at The Hawthorns and it was his left-wing cross that set up Allen again to give the Baggies the lead in the Final against Preston. George also netted seven League goals himself that season, including crucial ones in the away victories at Manchester United (3–1) and Sheffield Wednesday (3–2) and in the home triumph over Middlesbrough (2–1).

On three occasions George's goal-tally in a season with Albion reached double figures. In 1951–52 he scored 12 times, weighed in with 11 goals the following term and netted 13 in 1954–55 when only one other player, Allen, claimed more. After seven years as Albion's first choice left-winger – he appeared in 252 out of a possible 275 League games between February 1950 and September 1956 – George was eventually replaced by Roy Horobin early in 1956–57.

He remained at The Hawthorns for another season before joining Midland non-League side Lockheed Leamington in June 1958. After that George played briefly for Vauxhall Motors before returning to The Hawthorns as Albion's trainer/coach in June 1959. He stayed for another four years and after that, from 1963 until 1987, he served Norwich City, initially as first-team trainer/coach and then as second-team manager, working under future Albion boss Ron Saunders from 1969 to 1973.

Going back to his early days in football, George spent a season with Scarborough and was registered with York City from 1936 until 1947 when he transferred to Nottingham Forest for £7,500. In World War Two he served in the BAOR (British Army on the Rhine) and played as a guest for three different League clubs. He was the first footballer to score 100 goals for York, reaching that personal milestone with a penalty against Sheffield Wednesday in April 1943. He had earlier, in 1941, netted a four-timer in a 9–5 win over Middlesbrough and a hat-trick in a 3–3 draw at Hull. George played with some great players at York, including future Charlton goalkeeper Sam Bartram, England international Ronnie Dix and Frank O'Donnell. As a Forest player George finished up as the club's top scorer in 1948–49 with 10 goals. Finally, during his lengthy stay at Carrow Road, Norwich City twice won the Second Division championship, in 1972 and 1986, lifted the Football League Cup at Wembley in 1985 and finished runners-up in that same competition in 1973 and 1975.

RODDY McLEOD

'A short, bustling inside-forward, clever on the ball with a telling shot.'

Born:	12 February 1872, Kilsyth, North Lanarkshire
Died:	13 December 1931, Lambeth, London

Albion senior record:

Appearances:	League 149, FA Cup 20, Others 16
Goals:	League 50, FA Cup 7, Others 8
Senior debut:	FA Cup, 14 February 1891 v Sheffield Wednesday (a) won 2–0
Also played for:	Kilsyth & Kirkintillock Schools, Westburn FC, Partick Thistle, Leicester Fosse, Southampton, Brighton United, Southampton

After doing exceedingly well as a schoolboy, scoring plenty of goals, Roddy McLeod joined his local club Westburn FC in 1887 and two years later became a professional with Partick Thistle. In January 1891 he was signed by West Bromwich Albion for a fee of £50 and made an impressive debut the following month in a third-round FA Cup tie against Sheffield Wednesday, having a hand in Tom Pearson's goal, which clinched victory.

His arrival at Stoney Lane, however, came too late to prevent Albion finishing the 1890–91 season at the foot of the table and having to apply for re-election to the Football League, which was successful. Baby-faced, small in stature, chunky-looking and built like a piece of Scottish granite, Roddy was a splendid forward who had the ability to turn a game by using his deft footwork. He began the 1891–92 campaign with two goals in the opening match against Everton, but the remainder of the League season was again disappointing for both him and Albion, who struggled for long periods and eventually finished 12th (out of 14).

In the FA Cup, however, it was a completely different story as Albion enjoyed great success, reaching the Final for the fourth time in six years. Roddy scored in a 3–2 opening round win over Old Westminsters and then played his part in further victories over Blackburn Rovers, Sheffield Wednesday and Nottingham Forest in the semi-final, the latter taking three matches to complete before Albion produced a fine display to win 6–2 in a snowstorm at Derby.

The Final was against Aston Villa at the Oval in March 1892 and Albion's Cup experience proved the difference between the two Midlands sides. Roddy's telling cross to Jasper Geddes set up Albion's first goal and he also teed up Jack Reynolds to fire in a third goal to seal a comfortable 3–0 victory.

In the 1892–93 season Roddy was an ever-present for the first time in his career and finished with 10 League goals, two behind leading marksman Tom Pearson, as Albion finished in mid-table. He also registered his first Albion hat-trick, in a 7–1 home win over Burnley.

The following season Roddy scored in four of the first six League matches and continued to find the net on a regular basis thereafter, claiming his second Albion treble in a stunning 8–0 League victory over arch-rivals and reigning FA Cup holders Wolves at Molineux in late December 1893. The reporter covering that game for *The Weekly News* stated: 'The Albion forwards, simply made rings round the Wanderers and I have never seen the Cup holders so completely and hopelessly beaten. Bassett and McLeod were outstanding and besides his three goals the Scotsman (McLeod) twice hit the woodwork and was unlucky with two other shots.' Roddy ended the campaign as the Baggies' top scorer with a total of 24 goals, 14 in the League.

The perfect partner to England winger Billy Bassett on Albion's right flank, Roddy scored 11 times in 1894–95 but again it was a disappointing season for the Baggies, who managed only 13th place in the First Division but, as it had done three years earlier, the team battled hard and long in the FA Cup and again reached the Final to set up a repeat of the 1892 showdown with Villa. This time, despite having several scoring opportunities, two falling to Roddy, Albion went down 1–0, the goal coming after just 30 seconds play.

Unfortunately the 1895–96 season was yet again bitterly disappointing for Albion, who were very poor. They again finished at the foot of the table and stayed up only because of a Test Match victory over Liverpool. Roddy, though, worked his socks off up front. An ever-present once again, he was second top scorer behind Billy Richards with 10 goals.

Despite Albion's dismal League form – they had never looked like challenging for honours since 1889–90 – Roddy remained loyal to the club. The supporters loved him; he got on very well with the rest of his colleagues and was a regular in the team, only missing out on the action through injury or illness.

Just after scoring the winner in the Black Country derby against Wolves in October 1896, Roddy injured his right knee in a clash with the Wanderers' rugged centre-half Billy Malpass. Sidelined for almost three months, during which time Albion scored only 11 goals in 12 games and were battered 8–1 at Blackburn, he returned to first-team duty in January but played only two games before the injury flared up again. He contributed just four goals that season, which proved to be his last in an Albion shirt.

In his seven seasons with the Baggies, Roddy had made 169 appearances in all competitions, scoring 57 goals.

In the summer of 1897 he moved to Leicester Fosse and was the Foxes' top scorer with 13 goals in his only season with the club. Tempted by a good offer from Southern League side Brighton United, Roddy moved to the south coast in May 1898. He scored on his debut for the Seagulls but, despite finishing up as the club's top scorer, financial troubles resulted in his contract being cancelled in April 1899.

Persuaded to remain in the Southern League by Southampton, Roddy helped Saints win the championship in 1899–1900 and he also scored the winning goal in a 2–1 FA Cup victory over his former club, Albion, but had lost his place in the team by the time the Final was played in April, which Saints lost 4–0 to Bury.

In August 1900 Roddy joined Brentford and helped the London club win the Southern League Second Division title in 1901. Remaining at Griffin Park for six years, Roddy announced his retirement from professional football in May 1906. He subsequently fell on hard times and suffered from rheumatoid arthritis, a legacy from his playing days. In March 1911 Southampton made an appeal on his behalf for employment as a warehouseman. He later took employment in a brewery, was a civil servant, worked as a teller in a bank and then as a boiler mechanic in London. He was only 59 when he died in Lambeth in 1931.

BOBBY McNEAL

'Pertinacious and confident, he always gave good service to his left-winger.'

Born:	19 January 1891, Hobson Village, County Durham
Died:	15 May 1956, West Bromwich

Albion senior career:

Appearances:	League 370, FA Cup 30, FA Charity Shield 1, Wartime 2
Goals:	League 9, FA Cup 1, FA Charity Shield 0, Wartime 0
Senior debut:	League, 8 October 1910 v Leeds City (h) won 2–0
Also played for:	Hobson Wanderers; wartime guest for Fulham, Middlesbrough, Notts County and Port Vale; England (2 full caps), Football League (5 apps)

Although on the small side, around 5ft 6in tall, Bobby McNeal was a persistent, confident and thoughtful left-half who gave West Bromwich Albion wonderful service for a total of 16 years, 15 as a player. He had spent three years playing in the Tyneside & District League with his home-town club Hobson Wanderers before, as secretary manager Fred Everiss put it: 'One early evening in June 1910, Bobby came out of the pit from an afternoon shift to negotiate his transfer to Albion…and after talking for half-an-hour with myself and director Billy Bassett, he eventually agreed to move to the Midlands, signing the appropriate forms on a billiard table in a local miner's club.'

Costing Albion just a month's wages, around £25, within 12 months Bobby had gained a Second Division Championship-winning medal, played in an FA Cup Final in 1912, was capped twice by England, first against Wales (being one of four debutants in that game) and versus Scotland in 1914 and six years later was a key member of Albion's First Division Championship and FA Charity Shield-winning teams.

Bobby was introduced to League football four months after arriving at The Hawthorns. Taking over from the injured Freddie Buck at inside-left – the position he played in at school and during his early years with Hobson Wanderers – he helped Albion beat Leeds City 2–0 in a Second Division game at The Hawthorns in front of 13,149 fans, having a hand in Sid Bowser's opening goal.

He certainly played very well that afternoon and got high praise from his stand-in skipper Jesse Pennington and also from the local press, the *Midland Chronicle* stating: 'McNeal was always looking for an opening…his passing was thoughtful and his general all round performance was impressive.'

After reverting to his favourite position of left-half, Bobby went on to make 31 appearances that season, scoring his first Albion goal, a beauty, struck right-footed, in a 3–0 home win over Clapton Orient on April Fool's Day. At that time the race for promotion and top spot in the Second Division was hotting up. It went right to the wire. In their final game of the season Albion met Huddersfield Town at The Hawthorns. They knew they had to beat Huddersfield Town to become champions…and they achieved the required victory, just, by a goal to nil. Bobby had an outstanding game in midfield, completely bottling up the visitors' danger man and Scottish international Jim Howie. In the end Albion clinched the title with two points to spare over runners-up Bolton Wanderers (53–51) and Bobby had won his first medal as a professional footballer.

In 1911–12, playing in the top flight of English football, Bobby missed only one first-team game (against Everton, away in late April) as Albion finished a creditable ninth in the League and reached the FA Cup Final. After impressive victories in earlier rounds over Tottenham Hotspur, Leeds City, Sunderland (away), Fulham and Blackburn Rovers, the latter in a tightly-contested semi-final replay, Albion met Second Division Barnsley in the Final. They had most of the play at Crystal Palace but couldn't break down a tight and tough Tykes defence and, as a result, were taken to a replay. At Bramall Lane, the Baggies once more dictated the game for long periods but were undone in the very last minute of extra-time when Harry Tufnell raced past a tiring Bobby and then Jesse Pennington to score the winning goal and break Albion's hearts.

The last three seasons before World War One saw Bobby make 110 appearances for Albion and he also represented England and played five times for the Football League, indicating, to a certain extent, that he was one of the best left-halves in the country. A crowd of almost 128,000 packed into Hampden Park to see him play in front of his Albion teammate and captain Jesse Pennington against Scotland. Although finishing up on the losing side (3–1), reporter R.M. Connell of the *Daily Mail* wrote: 'McNeal played with heroic courage…he had one shot saved by Brownlee and generally held the clever McMenemy of Celtic at bay.'

During the war, when free from his duties as a private in the British Army, Bobby guested for four League clubs, and in 1918 starred for Fulham in their London Victory Cup Final win over Chelsea at Highbury. A year later he helped Albion win the Midland Victory League. Fit and raring to go when League football resumed after the hostilities, Bobby and Albion had a memorable 1919–20 season, winning the First Division championship in style with a record 60 points and a record goal tally of 104. Bobby was an ever-present and scored two goals – the first a booming penalty in a 4–0 win at Bradford, the second, and Albion's opener, in a last-match 4–0 home victory over Chelsea.

Retaining his fitness and his form, Bobby continued to impress as Albion battled to consolidate their place in the top flight. However, the 1924–25 season proved to be Bobby's last at The Hawthorns and, indeed, the last of his playing career. He started the campaign with 391 first-class appearances under his belt and only two players previously – England full-backs Joe Smith and Jesse Pennington – had made 400 or more for Albion. Although under pressure from Harry Dutton and Sammy Richardson for his place in the side, Bobby reached that milestone of 400 games in mid-October in the 1–1 draw with Birmingham. He played in three more matches after that before a knee injury ended his career.

When the final curtain came down at the end of that season, Bobby was presented with a runners'-up medal after Albion had finished second in the table behind Huddersfield Town. Leaving The Hawthorns in May 1925, Bobby took over a pub in West Bromwich and, once established, he returned to The Hawthorns as a part-time coach for the 1926–27 season. He continued to attend Albion's home matches whenever he could, and was a guest of honour at two FA Cup Final celebration dinners, in 1931 and 1954.

Bobby was taken ill at Easter 1956 and died soon afterwards, aged 65.

TOMMY MAGEE

'A "Pocket Hercules" who tackled strongly and gave splendid service to the attack.'

Born:	6 May 1899, Widnes
Died:	10 May 1974, Widnes

Albion senior career:

Appearances:	League 394, FA Cup 6, Wartime 6
Goals:	League 15, FA Cup 0, Wartime 3
Senior debuts:	Wartime, Midland Victory League, 5 April 1919 v Derby County (h) won 3–1 (1 goal scored)
	League, 30 August 1919 v Oldham Athletic (h) won 3–1
Also played for:	Widnes Athletic FC, Crystal Palace, Runcorn (player-manager), England (5 full caps), England international trialist, FA XI (tours in 1926 and 1931)

Originally an outside-right or inside-right, Tommy Magee was transformed into a short, stocky, nippy right-half, a midget on the football field, who played with evident enjoyment, tenacity, wonderful consistency and constructiveness. Nicknamed the 'Mighty Atom' by his playing colleagues and supporters alike, 'wee' Tommy appeared in over 430 games for Albion during 15 years of service with the club and he was good enough to win five full caps for England.

Besides enjoying football at school, Tommy was also a very enthusiastic Rugby League player, a sport he continued along with his football for two years after ending his education when he went to serve his country in World War One. In August 1917 Tommy was wounded at Sailly-Sailly and moved out of the front line. His new company had a 'pretty smoky' football team and Tommy went out and scored 48 goals in 24 games. A fellow soldier, Tom Brewer, who was an avid Albion supporter, contacted the club telling them about a very talented soldier-footballer, a wizard named Tommy Magee.

Albion's secretary-manager Fred Everiss received the letter and, in his own inimitable way, followed it up. Fred recalled in his *Memoirs*, published in the *Sunday Mercury* in 1949: 'We were always glad to hear of any up-and-coming youngsters, so I contacted the officer of the company, Lieutenant Hill, whose home was in Smethwick. I forwarded the necessary forms and asked him to obtain the boy's signature for us as an amateur. I learned later that he actually put his name on the dotted line in the trenches. The forms were returned, duly filled in, and when the lad (Tommy) was demobilised, I sent for him to play in a friendly against Aston Villa at The Hawthorns in March 1919. I found he was a chubby-faced, blue-eyed youngster aged 18 who actually joined the forces by giving a false age. Really, if he had told the truth then, I doubt whether he would have been old enough even to have been accepted as a drummer boy.'

One of Albion's smallest-ever players (he was just 5ft 2½in tall and weighed barely 10st) Tommy scored two grand goals in his first game, at the end of which he apologised for feeling 'a bit strange.' But Fred and team trainer Bill Barber, chairman Billy Bassett, former player Dan Nurse and captain Jesse Pennington saw something special, and knew that Albion had acquired a very talented player. The next day Tommy was upgraded to the professional ranks and he never looked back.

Tommy made his Football League debut at inside-right in Albion's opening game of the 1919–20 season at home to Oldham Athletic and went on to play his part in bringing the League championship trophy to The Hawthorns for the first (and so far only) time in the club's history, netting seven goals in 24 appearances as partner to flying winger Claude Jephcott.

Due to a niggling ankle injury, Tommy was called upon only five times the following season, but in 1921–22 he was brought back on the right-wing to replace broken leg victim Jephcott. When Jephcott returned, Tommy was moved back to right-half in place of Sammy Richardson and, apart from injuries, illness and international calls, he held that position for a decade, from August 1922 until October 1932 when Welshman Jimmy Murphy replaced him.

In March 1923, he won the first of five full caps for England, lining up in the 2–2 draw with Wales at Cardiff. Two months later he played in his second international against Sweden in Stockholm, when he had a hand in one of the goals in a 3–1 victory.

There were several quality wing-halves around at that time, with Frank Moss of Aston Villa being one of the best. It was he who tended to keep Tommy out of the England team. However, in December 1924 The Hawthorns played host to the England-Belgium game and once again Tommy was called into the team for his third cap, starring in a 4–0 victory. His fourth and fifth international appearances followed against Scotland at Hampden Park in April 1925 when 92,000 fans saw the Scots win 2–0, and in the 3–2 win over France in Paris a month later.

He then toured Canada with the FA party in the summer of 1926 and five years later made a return trip to North America, clearly emphasizing that at the time of both tours he was regarded as one of the best wing-halves in the country.

Continuing to play for Albion with wholehearted endeavour and total commitment, Tommy was an ever-present in 1926–27, but his efforts couldn't prevent the Baggies from being relegated to the Second Division. However, he rolled up his sleeves and with grim determination fought like a tiger with the rest of his teammates in an effort to regain top-flight status as quickly as possible. That finally arrived in 1930–31 when Albion completed the unique double, winning the FA Cup and finishing runners-up in the Second Division.

That season Tommy, who made 32 League appearances and played in all nine Cup matches, showed great spirit, feeling that every game could be won. He ran his socks off, covered every blade of grass in every game he played, and was an inspiration to everyone.

The editor of the *Albion News* wrote: 'Tommy is marvellous for his size. A stout tackler, full of dash and verve, his constructive ability is of the highest order and he always sets a fine example to the rest of the team…a wonderful professional to have around.'

Tommy, who also played in over 100 second-team games for Albion, gaining two Central League championship-winning medals, eventually left The Hawthorns in May 1934, moving to London to become player-coach of Crystal Palace. He never appeared in a first-class game for the Selhurst Park club and in May 1935 switched nearer to his place of birth by joining Runcorn as player-manager. Later taking over as coach, he remained with the non-League club until his retirement from football in April 1947, aged 48. At that point Tommy returned to Widnes, where he worked in engineering until 1954.

*The only player to have won both a League Championship and an FA Cup-winners' medal, Tommy is believed to be the smallest player ever to wear an England shirt and is certainly the smallest first-team player Albion have ever had.

LEN MILLARD

'A lithe and indomitable left-back who knew no fear – a splendid club man and captain.'

Born:	7 March 1919, Coseley near Wolverhampton
Died:	15 March 1997, Coseley

Albion senior career:

Appearances:	League 436, FA Cup 40, Charity Shield 1, Wartime 148
Goals:	League 7, FA Cup 0, Charity Shield 0, Wartime 11
Senior debuts:	Wartime League (South), 29 August 1942 v Northampton Town (a) (lost 2–0)
	FA Cup, 5 January 1946 v Cardiff City (a) drew 1–1
Also played for:	Wallbrook FC, Coseley Town, Bilston Town, Sunbeam FC, Bilston Borough (World War Two guest), Sedgley Rovers (World War Two guest), Stafford Rangers (player-manager)

Talking about Len Millard in an article published in the *Birmingham Gazette & Despatch* in April 1954, Albion's 1931 FA Cup-winning captain and then director, Tommy Glidden, said: 'I remember Len when he first came to the club as a youngster. As a matter of fact I was his coach at The Hawthorns. I've never met a keener youngster than he was, and he has gone on to be one of the finest servants the club has ever had. A superb team man, he has a wonderful temperament, is a grand footballer and is absolutely 100 per cent Albion.

'If every team had 11 Millards there would be no fear as to football's future. All I can say is, right now, that Len is one of the finest left-backs and captains in the Football League, and I would go so far as to say that there aren't many in the world who are better than him…he is England class, on par with the great Jesse Pennington who played for Albion either side of World War One and was of course an England international.

'Len was, of course, originally a wing-half but he could play anywhere really, even in goal if he wanted to. He was so adaptable and I have already seen him occupy five different numbered shirts and he's produced excellent displays in every position.'

Albion chairman Major H. Wilson Keys, who knew a bit about football and indeed about signing players, thought that Len was equally as good as Pennington, saying: 'When he beat Jesse's appearance record of 496 first-class appearances for Albion in 1953, I was one of the first men to congratulate him. He was 34 at the time, but looked as fit as any player at the club and I told him that he still had at least three or four more seasons left in him, so go on to reach the 600 appearance mark...but first make sure to bring back the FA Cup.'

Len did both. In fact, taking into account his exploits in wartime football, he went on to play in 625 games for the Baggies, a terrific record that stood for years until Tony Brown eclipsed it in the late 1970s. And he lifted the FA Cup at Wembley when Albion defeated Preston North End 3–2 in the 1954 Final.

A pupil at Christ Church School, Coseley, Len played for four local teams before joining Albion's groundstaff as an amateur in May 1937. Over the next five years he appeared in the club's third, fourth, fifth and sixth sides, finally making his first-team debut in a Wartime League South game at Northampton Town in August 1942. Three weeks later he signed professional forms and went from strength to strength after that.

Never dropped, he was fortunate to avoid any serious injuries and only a twisted ankle, sore knee and a couple of bouts of flu kept him out of action. He averaged over 42 games a season from 1942–43 until 1955–56, being an ever-present in 1947–48 and 1954–55. In fact, he missed only 14 competitive matches out of a possible 452 during the 10-year period from 1946–47. That's consistency of the highest degree.

In his first season in the senior side, Len actually lined up at right-half, left-half, centre-forward and inside-left, and he scored seven goals, including two hat-tricks, against Leicester City and arch-rivals Wolves in his third and sixth matches.

His first outing at full-back came in April 1944 and at the end of that season he helped Albion win the Midland Wartime Cup (v Nottingham Forest). After the hostilities had ended, Len occupied the left-half position throughout the 1946–47 campaign, before alternating between left-back and the two wing-half berths in 1947–48 and 1948–49 when he was in superb form as Albion secured promotion back to the First Division after a break of 11 years.

Taking over the number three shirt from Harry Kinsell, Len remained in the left-back position until the end of his Baggies career, which covered 21 years and one month. He was outstanding in 1953–54 when Albion came so desperately close to winning the coveted League and Cup double and, of course, he joyously skippered the team at Wembley when he completely blotted out the threat of the Preston captain and England winger Tom Finney.

Len's best goal return in League football came in 1946–47 when he netted three times. He also scored two vital goals in 1954–55 – a last-minute equaliser in the 3–3 draw at Chelsea in October when the attendance was almost 68,000 and the only strike of the home game with Cardiff City in late December. This second effort was a stunning 35-yard drive, struck high into the roof of Ron Howells's net at the Smethwick End of the ground. It was real gem.

In Len's penultimate season at The Hawthorns (1956–57), Welshman Stuart Williams and converted forward Wilf Carter both deputised for him at left-back. Len made 28 appearances that term, his lowest seasonal total as an Albion player up to that time He was given just one more League outing the following season by manager Vic Buckingham (in a 1–1 draw at Leeds when Williams was on international duty) before leaving the club to become player-manger of Stafford Rangers in June 1958. Retiring three years later, he spent the rest of his life relaxing in his native Coseley. In 1989 Len sadly had a leg amputated (a legacy of his playing days) and was confined to a wheelchair until his death in March 1997, at the age of 78.

Refereed to as 'Millard the Dependable' and 'The Agitator' by players and supporters alike, Len Millard would have shed the proverbial last drop of blood for West Bromwich Albion. He was a real 'honest-to-goodness' Black Country footballer who gave his all on the field of play, and I don't think there have been many more loyal and dedicated club men.

The great Stanley Matthews admitted that Len was one of the shrewdest full-backs he ever played against, confessing that he 'never had a good game' against him. And that was a huge feather in Len's cap.

DARREN MOORE

'A real strongman in defence, as hard as iron, who gave 110 per cent every game.'

Born: 22 April 1976, Handsworth, Birmingham

Albion senior record:
Appearances:	League 93+11 FA Cup 8, League Cup 4
Goals:	League 6, FA Cup 0, League Cup 0
Senior debut:	League, 15 September 2001 (sub) v Watford (a) won 2–1
Also played for:	Holly Lane Colts, Walsall (trialist), Torquay United, Doncaster Rovers, Bradford City, Portsmouth, Barnsley, Jamaica (3 full caps), Rest of the World (1 app)

A pupil at James Watt Primary and Holyhead Secondary schools in Handsworth, Darren had a trial with Walsall before becoming a trainee with Torquay United and, after doing well in the Gulls second XI, he made his League debut in March 1992 against Birmingham City. Turning professional eight months later, he established himself at centre-half and went on to play 124 times for Torquay before transferring to Doncaster Rovers for £62,500 in July 1995. Two years later he switched to Bradford City for £310,000, but a spate of injuries restricted his appearances during his first season at Valley Parade. Regaining his fitness, Darren helped the Bantams win promotion to the Premier League in 1999, but refused to sign a new contract and was left out of the team by manager Paul Jewell. Recruited by Portsmouth for £500,000 in November 1999, he spent less than two years at Fratton Park before returning to the Midlands to sign for Albion for £750,000 in September 2001.

Twenty-four hours after arriving Darren made his Baggies debut as a substitute in a 2–1 win at Watford. Slotting in alongside Larus Sigurdsson and Paul Gilchrist, he helped Albion gain promotion to the Premiership that season and had the pleasure of scoring the first goal 'to settle the nerves' in the decisive final game of the season against Crystal Palace. 'That was some game' he said. 'The atmosphere inside The Hawthorns was electric – we weren't going to lose, I can tell you that for nothing.'

A rock at the heart of the Baggies defence, Darren – 'Big Dave' to the fans – was named in the PFA Division One team that season and in August 2002 netted against Fulham at the Brummie End to earn Albion their first-ever win in the Premier League. Darren recalled: 'Things didn't go according to plan that season. We were always struggling and everyone at the club was bitterly disappointed when we were relegated. But we vowed to play our hearts out and try to get back up at the first time of asking.'

In fact, Darren suffered a serious knee injury in a clash with Jimmy-Floyd Hasselbaink during the home Premiership game against Chelsea in mid-March 2003, which kept him out of contention for some considerable time. 'I was sick of staring at the treatment room ceiling. I was in there for virtually six months. It was boring, real boring. I think I wore my ear-pieces out listening to my favourite music…much to the annoyance of physio Nick Worth.'

Darren returned to first-team duty in November 2003, as a late substitute in the win at Nottingham Forest, and was reinstated at the heart of the defence on a permanent basis by the end of December. Remaining in the side, he celebrated a second promotion-winning campaign following a 2–0 win over his former club, Bradford City, in late April.

Albion signed defender Darren Purse in June 2004 and this immediately put pressure on Darren. Thomas Gaardsoe was already bedded in at the back and it was Purse who got the nod to accompany him, leaving Darren somewhat annoyed, although he did win his third cap for Jamaica, having gained his first two with Portsmouth, and he also represented The Rest of The World (with teammate Jason Roberts) in a prestige friendly against an African XI.

Gritting his teeth, Darren plugged away and got back into Albion's League side in October, only to suffer another agonizing injury, which again saw him in the treatment room. He made only 17 appearances in 2004–05 and, with injuries continuing to affect his game, turned out just nine times the following season. Sent off at Wigan Athletic in mid-January 2006, his only dismissal in an Albion shirt, this proved to be Darren's 116th and last appearance for the club. Later that month he joined Derby County for £300,000, the fee rising to £500,000 after a set number of appearances.

During his time at The Hawthorns, Darren became a huge favourite with the fans and was mentioned in the third series of the BBC's satirical cartoon *Monkey Dust*. An Islamist group from West Bromwich planned to assassinate him, but failed and received a signed miniature shirt instead!

A pivotal figure in the Derby side in 2006–07, he helped the Rams gain promotion to the Premier League after a five-year absence by winning the Championship Play-off Final, ironically against his former club, Albion. This was the fourth time he had been part of a promotion-winning team, following on from his two successes with Albion and his achievement with Bradford City. And to put the icing on the cake, he was also named in the PFA Championship team for 2006–07. However, glory didn't last long and, after one season with the 'big boys', the Rams returned to the Championship, demoted in last place with just 11 points. Despite this Big Dave was voted Player of the Season.

Released in the summer of 2008, Darren was keen to rejoin his former club Bradford City, but in the end chose Barnsley, the Tykes fending off competition from several clubs to secure his services. Giving 100 per cent, as always, Darren helped keep the Oakwell side in the Championship while at the same time taking his career appearance record to almost 600.

Besides being called Big Dave (after a character in a Pot Noodle TV advert), Darren has also been referred to as Bruno (after boxer Frank Bruno), Dazza (at Derby) and also Mr T (from the A-Team). His manager at Derby, Billy Davies, called him Mooro, and occasionally Mooron if he had messed up on the pitch.

A devout Christian, Darren is active in the Christian charity Faith and Football. In 2005, along with Linvoy Primus, a former teammate, he walked along the Great Wall of China to raise money for children's causes. He has also raised thousands of pounds for Christian Aid and Oxfam and started to raise awareness about helping children in third-world countries. He organised a charity bicycle ride from the Valley (Charlton) to Fratton Park (Portsmouth) via Barnet and Reading, four clubs Primus has played for, to raise money for the Faith and Football charity, and in 2004 he received an award for 'Outstanding Contribution to Grass Roots and Community Football Projects' as part of the PFA's 'Let's Kick Racism Out of Football' campaign. Darren is also a current member of the management committee of the Professional Footballers' Association.

When Darren returned to The Hawthorns as captain of Barnsley in May 2010, he received one of the longest ovations, coupled with cheering, ever afforded to a former player, such was his popularity with the Baggies' supporters.

FRED MORRIS

'A highly skilled player with an extremely hard shot – a prolific goalscorer, one of the best of his era.'

Born:	27 August 1893, Tipton
Died:	12 July 1962, Great Bridge, Tipton

Albion senior record:

Appearances:	League 263, FA Cup 20, Others 4
Goals:	League 112, FA Cup 4, Others 2
Senior debut:	League, April 1912 v Sunderland (h) won 1–0 (scored)
Also played for:	Bell Street Primitives, Tipton Victoria, Redditch, Fulham (guest), Watford (guest), Tipton Excelsior (guest), Coventry City, Oakengates Town, England (2 full caps), Football League (1 app), FA XI (1 app), England trialist and junior international

In season 1919–20, Albion won the Football League championship for the first, and so far only, time in the club's history and they did so by recording 28 wins and netting 104 goals, 37 of which were scored by one player, Fred Morris. At the time Fred's total fell one short of the League scoring record held by Bert Freeman, who had struck 38 goals for Everton in season 1908–09. Yet Fred should have set a new record quite easily. In the last game of the season, at home to Chelsea, and despite his teammates continually creating chance after chance, he failed to hit the target as Albion romped to a 4–0 win. He actually missed two close-range sitters, the first a shot straight at goalkeeper Jim Molyneaux when clean through and the second when he headed Howard Gregory's centre over the top when it seemed easier to hit the net.

'That's how things go,' said Fred afterwards. 'One day you might score from 20 yards, the next day you will miss from point blank range, such is football.' Fred wasn't unduly worried about not scoring against Chelsea; Albion had already won the title and he had got his medal, as well as a new club scoring record.

Fred had a great ability. Two-footed, he displayed a rare degree of judgment in making passes to his colleagues, was quick off the mark, knew where the goal was (often shooting from distance and from any angle) and he was also a good header of the ball. Indeed, his marksmanship was the outstanding feature of his play. In his column in the *Birmingham Gazette*, Mavis once wrote 'Give Morris an opening, however small it may be, and he wouldn't hesitate a moment in taking advantage of it. He had the knack of shooting on sight, which is invaluable to any forward.'

Fred had plenty of off days. In a League game against Bolton Wanderers in September 1920 he missed five relatively simple chances. 'I was far too anxious,' he said. Six weeks later he couldn't do a thing right in the local derby against Aston Villa, fluffing two simple tap-ins, and then, during the first three months of the 1921–22 season, when Albion desperately needed some goals, he went 12 games without scoring and was actually dropped.

Fred came from an area where enthusiasm for Albion has always run high and it is a place made famous in pugilistic circles by an old-time boxer known throughout the Midlands as the 'Tipton Slasher.' Consequently Fred was imbued with that fighting spirit of local patriotism which makes it a distinction to play for the Baggies.

Fred played his early football in and around his native Tipton before spending two seasons, 1909–11, with Redditch, enticed there by a former Albion player, Harry Aston, who had certain connections with the non-League club. Occupying the centre-forward position, he scored over 30 goals for Redditch and was selected to represent Birmingham against Scotland in a junior international in April 1911.

Also starring in this same match was the Brierley Hill Alliance outside-right Claude Jephcott. Both players caught the eye of two Albion scouts and within a few weeks they had been signed up as professionals.

Fred's progress into the first team at The Hawthorns was rapid. He made a scoring debut in the home League game against Sunderland in April 1912 and ended that season with three goals to his credit in six starts. The following season he got into the first team in October and netted nine times in 22 outings while partnering Harry Wright, Bob Pailor and Sid Bowser.

Unfortunately he wasn't so effective in 1913–14 when playing alongside new signings Alf Bentley and Albert Lewis, managing only seven goals in 28 appearances, but in the last season before World War One, when he played mainly at inside-left, he reached double figures for the first time, netting 11 times in 29 appearances.

In an article written by Albion's secretary-manager Fred Everiss in 1913, he declared: 'Fred is one of the best shots in the League. He feeds his partners unselfishly and with uncanny artistry, which is rarely met with in so young a player.'

Now firmly established in Albion's forward line and averaging a goal every three games, Fred's progress, along with so many others, was halted when he enlisted in the RAF as a mechanic in the Ministry of Transport Base Depot, starting off in Northfleet before travelling overseas to Egypt via Ruislip and Bookham. During the hostilities Fred played as much football as possible. He scored 24 in 24 games as a guest for Fulham and assisted Watford and his local club Tipton Excelsior before helping Albion win the Midland Victory League in 1919.

Then, in 1919–20, when everything went right for Fred and Albion, his goal haul included a five-timer in an 8–0 home win over Notts County, making him the first player to achieve this for the club. He and his co-striker that term, Alf Bentley, netted 52 League goals between them and Fred's efforts earned him the first of two England caps, which he celebrated with a goal in a thrilling 5–4 victory over Scotland at Hillsborough in April. Gaining his second cap against Ireland six months later, he also netted twice for the Football League against the Scottish League and represented an FA XI.

Fred bagged 16 goals in 1920–21, and 11 the following season, and when he put away his seventh goal of the 1922–23 campaign in a 2–0 home win over Manchester City in early November he became the first player to score a century of goals for Albion at competitive level. He finished with a total of 14 that season, which included a stunning four-timer in a wonderful 7–0 victory over Arsenal.

Having scored 118 goals in 287 first-team appearances, Fred eventually left Albion for Coventry City in August 1924. He spent just 12 months at Highfield Road before having five excellent seasons with Oakengates Town, for whom he scored over 40 goals. Retiring in May 1930, he worked for a local engineering firm for several years before his death in 1962.

JIMMY MURPHY

'A sharp tackler with a huge appetite for hard work.'

Born:	27 October 1910, Ton Pentre, Glamorgan
Died:	14 November 1989, Manchester

Albion senior record:

Appearances:	League 204, FA Cup 19
Goals:	None
Senior debut:	League, 5 March 1930 v Blackpool (a) lost 1–0
Also played for:	Ton Pentre Boys, Treorchy Thursday, Treorchy Juniors, Mid-Rhondda Boys, Swindon Town, Morris Commercial FC, Wales (1 Schoolboy and 15 full caps)
Managed:	Manchester United (caretaker), Wales (international team)

The seventh child of a widowed Irish mother with six children by her first husband, Jimmy's early years in the Rhondda Valley were typically tough but leavened by his twin passions – football and music. His talent with the ball was soon spotted, and by 1924 he'd made a winning debut for Wales Schoolboys against England at Ninian Park, Cardiff.

This 'aggressive, little terrier', as the local paper put it, had his heart set on Cardiff City, but it was Albion who eventually saw off the attentions of several prospective suitors to secure his services in February 1928.

After overcoming 'terrible homesickness' his hard-tackling style and unquenchable spirit helped him make good progress at The Hawthorns and, after a handful of senior appearances, at inside-right and wing-half, he became a regular in Albion's League side halfway through the 1931–32 season, taking over the right-half position from Tommy Magee.

He went on to play in 223 first-class games for the club over the next eight years, appearing in the 1935 FA Cup Final defeat by Sheffield Wednesday and also gaining 15 full caps for his country, winning his first against England at Wrexham in November 1932 when skipper Fred Keenor was rested. In this game Jimmy – nicknamed 'Spud' and 'Twinkletoes' – marked his Baggies teammate Teddy Sandford and did a pretty good job in a goalless draw.

A very popular player at The Hawthorns, Jimmy had time for everyone, often staying behind for an hour after training to sign autographs for the young supporters. A very under-estimated player, and totally committed, Jimmy was one of the best right-halves in the First Division over a period of four years from 1932–36. 'His enthusiasm, drive and resilience made him a special player,' said

Albion's trainer at the time, Fred Reed. The man who signed him, secretary-manager Fred Everiss, described him as being 'a glutton for hard work', whereas his teammate in 1936, inside-right Tommy Green, said he was 'a tireless player, a real workhorse who never believed in defeat.'

In 1931–32 Jimmy made 27 League appearances, producing splendid displays in the home wins over Bolton Wanderers, West Ham United and Newcastle United. After the 2–1 victory over the latter club, the *Midland Chronicle* reporter wrote: 'Murphy was outstanding. He always had the upper hand in 50–50 challenges and United's inside-left, Ronnie Starling, was completely stifled.'

An injured knee sidelined Jimmy for the first six weeks of the 1932–33 season, but after that he was superb, producing many more outstanding performances as Albion claimed fourth place in the First Division, their highest League finish since 1925. Maintaining his form, he missed only 11 games out of a possible 145 played by Albion between 8 October 1932 and 23 November 1935 and, although he suffered a few niggling injuries, he always looked fit, sometimes running harder at the end of a game than he did at the beginning.

In 1935–36, he played in only 16 First Division matches. Jack Sankey had impressed in the second team and was pushing hard for a place in the League team, but Jimmy wasn't going to give up his position without a fight. Out of action with a twisted ankle and a hip injury, he returned as keen as ever and in his last two seasons at The Hawthorns made almost 50 appearances, including his 200th for the club against Charlton Athletic at the Valley in September 1937.

Albion were relegated at the end of that season and, with fellow Welshman Dougie Witcomb ready to fill the right-half position, Jimmy's last outing for Albion, at senior level, came in October 1938 in a 2–1 defeat away at Southampton.

After 223 first and 146 second-team appearances, Jimmy was transferred to Swindon Town for £140 in March 1939. He spent just four months at the County Ground and assisted Morris Commercial FC before serving in the Eighth Army during the war. In the summer of 1945, while stationed in Bari, Italy, he met Matt Busby and in the spring of 1946 Jimmy was invited along to Old Trafford to join Manchester United as a coach, the United boss describing Jimmy as '…my first and most important signing.'

Developing into a wonderful coach and brilliant motivator, he spent countless hours on the training ground in an old baggy tracksuit, drilling such talents as Johnny Carey, Charlie Mitten, Jack Rowley, Johnny Aston and Henry Cockburn, all of whom became internationals. He quickly helped guide United to FA Cup glory in 1948, and the League championship in 1952, as he continued to nurture along stars of the future like Duncan Edwards, David Pegg, Eddie Colman, Roger Byrne, Bobby Charlton and Tommy Taylor.

In October 1956, Jimmy took on the additional job of Welsh team manager, succeeding Wally Barnes, and he subsequently guided Wales to their only appearance in the World Cup Finals in Sweden in 1958. In the same year he also took Manchester United to their second successive FA Cup Final (beaten this time by Bolton Wanderers) having stepped into the breach in the aftermath of the Munich air disaster when Busby was lying seriously ill in a German hospital.

When Busby came home and returned to his day job at Old Trafford, Jimmy went back to coaching and serving as assistant manager. The United team was rebuilt and, with Denis Law, George Best, Charlton and others, won two League titles and the FA Cup. However, the pressure of having two jobs became too much for Jimmy and in June 1963 he gave up his position with Wales, continuing as assistant manger/coach at Old Trafford until 1972, seeing the coveted European Cup come to Old Trafford in 1968.

Engaged until 1982 as a locally-based scout and then as a senior scouting supervisor for the Reds, Jimmy spotted several 'future internationals' including Steve Coppell, Gordon Hill and Stuart Pearson, and he also recommended Gary Lineker to Old Trafford, although the board said 'no…he's far too lean!' Jimmy, who was associated with Manchester United for 36 years, was 79 when he died in Manchester in 1989.

STUART NAYLOR

'A terrific goalkeeper on his day, heavy in build, sound and courageous in performance.'

Born: 6 December 1962, Wetherby, Yorkshire

Albion senior record:

Appearances: League 354+1, FA Cup 13, League Cup 22, Others 20
Goals: None
Senior debut: League, 22 February 1986 v Manchester United (a) lost 3–0
Also played for: Leeds Boys, Yorkshire County Schools, Leeds United (trial), Yorkshire Amateurs, Lincoln City, Peterborough United, Crewe Alexandra, Bristol City, Mansfield Town, Walsall, Exeter City, Rushden & Diamonds, England (one Youth and 3 B caps)

Stuart Naylor's football career began, in earnest, as a 15-year-old when he represented Leeds Boys with another future Albion player, Martin Dickinson. At that time Stuart was attending Wetherby High School and actually played rugby and cricket as well as football. He did well at centre-forward for his school team but kept goal for both Leeds Boys and Yorkshire County before joining Yorkshire Amateurs in 1978, while also having a trial at Elland Road. 'I think I did okay at Leeds,' said Stuart, 'but I did not sign for Jimmy Armfield's team as something was not quite right.'

The following year, in February 1979, Stuart signed as a future professional for Lincoln City, whose manager, Colin Murphy, agreed to let him continue studying for his A-levels in history, geography, economics and general studies. In May 1980, Stuart played for England in a Youth international against Austria and when time allowed lined up in goal for the Imps at various levels.

During his time at Sincil Bank, Stuart

had loan spells at Kettering Town (during January and February 1983; two games), Peterborough United (another eight outings, as deputy to broken collarbone victim David Seaman, between February and April 1983) and Crewe Alexandra (from October 1983 to May 1984 and again from August to November 1984, appearing in a total of 62 competitive matches).

After making 61 appearances for Lincoln, including one as an emergency centre-forward away to Newport County in October 1982, Stuart was transferred to West Bromwich Albion, signed by manager Ron Saunders for £110,000 in February 1986. Replacing Tony Godden, he went on to serve the Baggies for 10 years, during which time he made 420 appearances (a record for an Albion goalkeeper), won three England B caps (v Switzerland, Iceland and Norway) and also went back for a brief spell on loan with his former club, Crewe (in August 1994).

After leaving The Hawthorns in August 1996, Stuart played, in turn, for Bristol City (46 appearances), Mansfield Town (six games on loan), Walsall (as experienced cover), Exeter City (38 outings) and Rushden & Diamonds (four matches) before announcing his retirement in May 2001, having made his final appearance at competitive level in a Football League Trophy game for Diamonds against Barnet in November 2000.

Moving quickly into coaching with Rushden & Diamonds, Stuart followed his former Albion teammate and manager Brian Talbot to Oldham Athletic in March 2004, acting as goalkeeping coach at Boundary Park for 15 months before taking up his current role as goalkeeping coach at Bristol City in July 2005.

Back in his Albion days, when Stuart arrived at The Hawthorns there were four other decent goalkeepers at the club: Tony Godden, Paul Barron, Mark Grew and Paul Bradshaw. He thought at the time 'bloody hell...I will have to work hard here.' Stuart was given his Baggies debut by Saunders at Old Trafford, where he was beaten three times, twice from the penalty spot, by United's Jesper Olsen.

Stuart recalled: 'I found that playing in the First Division was a far greater challenge than I had expected. But I quickly found my feet and although we went down that season I was confident I had joined the right club and vowed to play to my best ability in an attempt to win back our First Division place.

'Things weren't going all that well out on the pitch at that time. There was a bit of tittering among the players and occasionally articles would appear in the newspaper about our manager. Clive Whitehead, one of the senior players, told me to never slag off the boss in the press, because you don't know whether you'll ever need him again. I abided by what Clive said.

'However, quite a few things went wrong when Saunders was in charge. I remember one morning we were all waiting at the Moat House for the coach to arrive to take us to an away game at Luton. It never turned out and we had to drive to Kenilworth Road in three cars and a mini-bus. We lost 3–0!

'Then, ahead of a trip to Leeds, the coach was there at the Moat House when we arrived, but this time the directors were scheduled to come with us. When they turned up, there was no room on board and they had to travel to Elland Road by car. A few weren't too amused!'

During his time at The Hawthorns, Stuart played under seven different managers – Saunders, Ron Atkinson, Brian Talbot, Bobby Gould, Ossie Ardiles, Keith Burkinshaw and Alan Buckley – plus two caretaker managers, John Trewick and Stuart Pearson.

Stuart said: 'Saunders was one of the most upfront of the lot – he'd tell you if you'd done alright, and if you hadn't. I got on okay with him...I don't think he ever dropped me.

'As for Big Ron, I was okay with him. In fact, when he was in charge I was out of contract and was free to talk to other clubs, which I did, but I told Ron what was going on. He knew the score and in the end I signed a new deal.'

Stuart was having personal problems with a divorce in 1991. 'I was dropped by Talbot and thankfully missed the embarrassing FA Cup defeat by Woking,' he recalled. After that he played in 39 games under Ardiles in 1992–93. Stuart rated him highly, saying 'If he had asked us to jump off a cliff, we would have done so.' However, Stuart was obviously disappointed when the Argentinian signed Tony Lange from Wolves, who went on to play in that season's Play-off Final at Wembley.

An injured knee which required an operation and a lot of physio work affected Stuart's game from 1993 onwards, but he bravely battled on and in 1994–95 was an ever-present. A year later – after his testimonial match against Coventry City – he left The Hawthorns for pastures new. He is still enjoying the game, albeit as a coach rather than a player.

JOHNNY NICHOLLS

'A goal-poacher extraordinary — if there was a sniff of a chance, Johnny was there.'

Born:	3 April 1931, Wolverhampton
Died:	1 April 1995, West Bromwich

Albion senior record:

Appearances:	League 131, FA Cup 14
Goals:	League 58, FA Cup 6
Senior debut:	FA Cup, 23 February 1952 v Blackburn Rovers (a) lost 1–0
Also played for:	Heath Town FC, Heath Town Wesley, Heath Town United, Wolverhampton Wanderers, Cardiff City, Exeter City, Worcester City, Wellington Town, Oswestry Town, Sankeys Works, West Bromwich Albion Old Stars, England (1 Under-23, 1 B, 2 full caps)

Although Johnny Nicholls was an Albion player for only seven years, in my mind, and in the minds of thousands of Baggies supporters who saw him in action, he was a great goalscorer, a legend who formed a terrific partnership with Ronnie Allen. An instinctive 'poacher' who pestered defenders, Johnny was a real shooting star whose goals, for a brief period in the mid-1950s, helped brighten the firmament of the club.

Standing 5ft 8in tall and weighing under 11st, the son of a former Midlands bantamweight and featherweight boxer, Johnny was a real handful, with a quick eye and wonderful positional sense. He was brave, hungry for goals and was a thorn in most club's defensive structures. As so often happens, it took the prowess of a more talented footballer to bring out his qualities. The player who 'made' Johnny was Ronnie Allen. When Allen was switched from being a winger into a roving centre-forward, his partnership with Johnny took one's breath away.

During the 1953–54 season, when Albion came so near to completing the League and Cup double, Johnny and Allen — the 'Terrible Twins' — scored 66 goals between them, the biggest combined tally by two main strikers in the club's history.

Albion were on course to become the first club since 1888–89 to achieve the coveted double after defeating Port Vale in the Cup semi-final in March. But a spate of injuries eventually put paid to any hopes they had of winning the League. They did, however, make up for that disappointment by lifting the FA Cup, although Johnny was not at his best in a 3–2 victory over Preston at Wembley. 'I was too jittery,' he said.

Before the Final, Johnny and his buddy Ronnie Allen had played together for England against Scotland at Hampden Park. It was Johnny's first cap and he celebrated by scoring with a diving header from Tom Finney's cross in a 4–2 win. Reliving the occasion a few years later, Johnny said: 'It never stopped raining that day. The markings on the pitch were done in sawdust, not paint and the goalposts were square. Over 134,000 spectators packed into the ground…yet the atmosphere wasn't great – it all seemed the same as if 60,000 were there.

'It was my 23rd birthday and although a tad nervous, I soon settled down. I had a couple of chances in the first half before putting us 2–1 in front just after half-time. I didn't have a good game, but I was still chosen for the next international in Yugoslavia. We lost 1–0 and I was never chosen again. Well there were some decent forwards around besides me, Nat Lofthouse, Tommy Taylor and Dennis Wilshaw among them.'

Earlier that season, Johnny had played for England at Under-23 level against Italy and had come on as a substitute in the B international in Switzerland. 'I was sitting on the bench for the Swiss game – without a pair of shorts…that's the truth,' recalled Johnny. 'I was sent on in place of Ronnie (Allen) and yes, I had to play in my bleeding underpants, a pair of Y-fronts. That was embarrassing.'

As a youngster Johnny attended Molineux one week and The Hawthorns the next and scored goals galore in junior football. In 1946, Albion's manager at the time, Jack Smith, who lived in Wolverhampton, saw Johnny play and was obviously impressed, so much so that he sent his mate, Les Southall, round to see him. Asked if he would like to play for Albion, Johnny said yes straightaway. 'I played in a friendly which we won 7–0 and had a few games in the A team, but then I received a letter from Wolverhampton Wanderers who wanted me to sign for them. I told them that I had already signed amateur forms for Albion, but as a Wolves fan, I agreed to play a few games for Wolves.' Watched now and then by Stan Cullis, he scored a few goals for their A team before being called up to do his National Service in the Army.

Still undecided about which club to join, Albion or Wolves, in the end Jack Smith persuaded Johnny to sign for him, which he did in August 1950, with another year still to do in the Army.

Things moved fast for Johnny. He turned professional for £8 a week in August 1951, and made his senior debut for Albion in an FA Cup tie at Blackburn in 1952. Although not a regular in the first team, he appeared in over 40 games and scored 12 goals in two seasons, including strikes in both games against Wolves at Easter 1952. Then, under manager Vic Buckingham, he finally established himself as Allen's strike-partner in 1953–54. And what a terrific season it turned out to be.

Johnny cracked in his first Albion hat-trick in a memorable 7–3 League win at Newcastle, netted four important goals against the reigning champions Arsenal (two at home, two away), struck vital winners at Sheffield United and Manchester City and destroyed the Rotherham and Tottenham rearguards in the Cup.

In 1954–55 he netted 14 times in 19 outings, adding eight more goals to his tally in 24 starts in 1955–56, but failed to hit the target at all in his 17 appearances in 1956–57. By now Derek Kevan and Bobby Robson were playing alongside Allen and this meant that Johnny's Baggies career was over. Besides his first-class record, he had also scored 140 'other' goals for the club – 46 in 69 second XI matches, 52 for the intermediates and 42 for the juniors, 11 in one game.

Transferred to Cardiff City for £4,000 in May 1957, Johnny moved to Exeter City four months later before winding down with Worcester City, Wellington Town, Oswestry Town and Sankey's Works. Retiring in 1962, he continued to play in charity matches for the Albion Old Stars (up to 1985) and he attended Albion home matches right up until his sudden death from a heart attack while driving home after the Albion-Middlesbrough League game in 1995.

JOHN OSBORNE

'Albion's bionic goalkeeper...brave, brilliant at times, daring and consistent.'

Born:	1 December 1940, Barlborough, Derbyshire
Died:	2 December 1998, Worcester

Albion senior record:

Appearances:	League 250, FA Cup 24, League Cup 16, Europe 8, FA Charity Shield 1, others 13
Goals:	None
Senior debut:	League, 7 January 1967 v Nottingham Forest (h) lost 2–1
Also played for:	Chesterfield Boys, North East Derbyshire & District Schools, Barlborough Colliery Miners' Welfare, Netherthorpe, Chesterfield, Walsall, Coventry City, Shamrock Rovers, Preston North End, Telford United, Birmingham Post & Mail Rangers, West Bromwich Albion All Stars
Managed:	Corinthians FC (Birmingham)

John Osborne made 312 first-class appearances for Albion. Only five other goalkeepers have made more for the club: Tony Godden, Stuart Naylor, Harold Pearson, Joe Reader and Jimmy Sanders. Yet as a youngster he was an outfield player and represented England Schoolboys as a left-half. He took up goalkeeping as a 16-year-old and in July 1959 signed amateur forms for Chesterfield – just after Gordon Banks had left Saltergate for Leicester City. John did well in the second XI and in September 1960 Spireites boss Duggie Livingstone upgraded him to the professional ranks. He never looked back. He played over 120 competitive games for Chesterfield before transferring to Albion in January 1967, manager Jimmy Hagan paying just £10,000 for his services.

Taking over from Ray Potter, John missed that season's League Cup Final against Queens Park Rangers due to being Cup tied, but the following year he starred at Wembley, helping Albion beat Everton in the FA Cup Final.

'Ossie' was a goalkeeper right out of the top drawer. He was a character in many ways, often cracking jokes during a match, not only in front of his teammates but in the face of his opponents as well. He possessed enormous courage, was alert, quick off his line and wouldn't hesitate to use his feet to avert a dangerous situation. A safe handler (most of the time) he commanded his area with authority, although at times he did lose concentration, skipper John Wile once asking 'Where's he gone this time?'

Another of John's teammates, Bobby Hope, described him as being a 'great practical joker – the dressing room comedian', adding 'You need people to lift you when something goes wrong. Ossie was that kind of man, wonderful to have around.

'On the field, he would come out to the edge of his area if he had to, collect everything, or try to, but above all he was a good shot-stopper, a cracking goalkeeper, one of the best I've played with. Yet, surprisingly, he's the only player I've met who didn't enjoy playing football. He told me straight that he hated Saturdays and hated playing. He said that training was the best, turning out on a Saturday afternoon just seemed to spoil a week's hard work.

'He was often a bundle of nerves before a match and quite often he went missing just as we were about to walk down the tunnel. Someone had to dash off and look for him...finding him in the toilet, having a fag, twitching nervously. He was always the same – but once on the pitch, he was okay...and I will honestly say that he produced some terrific displays between the posts, especially during that 1967–68 Cup run. He deserved his winners' medal without a doubt.'

Ossie was also known around The Hawthorns as Giorgio Armani – because of the outrageous clothes he used to wear. Some of his gear – his ties especially – was unbelievable and he was often the butt of Jeff Astle's jokes. Despite his off-beat antics and over-elaborate dress sense, John suffered quite a few hand injuries and in the end had to have a strip of plastic inserted into one of his fingers, hence his nickname 'the bionic goalkeeper'.

He remained Albion's number one until May 1970, playing in that year's League Cup Final defeat by Manchester City. Then cricketer-footballer Jim Cumbes arrived from Tranmere Rovers, signed by manager Don Howe. Confined to the reserves, deep down John wasn't a happy chappie, but he stuck in there and regained his position 12 games into the 1971–72 season, only to announce that he was retiring at the end of the campaign.

That came as a shock to everyone, but in January 1973 he was persuaded to 'return' to The Hawthorns and, in order to get match fit, he was loaned out to Walsall. However, with new signing Graham Smith and young Peter Latchford both keen to make their mark in the first team, John knew he had to be at his best to win back his place. Reinstated between the posts for the home game with Chelsea on 10 March, unfortunately his experience, know-how and ability couldn't save Albion from relegation and for the first time since 1949 Second Division football came back to West Bromwich.

Out of favour for the duration of the 1973–74 season and for the first three months of the following term, John was brought back once again in October 1974. And this time he stayed put. 'Yo' can't keep a good 'un down for long,' said one ardent supporter.

Johnny Giles took over from Don Howe as manager in the summer of 1975 and in his first season in charge Albion gained promotion back to the First Division, John being quite outstanding. An ever-present, he conceded only 33 goals, kept 22 clean sheets and match after match produced some brilliant saves. Indeed, his displays at Blackpool, York and Portsmouth were all superb and on several other occasions he kept Albion in a game when realistically they should have been dead and buried.

John kept goal for another season before Tony Godden took over. After a deserved testimonial, which realised over £32,000, he eventually left the club for Shamrock Rovers in July 1978, teaming up once more with Johnny Giles, and after that was a non-contract player at Preston, Telford and Coventry before working for the *Birmingham Post & Mail*, based in the company's West Bromwich office. A non-contract player with Walsall in 1983, he then managed local non-League club the Corinthians and participated in several charity games for the Albion All Stars team before becoming commercial manager of Worcestershire CCC.

John was a keen ornithologist who also enjoyed quizzes and at one time ran a sports shop with fellow goalkeeper Jim Cumbes. He died of cancer at the age of 58 in 1998.

GARY OWEN

'A player with plenty of vision, he could switch the method of attack very quickly with his long passes.'

Born: 7 July 1958, St Helens, Lancashire

Albion senior record:

Appearances: League 185+2, FA Cup 12+2, League Cup 24, Europe 4
Goals: League 21, FA Cup 3, League Cup 2, Europe 0
Senior debut: League, 18 August 1979 v Derby County (h) drew 0–0
Also played for: Clockface Juniors, Glazeborough, Warrington & District Boys, Manchester City, Panionios (Greece), Sheffield Wednesday, Hammarby IF (Norway), Apoel (Cyprus), England (7 B and 22 Under-21 caps), Football League (1 app)

Midfielder Gary Owen had an excellent career which spanned 18 years. In that time he amassed 442 club and international appearances and scored 62 goals.

After doing exceedingly well as a schoolboy, Gary joined Manchester City as an apprentice in August 1972 and turned professional three years later. He made his League debut at the age of 17 against Wolves in March 1976 and scored his first goal against West Ham United soon afterwards.

He remained at Maine Road for seven years, during which time he netted 23 times in 124 first-class games, helping City finish runners-up in the First Division in his last season with the Sky Blues.

In May 1979, Len Cantello left Albion and immediately manager Ron Atkinson went out and signed Gary for a fee of £465,000, saying at the time: 'I will always have a ball player in midfield and Gary is the man for me.'

Around the same time Atkinson also signed Gary's City teammate Peter Barnes for a club record fee of £748,000, and they made their Albion debuts together in the opening League game of the 1979–80 season against Derby County at The Hawthorns.

Initially Gary partnered John Trewick and Bryan Robson in the engine-room, and as the season progressed he was joined by Remi Moses.

He played in 46 competitive games during his first campaign with Albion, scoring five League goals, one of them against his former club Manchester City in September when the Baggies won 4–0 at The Hawthorns.

In the 1980–81 season Gary made a further 42 appearances for Albion, netting six goals, four of them penalties, but then he, along with his teammates, was stunned when boss Atkinson left to become manager of Manchester United, eventually taking Gary's midfield colleagues Robson and Moses with him.

Ronnie Allen took over the reins at The Hawthorns and he quickly engaged another former Manchester City star, Steve Mackenzie, to take over from Robson in midfield. And shortly afterwards he recruited Andy King; however, the latter was in and out of the team and in fact Gary, the mainstay once more, had several assistants in the engine-room as he went on to appear in 54 of Albion's 58 competitive matches.

Although Albion's League form was not brilliant in 1981–82 – they only escaped relegation by two points – the team did reach the semi-final of both domestic knock-out competitions, losing to Tottenham Hotspur over two legs in the League Cup and to Queen's Park Rangers in the FA Cup.

Gary recalled: 'To lose a semi-final is a sickening experience. To lose in two was earth-shattering. I was confident we would reach the League Cup final, but we didn't play well in the first leg against Spurs and although we perhaps played the better football at White Hart Lane we simply couldn't find a way through.'

'I was substitute for the FA Cup semi-final encounter with QPR at Highbury, and although we were expected to win, again our form eluded us and on a dusty pitch we fell short on the day and lost to a flukey goal.'

In 1982–83, with Ron Wylie in charge, Gary was again one of Albion's most consistent players, adding another 41 senior appearances to his tally, but his Baggies career was under discussion throughout the campaign as both Wolves and his former club Manchester City came sniffing around.

Thankfully, Gary agreed to sign a new contract in readiness for the start of the 1983–84 season, and when Johnny Giles returned for a second spell as Albion manager, he began to mould his side around the midfielder. But it was hard going on the pitch. Albion struggled in the League and to make things worse Gary fractured his right shin in a 1–0 defeat at West Ham in December. Close to regaining full fitness, he then had the misfortune to break his shin again (also requiring a skin graft) as well as twisting his knee and suffering from a bout of meningitis. In fact, he was out of action for a combined total of 14 months, eventually returning in February 1985.

Unfortunately he was never the same player again and, following Albion's relegation from the top flight, he left The Hawthorns in July 1986, signing for the Greek club Panionios for a fee of £25,000, having scored 26 goals in 229 first-class appearances and once in 31 Central League games for Albion over a period of seven years.

After a year in Greece, Gary returned to England and spent the 1987–88 season with Howard Wilkinson's Sheffield Wednesday, and after two games for the Swedish club Hammarby IF and 16 for Apoel in Cyprus, he reluctantly announced his retirement in May 1990, two months before his 32nd birthday.

Away from his club football, Gary gained 22 Under-21 and seven B caps for England, but he never made it into his country's senior team despite being named in the squad for a major international on three occasions.

He helped England win the 1982 UEFA European Under-21 Championship, scoring two goals in the Final against West Germany. In fact, his total of 22 Under-21 caps remained a record for several years and to this day only 11 players have won more caps for England at this level than Gary.

Currently, Gary works as a freelance journalist in Manchester, providing opinion on his beloved Manchester City in the *Manchester Evening News* and on the local radio station, Century FM. He also has an art dealership, called Gary Owen Fine Art.

HAROLD PEARSON

'A natural between the posts,"Algy" was sound rather than showy, and difficult to beat.'

Born:	7 May 1908, Tamworth
Died:	31 October 1994, West Bromwich

Albion senior record:

Appearances:	League 281, FA Cup 21, Charity Shield 1
Goals:	None
Senior debut:	League, 26 September 1903 v Liverpool (a) won 3–1
Also played for:	Glascote United, Glascote Methodists, Belgrave Working Men's Club, Belgrave United, Two Gates FC, Nuneaton Borough, Tamworth Castle (guest), Millwall, West Ham United (guest), international trialist, England (1 Junior, 1 full cap), FA XI (1 app)

At the peak of his career, goalkeeper Harold 'Algy' Pearson stood over six feet tall and weighed almost 14 stone. He was sound rather than spectacular, difficult to beat in the air and to a certain extent on the ground, and his playing days spanned more than 20 years.

He had played for several different local clubs in and around the Tamworth area before joining Albion as a 16-year-old amateur in April 1925, his father Hubert having a big say in the transaction. In fact, Harold's father was still a member of Albion's playing staff at the time and would remain at The Hawthorns for 12 months before announcing his retirement. Even then he regularly attended training sessions, giving his son advice and generally passing on all the experience of being a top-class goalkeeper himself.

In an interview I did with Harold in 1981, he told me that he was sure he would follow in his father's footsteps and become Albion's goalkeeper. 'I knew I would make the grade,' he said. 'I was confident from the first day I joined the club and I knew as well that my father was always there to give me encouragement.'

Albion's secretary-manager Fred Everiss, who signed Harold, said at the time: 'We had an early option on young Harold. When the team coach called at Tamworth to pick up his father for away games, Harold, a babe in his mother's arms, was usually there to wave dad goodbye. The players insisted, even then, that one day young Harold would play for Albion, one of them saying "Make sure you keep on eye on him, gaffer".'

Harold quickly settled in at The Hawthorns and after a season in the intermediate team he broke into the Central League side in 1926–27 and was loaned out to Tamworth Castle, whom he helped win the Bass Charity Vase Final as well as representing England in a junior international.

However, with George Ashmore and Tom Sproson ahead of him in terms of selection, Harold had to wait until a week before Christmas 1927 before making his Football League debut in the home Second Division match against South Shields. Harold recalled: 'I was told that I would be playing after training on the Friday lunchtime. George (Ashmore) got injured the week before at Manchester City and with Tom (Sproson) suffering with a bout of flu, I was selected ahead of another young 'keeper, William Vaughan. I will admit that I was nervous before the kick-off, but as soon as the game got going and I had touched the ball a couple of times, I was fine. And we went on to win 3–0.'

Harold made 10 more first-team appearances that season, ending with a five-match unbeaten run. He played in the opening two games and the last 12 of the 1928–29 campaign.

At this time Ashmore was still playing very well and Harold, although keen to get regular first-team action, was still effectively learning the trade in the 'stiffs'. In 1929–30 he played in half of Albion's 42 League games, but by now another 'keeper, Jimmy Adams, had arrived on the scene to put extra pressure on himself and, of course, Ashmore.

As things turned out, Harold became first choice between the posts the very next season, when he helped Albion achieve something that had never been done before (or since)…winning the FA Cup and gaining promotion to the top flight of English football in the same season.

With a settled back division of himself, full-backs Bert Trentham and George Shaw and centre-half Bill Richardson, along with Jimmy 'Iron' Edwards, Albion finished runners-up in Division Two behind Everton and defeated Birmingham 2–1 in the Cup Final at Wembley. In goal for Blues that day was Harold's cousin, Harry Hibbs, who was also first-choice in the England team. And when Harry was injured during a game against Bolton in March 1932, Harold was called up as his replacement for the home international against Scotland at Wembley the following month. With his Baggies teammate George Shaw also in the side, both did a fine job as the Scots were defeated 3–0.

Unfortunately, that was Harold's only major representative honour, although he did return to Wembley for a third time in 1935 when Albion lost 4–2 to Sheffield Wednesday in the Cup Final, and he also helped the second XI win the Central League title in 1934, when he played in 12 games. By this time Ted Crowe and Adams were Albion's other two main goalkeepers and in 1936 Billy Light arrived at the club from Southampton. However, Harold was still good enough to compete with them all and hold his place in the first team.

In August 1937, Millwall's manager Charlie Hewitt, a former Albion player, enquired about Harold's availability. After a couple of days of negotiations a deal was agreed and Harold – after 303 appearances for the club – was transferred to the Londoners for £300. He bedded in immediately at the Den and helped the Lions win the Third Division South Championship in his first season. Registered with the club during the early part of the war, he made a guest appearance for West Ham in a 5–0 win over Watford in November 1939 before announcing his retirement in May 1940 when he returned to the Midlands.

For four years from 1948 to 1952 he was employed as a coach at The Hawthorns and for two seasons under manager Vic Buckingham, 1953–55, he acted as Albion's regional scout before taking up full-time employment at W.J and S. Lees, iron founders in West Bromwich, where he worked until he was 65, staying on as a labourer for a few years after that to earn some money for his pipe tobacco! Harold was 86 when he died in 1994.

HUBERT PEARSON

'His safe and supple goalkeeping was marked by certainty and brilliance.'

Born:	16 May 1886, Kettlebrook, Tamworth
Died:	26 October 1955, Kettlebrook, Tamworth

Albion senior record:

Appearances:	League 341, FA Cup 29, Others 7
Goals:	League 2, FA Cup 0, Others 0
Senior debut:	FA Cup, 15 January 1908 v Birmingham (a) won 2–1
Also played for:	Kettlebrook Oakfield, Tamworth Castle, Tamworth Athletic, Oldbury Town (guest), England (Junior international), Football League (2 apps), Football League XI (1 app)

The only goalkeeper to have scored for Albion in a major competition, Hubert 'Joe' Pearson took over the number one spot at The Hawthorns from Jimmy Stringer during the 1909–10 season, having made his debut two years earlier in an FA Cup replay at St Andrew's. Broad-shouldered, well-balanced, agile, daring, full of confidence and utterly dependable, he joined the club as a 19-year-old amateur in February 1906, actually signing the appropriate forms on platform one at Glasgow's main railway station shortly after starring for England in a Junior international match against Scotland at Celtic Park.

Said Albion's secretary-manager Fred Everiss, who attended the match: 'I was very impressed with Hubert. I had to sign him there and then.' In fact, the Albion official learned later that representatives from Aston Villa had been waiting at Birmingham's Snow Hill station for Hubert's train to arrive from Scotland and were ready to offer him a lucrative contract.

Upgraded to professionalism within a month, Bert performed with confidence and no mean skill in Albion's second team before making a competent debut for the senior XI in a local derby against Blues, the first of 12 senior outings he was given that term.

The following season he made only two appearances before playing 18 times in 1909–10 when Stringer was still a strong challenger between the posts. But it was Bert who took control and he would remain as first choice 'keeper at The Hawthorns until 1923, when George Ashmore replaced him.

In 1910–11, when Albion gained promotion as Second Division champions, Bert missed only four matches, due to a back strain. He actually conceded only 32 goals in 34 appearances and at times was quite superb, especially in the away wins at Fulham, Glossop, Lincoln and Stockport and during the home victories over Burnley, Gainsborough Trinity and Wolves.

Playing in the top flight for the first time in his career, Bert produced some excellent displays as Albion powered their way to the FA Cup Final. He helped keep Barnsley at bay in the first game at the Crystal Palace, and for 119 minutes of the replay at Sheffield, but then, after a slip by full-back Jesse Pennington, he was beaten by a late strike from Harry Tufnell and the trophy went to Oakwell instead of The Hawthorns.

Bert scored two League goals for Albion in 1911–12, both from the penalty spot. The first was against Bury at home on Boxing Day, which set up a 2–0 win, and his second was against Middlesbrough, also at The Hawthorns, over the Easter period when the Baggies won 3–0.

In and out of the team owing to injury and illness in 1912–13, Bert was an ever-present the following season and missed only two games in 1914–15. During the war he served in the AA Reserve Regiment, based on the Isle of Wight, and when on leave played a few games as a guest for Oldbury Town (1915–16) and also turned out for Albion, whom he helped to win the Midland Victory League at the end of the 1918–19 season.

League football resumed in earnest in August 1919 and what a terrific first post-war season it turned out to be for Albion! They won the First Division Championship in style, scoring over 100 goals and conceding only 47. Bert played in 39 of the 42 matches, missing the 2–1 and 8–0 wins over Bolton away and Notts County at home and the 2–0 defeat at Notts County. He was brilliant in the 3–0 and 5–1 victories over Derby and Blackburn respectively and he also saved Frank Hudspeth's penalty in the 2–0 win at Newcastle.

Holding his form for the majority of season 1920–21, Bert was injured at Preston in April and missed the last six matches and the first 14 of the following term. He returned to the fold in November 1921 and held his place until the final weeks of the 1922–23 campaign when Ashmore took over.

Bert had been playing quite splendidly during the final weeks of the 1922–23 season, so much so that he was selected to play for England against France in a full international in Paris in May. The regular 'keeper at the time, Ted Taylor of Huddersfield Town, had been carrying a thigh injury for several weeks and pulled out of the team. Bert was called up as his replacement but, agonizingly for him, he too had to withdraw at the 11th hour due to a knee problem. Jack Alderson of Crystal Palace took over and Bert never got another chance.

Over the course of the next two seasons – 1923–24 and 1924–25 – Hubert made only eight first-team appearances for Albion. At this juncture Ashmore was firmly established between the posts, Joe Sproson was a capable reserve and Hubert's son, Harold Pearson, was slowly but surely making headway in the club's third team.

Officially announcing his retirement as a player in May 1926, having spent a season on the coaching staff at The Hawthorns, during which time he passed onto his son some very helpful tips, Hubert was associated with Albion for a total of 20 years. He made 377 first and 100 second team appearances for the club and in fact only two other goalkeepers have played in more games for the club than Hubert – Stuart Naylor (410) and Jimmy Sanders (391). After quitting football he worked briefly for a local engineering company but was always a welcome guest at Albion's home matches.

Hubert, who in 1919 saved a 12-year-old girl from drowning in the sea off Whitley Bay, was a guest at Albion's FA Cup-winning celebration dinners of 1931 and 1954.

Between them, Albion's Tamworth-born goalkeepers, father (Hubert) and son (Harold), gained First, Second and Third Division South championship-winning medals, First and Second Division runners'-up medals, FA Cup-winners' and runners'-up medals, FA Charity Shield winners' and losers' medals, Central League championship-winners' medals, represented England in Junior and full internationals and played for the Football League and the FA.

TOM PEARSON

'A refreshingly direct player with an eye for goal.'

Born:	20 May 1866, West Bromwich
Died:	4 July 1918, West Bromwich

Albion senior record:

Appearances:	League 138, FA Cup 26, Others 7
Goals:	League 72, FA Cup 12, Others 4
Senior debut:	FA Cup, 19 February 1887 v Notts County (a) won 4–1
Also played for:	Oak Villa, West Bromwich Sandwell

Sadly – and annoyingly – Tom Pearson's football career came to an abrupt end in May 1894 when he was forced to retire with a serious knee injury which, he admitted, had been troubling him for at least 12 months. Aged only 28 at the time, his enforced retirement proved a huge disappointment, not only for Tom himself but also for the club and the Albion supporters, who had seen him destroy some pretty solid defences and beat some of the game's finest goalkeepers with his wonderful scoring technique.

With a distinctive short gait, Tom was Albion's first real high-quality marksman, a natural goalscorer who played mainly as an inside-left and had been quite outstanding for six years. Indeed, his speed over short distances, his clever footwork, his endurance and his wonderful anticipation, as well as his 'flashing shots', made him one of the best strikers in the game during the late 1880s and early 1890s.

In his first season with Albion, 1886–87, he made his senior debut, scored plenty of goals in various local competitions and friendlies and also appeared in an FA Cup Final. Not many players have done that!

He was twice on target in an excellent 3–1 victory over the Cup favourites Preston North End in the semi-final, but unfortunately he and his co-forwards all had an off-day in the Final, which went in favour of Aston Villa by 2–0.

The following season Tom was again in superb form, and although he didn't score half as many goals, he made several for his fellow forwards. He struck twice himself in the Birmingham Senior Cup Final defeat by Villa, helped Albion reach the Final of the Staffordshire Cup (which they lost to Wolves) and more importantly he gained an FA Cup-winners' medal.

After scoring in the first round victory over Wednesbury Old Athletic, he sent centre-forward Jem Bayliss racing clear to set up the second goal in the third round win over Wolves, had a helping hand in two of Bayliss's four goals against Stoke in round five, grabbed two himself in an excellent quarter-final triumph over Old Carthusians and then assisted in the build up to Joe Wilson's goal in the semi-final win over Derby Junction.

The Final, in front of a record crowd at the Oval, was against Preston North End, known at the time as the 'Invincibles', who had actually asked to be photographed with the trophy before the match had kicked off. Tom and his colleagues were the underdogs, but as a team they produced a great fighting performance to beat the Lilywhites from Deepdale by 2–1, Tom twice coming close to scoring in the second half.

League football began the following season and Tom, with 10 others, made his debut in the competition away at Stoke on 8 September 1888. He was an ever-present during the campaign and finished up as joint top scorer with Billy Bassett, each with 11 League goals. Yet how he had wished he could have scored in the semi-final of the FA Cup…a game Albion, as holders of the trophy, lost 1–0 to their 'Lancashire Enemy', Preston North End.

In 1889–90, Tom scored 19 League goals including Albion's first League hat-trick, a four-timer in fact, in a resounding 6–3 home victory over Bolton Wanderers in late November. One newspaper report of this game stated: 'Pearson's pace, dribbling, passing and kicking with great accuracy, was so remarkable it thoroughly baffled his opponents.'

Continuing to torment defenders and goalkeepers up and down the country, Tom bagged another 13 League goals in 1890–91, including two outstanding efforts in a 4–1 away win at Burnley and another beauty in a resounding 5–1 home victory over Accrington. And then, in 1891–92, he perhaps played the best football of his short career, helping Albion once again to lift the FA Cup.

As a unit, Albion didn't perform all that well in their 26 First Division matches. Tom, though, was by far the team's best forward, playing better on most occasions than England's flying winger Billy Bassett. He claimed another 13 League goals, four of which came in a record-breaking 12–0 home win over hapless Darwen in early April. His first in this one-sided game was described as being 'a low drive with direction'; his second was a 'close-range shot after a mazy run by Bassett'; his third was 'a firm header from Bassett's centre' and his fourth was a wonderful individual effort, the match reporter stating: 'Winning possession in the centre, he took the ball fully 40 yards downfield before firing past goalkeeper McOwen.'

In the Cup, however, it was a different story. Tom scored in the first two rounds against Old Westminsters and Blackburn Rovers and he also assisted with the scoring of two in the 6–2 semi-final second replay victory over Nottingham Forest, although he believed he might well have touched the ball over the line simultaneously with winger Jasper Geddes for Albion's third.

In the Final against Aston Villa Tom came close to scoring twice but he cared not, as Albion eased to a 3–0 victory, which meant a second winners' medal in four years for local lad Tom.

After a very good 1892–93 season, in which he scored a total of 12 goals, Tom was jogging along nicely the following term before he got a nasty kick on his already troublesome right knee during a League game against Sheffield United. Annoyingly, he missed the next match against Wolves, returned for the away fixture at Everton but sat out the next two. Despite lengthy treatment he managed only two more outings towards the end of that season and, sadly, that was the end of his Albion career.

He had scored more than a goal every two games at senior level – 88 in 171 appearances – and in fact had notched somewhere in the region of 150 goals in 250 games overall. His departure from the game proved a big loss to Albion, who never really found a true replacement until Chippy Simmons came along in 1899.

Sadly, Tom never recovered his fitness and by the age of 30 was confined to a wheelchair. He died in West Bromwich at the age of 52.

JESSE PENNINGTON

*'The doyen of England full-backs, "J.P." was a wonderfully consistent defender,
admired by many for his unselfish and clean displays.'*

Born:	23 August 1883, West Bromwich
Died:	5 September 1970, Kidderminster

Albion senior record:

Appearances:	League 455, FA Cup 39, Charity Shield 1
Goals:	None
Senior debut:	League, 26 September 1903 v Liverpool (a) won 3–1
Also played for:	Brasshouse Lane & Devonshire Road Day Schools, Summit Star, Smethwick Centaur, Langley Villa, Langley St Michael's, Dudley Town, Kidderminster Harriers, Oldbury Town (World War One guest), Notts County (World War One guest), England (25 full caps), England XI (5 apps), Football League (9 apps), England international trialist
Managed:	Kidderminster Harriers (and coach)

Left-back Jesse Pennington joined
Albion as a professional in March
1903 and made 20 League
appearances in his first full season,
followed by 23 in 1904–05 and 31
in 1905–06. Thereafter he hardly
missed a game, being absent only
through injury, international call-
ups and when he was in a pay
dispute with the club in 1909–10
and went off to play briefly for
Kidderminster Harriers. When he
retired in May 1922 he had played
in 495 senior games for the
Baggies, a record that stood for 53
years until it was topped by Tony
Brown in 1975–76.

During his time at The
Hawthorns, Jesse – who was
known as 'Peerless', meaning that
he had no equal – captained Albion
for 11 seasons either side of World
War One. He took them into the
1912 FA Cup Final and then guided
them to their first and only League
championship triumph in 1920. He
was vice-captain (to Freddie Buck)
when the Second Division title was
won in 1911.

Unfortunately, it was his 'fairness' as a defender which handed the FA Cup to Barnsley in 1912. With the clock running down at the end of extra-time in the Sheffield replay, Harry Tufnell, the Barnsley inside-right, raced away from the halfway line with Jesse in pursuit. The Albion skipper could have impeded Tufnell, even committed a 'professional foul' by bringing him down well before the penalty area, but he failed to do either. Tufnell went on to score the winning goal and so stun Albion and their travelling supporters. Talking after the game, a rather deflated Jesse said: 'I hadn't got it in me to commit a foul. If I had I am sure referee Mr Schumacher, whom I had come in contact with several times before, would have sent me off.'

Jesse was never showy and not very conspicuous, but was immensely impressive, tackling with perfection, kicking accurately and a master in positional play. He won 25 full caps for England between 1907 and 1920, forming a splendid partnership with Blackburn Rovers' Bob Crompton. Indeed, the pair played together in 23 internationals, 18 of them in front of legendary goalkeeper Sam Hardy. Together this trio was universally rated as the safest England defence of all time, with Jesse being perhaps the coolest of the three. England lost only four times with Jesse in the team.

Born within walking distance of The Hawthorns, Jesse played for several local teams before signing amateur forms for Aston Villa. Surprisingly he was rejected at Villa Park and, after a spell with Dudley Town, he signed for Albion. He made his League debut against Liverpool in April 1903 and 19 years later appeared in his last game for the Baggies against the same opposition.

In 1913 Jesse was approached, in casual circumstances, by a man who asked him if he could fix the result of the Albion-Everton League game, soon to be played at The Hawthorns. If Everton did not lose then Jesse would be paid £55. The Albion captain immediately informed club officials, who in turn notified the police. A trap was set and, on the day of the match – 29 November 1913 – Pascoe Bioletti (alias Samuel Johnson and Frederick Pater) – was arrested near the ground. He was charged under the Corrupt Practices Act with attempted bribery and was later found guilty and sentenced to five months imprisonment by Lord Justice Lush at Stafford Assize Court.

That incident apart, probably Jesse's most ironic experience came at the height of his career. Arriving for a League game at Villa Park in 1919 without his official players' ticket, the gateman, although knowing him quite well, would not allow the Albion captain into the ground. 'You must have a pass' said the stern official – and neither Jesse's face nor his reputation could over-rule that! Jesse hung around until an Albion director came along and took him inside. Albion went on to win the game 4–2.

After retiring as a player, Jesse spent 18 months as a coach at The Hawthorns. He then did the same job at Kidderminster, whom he managed briefly in 1939–40, and also coached football at Malvern College. For a while he did some scouting for Wolves and also Albion (1950–61). He became a Life Member of West Bromwich Albion FC in 1969.

I had the pleasure of meeting Jesse twice – initially when he opened the Throstle Club (for supporters) on the Birmingham Road in 1964 and again in 1968. On both occasions he never stopped talking football, chatting mostly about the Albion. He was a brilliant full-back, as comments made by two of his former colleagues will attest.

In 1928, Bob Crompton wrote in a Blackburn Rovers programme: 'Jesse Pennington of West Bromwich Albion made full-back play look easy. Never out of position, always focused on the game, he was one of the very best in his position.'

In a newspaper article published in 1935, former Albion wing-half Sammy Richardson described Jesse as 'A wonderfully consistent player, unsurpassed in tackling and retaining his composure. I never saw a better full-back anywhere.' '

CHARLIE PERRY

'A fine defensive centre-half, skilled in holding his side together.'

Born:	3 January 1866, West Bromwich
Died:	2 July 1927, West Bromwich

Albion senior record:

Appearances:	League 171, FA Cup 39, Others 9
Goals:	League 12, FA Cup 3, Others 1
Senior debut:	FA Cup Final, 3 April 1886 v Blackburn Rovers (at the Oval), drew 0–0
Also played for:	West Bromwich Strollers, England (3 caps), Football League (1 app), international trial (4 apps)

In the history of football, there haven't been too many players who have made their senior debut for a club in an FA Cup Final, but Charlie Perry was one. Joining the club in March 1884, he played in several second-team matches and in quite a few first-team friendlies and local Cup competitions for Albion.

Regular centre-half Fred Bunn had injured his thigh tripping over a hurdle during a training session and failed to recover in time to play in the Final. So, rather than rearranging the defence, it was decided by the committee, with a major input from a handful of senior players, including Jem Bayliss and Ezra Horton, that 20-year-old Charlie should be given his chance against the favourites and holders of the trophy, Blackburn Rovers, who were chasing their third successive Final win.

A record crowd of over 15,000 attended the Oval to watch the Final, which ended goalless. A reporter, covering the game for the *Blackburn Standard*, wrote: 'After 15 minutes play Albion's Perry went off with a wound over his right eye, received in a clash with Sowerbutts, the Blackburn centre-forward. He had been playing well and returned quickly, immediately setting up an attack from which his side almost scored.'

Later on in the report it said: 'Some clever play by Perry and Horton evoked loud applause…a long shot by Perry was kicked away by Arthur…and towards the end of the game, when everybody thought that Rovers had forced the ball between the posts, Perry came along and cleared the leather behind.'

Unfortunately Albion lost the replay at Derby a week later by 2–0. Charlie, who had kept his place, came close to equalizing with a long-range drive after Rovers had taken the lead and late in the game he headed a Loach centre just wide.

A fighter to the end, Charlie gave Albion 12 years of dedicated service. He appeared in 219 first-class matches and in more than 280 at a lower level, although during the 1880s/90s local Cup tournaments were very competitive. One of the first players to sign as a professional for Albion when that was introduced to the game in August 1885, Charlie was a regular at the heart of Albion's defence from 1886 until 1895.

A superb player, with a polished style, he was confident in everything he did. He was cool under pressure, he organised his defence splendidly and, as captain of the team, his encouragement was excellent. One paragraph from a newspaper report on Albion's 4–1 victory over Notts County in the sixth round of the FA Cup in February 1887 read: 'Albion's centre-half Perry showed far more dash and vigour than the whole of the Nottingham team. He was always there to stem a threatening raid and he was more than useful when he went forward into the opposition half of the field.'

In 1887, Charlie suffered disappointment yet again when Albion lost in the FA Cup Final for the second year running, this time going down 2–0 to arch-rivals Aston Villa. But the following season it was third time lucky for Charlie as Albion beat the 'Invincibles' of Preston North End 2–1. Preston had gone into the game full of confidence. They had even asked if they could be photographed with the trophy before kick off, having scored a total of 47 goals in the previous rounds, 26 in one game against Hyde. However, Albion had done their homework and, with a strong defence, marshalled superbly by skipper Charlie Perry, they pulled off a wonderful victory.

The report in the *Birmingham Daily Post* stated: 'As the game progressed at a fast pace, North End's backs looked fatigued, while Albion's trio of Horton, Perry and Timmins played with unflagging spirit, Perry twice heading clear dangerous centres and once using his weight to deny Goodhall.'

Soon after that triumph Albion entered the newly-formed Football League and Charlie played in the opening game, a 2–0 win at Stoke. He was absent from just two games in each of the first three League seasons, the third ending in another FA Cup Final victory, this time 3–0 against Aston Villa – sweet revenge for the defeat six years earlier.

Charlie, again acting as captain, had a good, solid game against Villa's strong attack of Jack Devey, Dickson and Dennis Hodgetts. He twice cleared off his own line and came close to scoring himself with a shot from fully 25 yards, which 'keeper Warner saved at full length.

In March 1890, Charlie gained the first of his three England caps against Ireland; his others followed against the Irish in 1891 and Wales in 1893. He perhaps deserved more, but there were some pretty good centre-halves around at that time including Jack Holt (Everton), Bill Winkworth (Old Etonians) and Harry Allen (Wolves).

An ever-present in 1892–93, Charlie missed just one game the following season and six in 1894–95 when once again, for the fifth time in nine years, Albion reached the FA Cup Final.

Unfortunately Charlie, who by now had switched to right-back so that his brother Tom could come into the side at centre-half, was forced to miss the all-Midland clash at Crystal Palace with a badly twisted knee, suffered in a Birmingham Cup semi-final win over Small Heath a month earlier. Jack Horton took Charlie's place at full-back as Albion, sadly, lost to a goal scored inside the first minute.

That knee injury plagued Charlie for the rest of his career. He made only three more first-team appearances before announcing his retirement in May 1896. He was still a very fit man, as he regularly played tennis. Almost immediately Charlie became a director of the club, and retained his position on the board for six years.

In the meantime he had entered the licensed trade and was landlord of the Globe Cup public house in Cross Street, West Bromwich, until 1905, when his former teammate George Woodhall took over the licence.

Charlie was 61 years of age when he died. Two weeks later his brother Tom also passed away, while a second brother, Walter, who also played for Albion, died in September 1928.

TOM PERRY

'A most capable and efficient footballer who had an enthusiastic and hard-working approach.'

Born: 5 August 1871, West Bromwich
Died: 18 July 1927, West Bromwich

Albion senior record:

Appearances: League 248, FA Cup 29, Others 14
Goals: League 14, FA Cup 0, Others 1
Senior debut: League, 13 September 1890 v Preston North End (a) lost 3–0
Also played for: Christ Church FC, West Bromwich Baptist, Stourbridge, Aston Villa, England (1 cap), Football League (3 apps), Football League XI (1 app)

An entry in an 1892 'international' file from the FA described Tom Perry as being 'A most capable and efficient half-back and something of a utility man, who has an enthusiastic and hard-working approach.' Tom was certainly that. He was a real stalwart for Albion during his 10-year association with the club, during which time he appeared in almost 300 competitive matches (the majority in the right-half position – his best), scored 15 goals, played in the 1895 FA Cup Final, gained one England cap (versus Wales in March 1898), represented the Football League on three occasions between 1893 and 1897 and starred for a League XI against Aston Villa in 1894. And he also turned out in around 170 'other' matches for the club (friendlies, local Cup competitions and the like).

Wholehearted in every sense of the word, Tom actually made his senior debut for Albion at the age of 18 as an emergency outside-left against Preston in September 1890. Joe Wilson had left the club for Kidderminster Harriers a few months earlier and to replace him Albion had signed Alf Burns. Unfortunately Alf was injured in training and for the opening game of the season against Everton at home, Harry Roberts played on the left wing. He didn't do too well, so Tom was tried there in the next match and, alas, he fared no better. Burns returned and retained his place for virtually the rest of the season.

Tom, who had joined Albion as a professional from Stourbridge in July 1890, was still regarded as a reserve, although he featured in the next four matches at inside-right, with his elder brother Charlie behind him at centre-half. He scored his first senior goal in a 3–2 defeat at Notts County in mid-October 1890, and made one more senior appearance that term.

He was called into action only twice in 1891–92 (at inside-left and outside-left) before having 16 outings in the League and one in the FA Cup in 1892–93 when, after just one game on the left flank, he went on to occupy all three half-back line positions. In fact, at this juncture (April 1893) Tom had already appeared in six different outfield positions for the first team, emphasising the point made earlier in the FA's file, that he was a 'utility man.'

However, it was in the middle line where Tom excelled and over the next seven seasons, from August 1893 until April 1900, he missed only 12 first-team games out of a possible 254, being an ever-present on three occasions, in 1894–95, 1896–97 and 1898–99.

He occupied the right-half berth most often, but was asked to play at inside-right, and even centre-forward, during the 1899–1900 season when several players were either injured or out of form.

Tom, who helped Albion destroy neighbours Wolves 8–0 at Molineux in December 1893, scored in a 6–0 last-match home win over Sheffield Wednesday in April 1895 – a game Albion had to win to avoid automatic relegation. He then played his heart out the following season when Albion were again in danger of losing their top-flight status. He produced three wonderful performances in two Test Matches against Manchester City and one against Liverpool to help Albion stay up. He actually scored the decisive goal to earn a draw in the opening match against City and then played his part in a resounding 6–1 win in the return fixture before assisting in a 2–0 win over the Merseysiders. Tom also battled hard and long, to no avail, when Albion lost to Aston Villa in the FA Cup Final in 1895.

Albion certainly appreciated Tom's all-round displays and, for an FA Cup tie at Luton in January 1897, the club went as far as to hire a special train to take him to the Bedfordshire town. Earlier in the day he had misunderstood the time of departure of the pre-booked train from Birmingham's New Street station. So secretary-boss Frank Heaven waited for Tom to turn up at the station and they travelled down together in a special carriage, which cost the club £50. It was worth the effort in the end as Albion won the game 1–0.

Tom's international appearance for England came at a time when the team was in the process of 'change.' No fewer than five different players had been used in the right-half position in the previous six games, including former Albion star Jack Reynolds. Tom was introduced for the clash with Wales at Wrexham. His Baggies teammate Billy Williams was also in the side, which won comfortably by 3–0, Tom setting up a goal for future Albion player Fred Wheldon. Unfortunately he never got another call from the England selection committee as Frank Forman (Nottingham Forest) and Ernest Needham (Sheffield United) took over the wing-half positions.

After playing 18 games at Albion's new ground, The Hawthorns, and captaining the side, Tom chose to leave the club in October 1901, signing, perhaps surprisingly, for Aston Villa for £100. He was 30 at the time and spent just eight months at Villa Park, retiring in May 1902 after 29 outings in the claret and blue strip. Soon afterwards he took employment as an accountant and stayed in that line of work until his death in 1927.

Tom and his brother Charlie played together 98 times for Albion at senior level. The Perry family certainly served Albion well over the years. Besides the three brothers already named, two more, William and Edward, also played for the club, albeit as reserves, while in later years Tom's two nephews (Charlie's sons), Arthur and Eric, were both professionals at The Hawthorns. Douglas, son of Arthur, became an Albion shareholder.

TED 'COCK' PHEASANT

'Very few forwards got the better of "Cock" Pheasant in 50–50 challenges. He was tough, very tough.'

Born: 15 February 1877, Darlaston
Died: 15 July 1910, Wolverhampton

Albion senior record:
Appearances: League 140, FA Cup 12
Goals: League 20, FA Cup 2
Senior debut: League, 5 November 1904 v Manchester United (h) lost 2–0
Also played for: Wednesbury Excelsior, Wednesbury Old Athletic, Wolverhampton Wanderers

Ted 'Cock' Pheasant was a great Black Country character. As hard as nails – 'as tough as a piece of old iron' as one supporter said – and equally big-hearted, he was typical of all local sportsmen at that time, knowing no fear, ready for anything and everything and the happy possessor of a wonderful and jolly sense of humour.

It was said that when Albion were faced with a particularly tough match, Ted would go to the barber's shop and get his hair cut right down to the scalp, leaving only a small frontal fringe. Then, on the day of the match, he would gee-up his teammates in the dressing room before running on to the field with his sleeves rolled right up to his armpits, irrespective of the weather conditions, yelling out 'Come on, let's get stuck in to this lot!' He was a real tough guy all right, a wonderful competitor who thoroughly enjoyed his football, often returning to the changing rooms with bruises and cuts to his head and knees to prove he had been involved in a battle.

Ted also enjoyed the daily training sessions, regularly putting the younger players through their paces with some tough routines. Frequently involving them in robust play, including tackling, he loved the shoulder-charge and once bowled over right-winger Ernie Perkins, causing him to miss three matches. Ted, who rarely missed training, was nowhere to be seen one day and, as a result, the next day Albion's secretary-manager Fred Everiss called him into his office and asked him to give a good reason for being absent. Ted replied: 'Oi was out shooting rabbits and oi fell down a hole about noine feet dape, gaffer.' Mr Everiss laughed and Ted was let off with a reprimand.

Ted was six feet two inches tall and, in his prime, tipped the scales at 15 stone, making him one of the biggest and weightiest defenders in the game. And as well as playing centre-half he could always throw his weight around as a centre-forward, which he did to good effect with his first League club, Wolverhampton Wanderers.

A pupil at Joseph Edward Cox County School, Wednesbury, he spent a season with Wednesbury Excelsior and two with Wednesbury Old Athletic before joining Albion's arch-rivals Wolves as a professional in August 1895. He spent nine years at Molineux, amassing 168 appearances and scoring 19 goals, including a hat-trick from the centre-half position against Newcastle United in March 1902. He also skippered the team on several occasions and was said to have been the club's highest-paid professional, earning £3 10s a week during a season and £3 in the summer. He was once selected for the Football League side but turned down the offer and played for Wolves instead, such was his dedication to club football. In fact, he missed only one match in three seasons (1899–1902).

In November 1904, Ted moved across the Black Country to The Hawthorns, signed by Albion for what was to prove a bargain fee of just £500. Taking over from Jack Bowden, he played 'okay' on his debut at centre-half against Manchester United and remained in the team, injuries apart, for almost four years, until October 1908, helping Albion reach the FA Cup semi-final in 1907 when they were beaten 2–1 by Everton.

Forming part of an exceptionally fine half-back line of Arthur Randle, himself and Jack Manners, Ted netted seven goals in 25 appearances in his first season, which ended with him playing four games at centre-forward at a time when there was only one fit goalscorer at the club (Walter Jack). Then Fred Shinton arrived on the scene and Ted moved back into the defence, being an ever-present with eight goals to his name in 1905–06. The following season, as captain, he missed a few games through injury and managed to score just three times in 31 starts, while in 1907–08 he was an absentee three times out of the 41 games played.

After nine outings at the start of the 1908–09 season Ted suffered a serious knee injury playing against Leeds City. This kept him out of action until the end of September, Albion filling his position with first Sammy Timmons, then George Harris and also a converted centre-forward, Billy Garraty.

Ted returned, albeit not 100 per cent fit, halfway through September 1909, but after three games he broke down again. He came back for another try later in the season, but was always struggling and in the end gave up, allowing Frank Waterhouse to take over as centre-half. Although he worked hard on his fitness for a couple of months, it came as a huge surprise to a lot of supporters when, on 1 July 1910, Ted packed his bags and left The Hawthorns for Leicester Fosse for a mere £100. Admittedly he was 33 years of age at the time, but he believed he still had a couple more years left in him. He was certainly as keen on the game as he had ever been, but Waterhouse was in good form and had not let the side down, and Albion thought it was the right time to let Ted depart for pastures new.

One reporter in a local paper wrote: 'Ted Pheasant's departure will leave an enormous hole in the Albion team. We wish him well for the future.' An Albion spokesman said: 'Ted has been a terrific player for us. He always gave it his best shot; he used to put everything into a game of football. He will be missed, not only on the pitch but also in the changing room.'

Just two weeks after moving to Filbert Street and before he could play a single game for Leicester, Ted was rushed to the Royal Hospital, Wolverhampton, with peritonitis. Although allowed home (to Wolverhampton) he never got over the illness and died on 15 July 1910.

An expert bee-keeper and keen gardener who loved roses, Ted made a combined total of 320 appearances for Wolves and Albion and scored 41 goals, including eight viciously-struck penalties.

JOE READER

'A wonderful goalkeeper whose proficiency was enhanced by fine consistency and his courage was noteworthy.'

Born: 27 February 1866, West Bromwich
Died: 8 March 1954, West Bromwich

Albion senior record:

Appearances: League 315, FA Cup 39, Others 16
Goals: None
Senior debut: League, 26 October 1899 v Aston Villa (a) lost 1–0
Also played for: England (1 cap), Football League (3 apps), League XI (1 app), Staffordshire (2 apps)

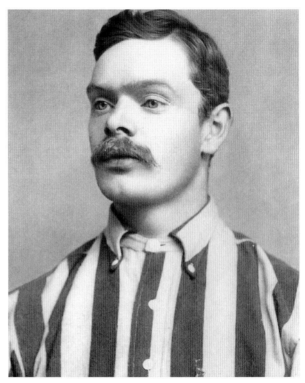

Josiah (Joe) Reader was a very talented goalkeeper who joined Albion as an 18-year-old amateur in January 1885 and turned professional seven months later. Playing second fiddle to the great Bob Roberts, Joe initially suffered from a disease called erysipelas and when he took to the field his face was often wrapped up in a flannel to protect the skin. This gradually disappeared after treatment.

After playing in several friendly matches and the odd local Cup tie, Joe eventually gained a regular place in the Baggies team in 1890, after Roberts had departed, and held his position almost unchallenged for the next 11 years. A superb handler of the ball, he possessed expert reflexes and used his feet as much as anyone to divert shots and headers away from the danger-zone. Indeed, he quite often raced outside his area to fly-kick the ball to safety when required, but on occasion he would control it, sometimes beat an opponent and pass it coolly to a colleague. Doing something like that today wouldn't go down too well with his manager. Nicknamed 'Kicker' by his teammates for these goalmouth antics, Joe was a great character, a real joker in the dressing room. He got on with everybody – even some opponents.

Joe once turned out in a friendly game for Albion with his arm in a sling and had the misfortune to be the first Baggies goalkeeper ever to be sent off, dismissed for 'defending' himself during a League game at Bolton in April 1895. He also managed to score twice as an outfield player in an

11–6 win over the touring South African side, the Kaffirs, in 1899, and he was probably the last goalkeeper of the 'old school' to discard the long white cricket trousers he used to wear from the day he joined the club. That decision came after the away League draw with Liverpool at Anfield in January 1898.

Still available from the BBC Archive Library today is a short clip of film – possibly the oldest in the world featuring a football match – showing Joe strolling around his goal area during Albion's 4–1 League defeat at Blackburn in September 1898.

Joe, who was a huge favourite with the supporters, appeared in one full international for England, doing well in a 2–2 draw with Ireland in March 1894. He represented the Football League on three occasions and played for a League XI once. He also played in the 1892 and 1895 FA Cup Finals for Albion, both against rivals Aston Villa. He gained a winners' medal in the first and a runners'-up prize in the second. But deep down Joe knew it should have been two winners' medals! He admitted some years later: 'In Villa's first attack of the 1895 Final, I let the ball escape from my grasp, allowing Bob Chatt to somehow scramble it over the line for the only goal of the game.'

In his book, *The Association Football in Victorian England*, Philip Gibbons, commenting on Albion's emphatic victory in the 1892 Final, wrote: 'Reader made several excellent saves and WBA ended up 3–0 winners.'

In another book, *The Essential History of West Bromwich Albion*, author Gavin McOwan describes an Inter League game that Joe played against the Irish League: 'With Reader's defence caught out by a counter attack, he rushed 50 yards out of his goal to thwart the Irish charge. But rather than merely booting the ball away, Reader coolly controlled it, beat his man and then played the ball forward to a teammate.'

During his time as the last line of defence, Joe was the only player to appear in a first-class game on three different Albion grounds – the Four Acres, Stoney Lane and The Hawthorns. However, unfortunately his Baggies League career left a lot to be desired, despite Joe producing some terrific performances. In fact, such was his consistency that he was an ever-present a club record five times – in 1890–91 when the team finished bottom (before there were any relegation or promotion issues to contend with), in 1892–93, in 1894–95, again in 1897–98 and finally in 1899–1900. He missed only one game in seasons 1893–94, 1898–99 and 1900–01, and was absent from just three matches in 1895–96 and 1896–97.

He didn't play at all well in season 1900–01, Albion's first at The Hawthorns. His reputation wasn't quite the same as it used to be and he certainly wasn't getting any younger. After some unusually poor displays, in which he conceded five goals at Liverpool, six at Bury and another six at home to Nottingham Forest, he was eventually dropped for the first time in his career for the trip to Derby in December, reserve 'keeper Joe Lowe taking over. But he was beaten four times and, with no other options available, Joe was recalled after just one game. He stuck in there as best he could, but Albion, although going through to the FA Cup semi-finals, couldn't find a winning formula and disappointingly slipped into the Second Division for the first time in the club's history.

Joe immediately announced his retirement. Albion secured the services of Ike Webb from Small Heath (Birmingham) to take over the number one spot. Joe called it a day having made 370 appearances at senior level for Albion as well as playing in more than 105 'other' games, including local Cup competitions and friendlies.

After deciding to terminate his playing career Joe, a dedicated club man who loved the Albion, stayed at The Hawthorns as first-team trainer-coach, a position he held for almost 40 years, right up to the start of World War Two. After that he worked as a steward and odd-job man and, when he finally quit his day job in May 1950, he had served West Bromwich Albion football club honestly and professionally for a total of 65 years – the longest anyone has ever been associated with the Baggies.

CYRILLE REGIS, MBE

'A powerful, all action-striker, strong in the air and on the ground, Cyrille scored some absolute beauties for Albion.'

Born:	9 February 1958, Maripiasoula, French Guyana

Albion senior record:

Appearances:	League 233+4, FA Cup 25, League Cup 27+1, Europe 10, Others 2
Goals:	League 82, FA Cup 10, League Cup 16, Europe 3, Others 1
Senior debut:	League Cup, August 1977 v Middlesbrough (h) won 2–1
Also played for:	Ryder Brent Valley, Moseley, Hayes, Coventry City, Aston Villa, Wolverhampton Wanderers, Wycombe Wanderers, Chester City, England (5 full, 6 Under-21, 3 B caps), England XI (1 app)

Cyrille Regis's career in competitive League football spanned 19 years – from May 1977 until May 1996. During that time he scored no fewer than 205 goals in 741 appearances for six different clubs, played for England at three different levels and toured the world.

Brought up in north-west London, Cyrille played his schoolboy, junior and intermediate football in and around the Harlesden, Kensal Rise, Brent and Kilburn areas before joining Hayes as a semi-professional in July 1976. Blessed with power and strength, he scored 24 goals in his first season in the Isthmian League and as a result was invited to attend training sessions with Tottenham Hotspur. 'I declined the offer because it would disrupt my evening classes at Harrow Technical College where I was studying for my City & Guilds diploma as an electrician,' recalled Cyrille. He did receive his diploma and it coincided with him signing as a full-time professional for West Bromwich Albion.

Baggies scout Ronnie Allen had watched Cyrille several times and was impressed with what he saw. He told the Albion board that they should buy the 'promising striker', saying 'He's got everything – power, ability, pace and attitude.' Nothing came of this at first but then, after manager Johnny Giles had left The Hawthorns to be replaced by Allen himself, things moved quickly. 'What sort of money would he cost?' asked one director. 'It won't be a lot,' replied Allen, 'perhaps £3-£4,000, maybe £5,000, not much more.' No decision was made, so Allen signed Cyrille himself, paying £5,000 out of his own account to Hayes on 12 May 1977. It was also agreed that a further payment of £5,000 would be made (by the club) after the player had made 20 appearances.

Hayes manager Bobby Ross said: 'Cyrille's got wings – let him fly.' And fly he did – straight into the record books in his first season with Albion. The last 'King' at The Hawthorns had been Jeff Astle, but Cyrille was the new one, and he became an instant hero, scoring some spectacular goals. He netted in his first game for the reserves against Sheffield Wednesday, bagged a brace on his League Cup debut v Rotherham United (one a penalty), fired home a beauty after a mesmerizing run in his first appearance in a Football League match against Middlesbrough and scored again in his first FA Cup outing versus Blackpool. He hit 18 goals in his first season, followed up with another 18 in 1978–79 and also played his first game in an England shirt, winning a B cap. More honours were soon to follow.

Several of Cyrille's goals were quite stunning efforts. He brought the house down with classic strikes in League games against Manchester City at Maine Road and Everton at The Hawthorns in April 1978 and also with a rocket which flew past Nottingham Forest 'keeper Peter Shilton in an FA Cup tie. The following season he continued to bulge nets up and down the country, whipping in beauties in League games at Norwich, Derby, Southampton and Manchester United. His right-foot shot stunned the Old Trafford faithful as Albion recorded a magnificent 5–3 victory there in December 1978. He also set Europe alight with some more marvellous goals, helping Albion reach the quarter-finals of the UEFA Cup.

In April 1978, soon after Albion had succumbed to Ipswich in the FA Cup semi-final, Cyrille admitted that he had been approached by French club St Etienne, who were willing to pay Albion £750,000 for his transfer. 'No way am I going to lose Cyrille,' said his manager Ron Atkinson and, with the backing of the board, he quickly offered the big fellow a new and much-improved contract. Atkinson described Cyrille as 'Black gold' and added 'With so much natural talent, I shudder to think how valuable he will become.'

After a relatively lean period in 1979–80 as far as goalscoring was concerned (he netted only nine times) Cyrille was, nevertheless, voted PFA Young Player of the Year before bouncing back in style in 1980–81, scoring 17 goals, including a brilliant header to win a League game at Crystal Palace.

The following season turned out to be his best in terms of goals scored. He bagged 25 in total, two of them superb efforts in home FA Cup ties against Norwich and Coventry. Sadly Albion again missed out on a trip to Wembley, losing in both domestic Cup semi-finals. These defeats sickened Cyrille, who took several weeks to get over the double disappointment.

His last two full seasons with Albion yielded 24 goals, bringing his overall tally to 112 in 302 appearances. He had also added four full caps to his collection, played in two more B internationals, appeared in six Under-21 internationals and was runner-up to Steve Perryman as PFA Footballer of the Year in 1982.

In October 1984, after seven wonderful years at The Hawthorns and much to the anger of some supporters, Cyrille left to join Coventry City for £300,000, and within three years had gained an FA Cup-winners' medal. Moderate spells with Aston Villa, Wolves, Wycombe Wanderers and Chester City preceded his retirement in May 1996. Nine months later he returned to The Hawthorns as reserve-team coach, staying until 2000 when he became a football agent, later joining the Stellar Group Ltd.

A born-again Christian, Cyrille was awarded an honorary fellowship by the University of Wolverhampton in 2001 and three years later was voted West Bromwich Albion's all-time Cult Hero, gaining 65 per cent of the vote. Also in 2004 he was named as one of Albion's 16 greatest players, in a poll organised as part of the club's 125th anniversary celebrations.

Cyrille, who, with his second wife Julia, visited water-related projects in Ethiopia in 2007 as part of their continued support for WaterAid, was awarded the MBE in the 2008 Birthday Honours List.

The uncle of former Albion striker Jason Roberts, for whom he has acted as an agent, Cyrille is also the cousin of sprinter John Regis and brother of former footballer Dave Regis.

JACK REYNOLDS

'A player of infinite variety, fast, two-footed, skilled in heading, a sure shot and a strong in the tackle.'

Born: 21 February 1869, Blackburn
Died: 12 March 1917, Sheffield

Albion senior record:

Appearances: League 37, FA Cup 7, Other 2
Goals: League 3, FA Cup 2, Other 1
Senior debut: League, 3 October 1891 v Blackburn Rovers (h) drew 2–2
Also played for: Portglenone & Ballymena Schools, Park Royal, Witton, Blackburn Rovers
(reserves), East Lancashire Regiment, Distillery (guest), Ulster, Droitwich Town
(loan), Aston Villa, Celtic, Southampton St Mary's, Bristol St George's, Grafton
FC (New Zealand), Royston, Willesden Town, Stockport County, Ireland (5
caps), England (8 caps), Football League (3 apps), England international trialist

While on a scouting mission to Northern Ireland in March 1891, Albion's secretary Louis Ford spotted a player whom he believed was the finest half-back playing on the Emerald Isle. His name was Jack 'Baldy' Reynolds, the 5ft 4in star of one of Ireland's strongest clubs, Ulster.

It was learnt that Jack wanted to try his luck in the Football League and, following this up, Ford persuaded him to come to England and talk with Albion. Jack agreed and duly signed the appropriate forms to become a Baggie, but before he could get started, he expressed a desire to return immediately to Ireland so that he could play for Ulster in the Irish Cup Final against Linfield in Belfast. Albion granted him his wish, but sadly his efforts were all in vain as Ulster lost 4–2 and Jack had to be content with a runners'-up medal.

Back with Albion, Jack played his first game for the club against Wednesbury Old Athletic in the Final of the West Bromwich Charity Cup – and this time he ended up a winner, scoring the deciding goal 15 minutes from time to seal a 3–2 victory.

Jack's impressive displays had been so well reported that several other clubs had shown interest long before Albion acquired his services. And in fact, at a board meeting held soon after Jack had been signed, the Albion directors were forced to turn down an offer from Burnley for his signature.

Suffering with a rheumatic hand, Jack missed the start of the 1891–92 season and had to wait until 3 October before making his League debut against the team he had earlier had trials with, Blackburn Rovers. Starting in his preferred right-half position, as the season progressed he was asked to play at centre-half, centre-forward and left-half. He never moaned; he simply got on with the job in hand – that of playing football – and he did that majestically.

Albion were not playing at all well in the League, but in the FA Cup they were much better and with Jack in the team they made steady progress, reaching the Final for the fourth time in the club's history. This time they came up against Aston Villa and, in front of a record Oval crowd of 32,710, the Baggies won in style by 3–0, Jack scoring the third goal on 65 minutes with a speculative long-range shot. There is no doubt that the Villa directors made a careful note of Jack's performance that day and a year later they secured his transfer – much to Albion's disgust.

Well before then, however, and soon after that Final triumph, Jack was selected to play for England against Scotland. It was something of a surprise for the football supporter in general, because prior to that Jack, whom it was discovered had been born in Blackburn, had already played in five full internationals for Ireland, where he had grown up as a lad, and where everybody thought he was Irish! Therefore when he lined up against the Scots, he went into the record books as the first player to represent two home countries. He went on to play in seven more games for England, thus winning a total of 13 caps overall.

On 4 April 1892, Jack had the pleasure of scoring twice in Albion's (and the League's) record win – 12–0 against Darwen. Jack played his heart out in that game and was 'rested' for the next fixture – which Albion lost 7–0 at Everton. Around this time Jack began to have an attitude problem – so much so that he was dropped for insubordination, or as Jack himself put it 'Because there's a snake in the grass!'

Albion finished third from bottom in Division One in 1891–92, but were excused from having to apply for re-election due to their Cup success. Jack would not have been happy if the team had been relegated.

At the start of the 1892–93 season Jack had the honour of scoring Albion's first-ever penalty in a friendly against Coleshill, but after that things started to go wrong. Injured several times, he was carried off with a suspected broken leg in an 8–1 League defeat by Notts County and his general play 'was not up to standard' said one club official.

Jack was told by Albion that he would be fined £1 a week until his play improved and as a result was banished to the reserves. He returned to the first team and was used as a right-back in one game before reverting to his favourite right-half spot.

On 3 April 1893 Jack netted Albion's first penalty in a League game against Nottingham Forest and soon afterwards he made his last appearance for the club in a 6–0 drubbing by Aston Villa in the semi-final of the Lord Mayor of Birmingham Charity Cup. Jack conceded an own-goal in that game.

He refused to re-sign for the next season and at one point was all set to join Blackburn Rovers before Villa stepped in and secured his services for just £50. Ironically he made his debut for his new club against the Baggies, scoring from the spot in a 3–2 win. That was one of 17 goals he netted in 110 appearances for Villa, with whom he gained three League championship-winners' medals and two more FA Cup-winners' medals, playing a big part in Villa's double-winning season of 1896–97. He left Villa Park for Celtic in May 1897 and added a Scottish League winners' medal to his collection before slowly winding down his career. He also coached in New Zealand and held a similar position with Cardiff City before retiring from football in 1908 to become a miner in Sheffield.

Jack sadly died from heart failure at the age of 48.

BILL 'W.G.' RICHARDSON

'One of the most-feared centre-forwards of the 1930s, W.G. was quick off the mark with an accurate shot.'

Born:	29 May 1909, Framwellgate Moor, County Durham
Died:	29 March 1959, Small Heath, Birmingham

Albion senior record:

Appearances:	League 320, FA Cup 34, FA Charity Shield 1
Goals:	League 202, FA Cup 26, FA Charity Shield 0
Senior debut:	League, 26 December 1929 v Millwall (h) won 6–1 (scored)
Also played for:	Durham Schoolboys, Horden Wednesday FC, United Bus Company (Hartlepool), Shrewsbury Town, Derby County (World War Two guest), Walsall (World War Two guest), England (1 cap)

When centre-forward Bill Richardson joined Albion from Hartlepool United in June 1929, he became the second player by that name at the club. The other was a centre-half. So, in order to avoid confusion with newspaper reporters, programme editors and other players, new signing Bill was given the nickname 'W.G.' – the 'G' referring to his ginger hair. However, it could well have been 'G' for goals, as he scored over 320 for the Baggies during his time at The Hawthorns. His tally of 202 League goals remained a club record for 20 years, until Ronnie Allen bettered it in 1959.

Prior to arriving at the club W.G. had never heard of West Bromwich Albion. He admitted that he took a gamble when moving to the Black Country at a time when the Baggies were preparing to start their third season in Division Two. An England schoolboy trialist, W.G. had a miner father who was an ardent Sunderland supporter and who approached the great Charlie Buchan for advice about his son's career. 'Don't let him play at a competitive level for three years when he leaves school. His muscles will adjust themselves to his physical growth by then and he will be all the better for it,' warned Buchan.

Dying for a game, W.G. took a job with the United Bus Company in West Hartlepool and worked shifts on a Saturday afternoon instead of playing football. It should be remembered that in those days there was little 'bridging' football for young boys. If they wanted to play they had to do so against grown men. W.G. chose to play in the local Sunday League for Horden Wednesday and his prolific scoring feats soon brought him to the attention of Hartlepools United, who signed him as a part-time professional in August 1928.

In the summer of 1929, former Albion full-back Jesse Pennington was spending his holiday with another ex-Baggies star, Bob Pailor. Jesse got to hear about W.G.'s ability to score goals and recommended him to his old club. In double-quick time Albion's secretary-manager Fred Everiss and director Lou Nurse travelled north to meet W.G., who had just finished his tour of duty as a bus inspector. W.G. later recalled: 'All three of us trooped off to my house where mother was getting my meal out of the oven. We talked and I agreed to join Albion, signing the paperwork in the front parlour by the aspidistra. I wanted to play for Sunderland whom I had followed for some time. But in the end I was pleased to join Albion.' A fee of £1,250 was agreed with Hartlepools boss Will Norman, who was Barnsley's trainer when they beat Albion in the 1912 Cup Final.

W.G. spent the first half of the 1929–30 season in the reserves before making a scoring debut in place of the injured Jimmy Cookson in a 6–1 win over Millwall on Boxing Day. Cookson had been in superb form and eventually returned to the side, W.G. slipping back into the second XI. He made only nine League appearances in his first season but was quite brilliant in the reserves, bagging 50 goals, including eight hat-tricks, in 33 starts. He went on to net 83 goals for the 'stiffs' in 79 games.

Albion had found a gem. W.G. gained a regular place in the first team in November 1930 and it was his goals that enabled the Baggies to become the first and so far only team to complete the unique double of winning promotion and the FA Cup in the same season. W.G. netted 18 League goals and six in the Cup in 1930–31. Nine came in the last seven matches, including vital winners against Charlton and Stoke in the League and two against Birmingham in the Cup Final.

The question everyone was asking now was whether or not W.G. could continue his lethal marksmanship in the top flight. The answer was yes, as his 27 goals in 40 games helped Albion finish sixth in the table.

At West Ham in November 1931, W.G. equalled the League record by scoring four goals in five minutes in a 5–1 victory. Thereafter he continued to destroy defences, scoring 31 goals in 31 games in 1932–33 and 26 in 42 outings in 1933–34.

The following season he struck 33 times in 49 starts, but annoyingly failed to score in the Cup Final defeat by Sheffield Wednesday, and then, in 1935–36, he netted a club record 40 goals in 45 matches, four coming in a 7–0 win at Villa Park. He subsequently weighed in with another 24 goals in 44 games in 1936–37, fired home 17 in 31 fixtures in 1937–38 when relegation was suffered, and claimed five in 15 outings in 1938–39 when he struggled with injury.

More was to follow. During the 1939–45 hostilities, when on leave from the Army, W.G. was magnificent, rattling in 100 goals in only 90 competitive appearances and helping Albion win the Midland War Cup in 1944.

Not a rough and ready sort of centre-forward – far from it – W.G. was nimble, quick, alert and positive. He had the knack of being in the right place at the right time, his anticipation was second to none and he was pretty good in the air as well. He was certainly one of the most feared strikers in the game during the early to mid-1930s, but for all his efforts W.G. gained only one England cap, against Holland in 1935. He certainly deserved more and would probably have had more chances if he'd been with a more popular club.

W.G. joined Shrewsbury Town for £250 in November 1945, but returned to The Hawthorns as assistant trainer-coach in June 1946. He saw the Baggies regain their First Division status in 1949 and win the FA Cup five years later, and was still a member of the backroom staff when he collapsed and died playing in a charity match at the BSA Sports Ground, Birmingham, in 1959.

Over the years many people have asked the question: who has been Albion's greatest-ever goalscorer? Ronnie Allen, Jeff Astle and Tony Brown are all candidates, but there is no doubt that W.G. Richardson is high on the list.

BILLY RICHARDSON

'A solid centre-half, always alert, who had no need to resort to vigorous methods.'

Born:	14 February 1908, Great Bridge, Tipton
Died:	12 August 1985, West Bromwich

Albion senior record:

Appearances:	League 319, FA Cup 32, FA Charity Shield 1
Goals:	League 1, FA Cup 0, FA Charity Shield 0
Senior debut:	League, 1 December 1928 v Middlesbrough (a) drew 1–1
Also played for:	Greets Green Boys, Greets Green Prims, Great Bridge Celtic, Swindon Town, Dudley Town, Vono Sports FC

No relation to W.G., centre-half Billy 'Steel' Richardson was born and bred in the Black Country and, like most sportsmen from that area, he was a tough competitor who possessed a strong but fair tackle, was positive in his approach to the game and above all was very consistent, hardly missing a game. And for a defender he was as fair as they come, hardly ever spoken to by a referee and never sent off.

Perhaps a shade casual at times, he was not the fastest of centre-halves, but nevertheless he was unflagging, especially good in the air and on the ground, and he had excellent positional sense. After doing well in local football circles, when he played in every defensive position, once scoring three times in one game as a left-half, Billy was 18 years of age when he joined his elder brother, Sammy, at The Hawthorns, signing as a full-time professional in November 1926.

He bided his time in the reserves and played in 22 games that season, helping the second XI win the Central League title. He was again a regular in the team during the early stages of 1927–28 before being handed his first-team debut in the Second Division fixture at Middlesbrough.

At the time the centre-half position was causing Albion some concern. In fact, the club had not found a direct replacement for pivot Joe Evans and as a last resort had switched inside-forward Harry Chambers into the heart of the defence, but he was now into his thirties, well past his best and he wasn't the tallest player anyway.

After conceding 12 goals in four games, Chambers was moved back into the forward line, allowing Billy to step up for his first senior game – and he did well. One newspaper report stated: 'Albion's new centre-half Richardson made full use of his height and weight and performed cleverly, his tackling and heading being of the highest order.' Billy retained his place in the side for the duration of that season, switching to the right-half position from mid-March onwards when Tommy Magee was injured, thus allowing Evans to return to the centre of the defence.

An ever-present in 1929–30 when, in fact, he played in all three middle-line positions, Billy was outstanding again the following term, playing in every game as Albion completed the unique double of winning the FA Cup and gaining promotion to the First Division. With his bosom pal from the Black Country, Jimmy 'Iron' Edwards, on his left and 'wee' Tommy Magee on his right, Billy marshalled the Baggies defence splendidly and at one point in the season it was reported in the press that he was being watched by an England selector.

He was quite superb in some games, completely blotting out the goal threat of Everton's Dixie Dean in the Cup semi-final and then doing likewise to another brilliant marksman, Joe Bradford of Birmingham, in the Final. He also held firm against the likes of George Beel (Burnley), Billy Hartill (Wolves) and Johnny Dent (Nottingham Forest), all of whom scored 25 or more goals apiece that season.

The only player to cause Billy trouble that term was Jack Vidler of Plymouth Argyle, who scored a hat-trick in the Pilgrims' surprise 5–1 win at Home Park in January. A reporter in the local paper wrote: 'Fidler gave Richardson, the Albion centre-half, a torrid time.' Such comments, however, were rare, and overall Billy's performances for the Baggies down the years were solid and steady. In 1931–32, when he tasted top-flight football for the first time, he missed only one game (at Blackburn), was absent four times in 1932–33, played in 37 out of the 42 League matches in 1933–34, was sidelined for five in 1934–35 and missed seven in 1935–36. That's consistency for you.

Billy was in good form when Albion reached the 1935 FA Cup Final, which they lost to Sheffield Wednesday, who scored two late goals in a 4–2 victory. After that game he admitted that he should have been closer to Ellis Rimmer when the winger headed in from close range to make it 3–2 with three minutes remaining, and he also owned up to not reacting quick enough when the ball rebounded off goalkeeper Pearson to allow the same player to net again with virtually the last kick of the game.

Two seasons later, in October 1936 and in his 338th match, Billy scored his one and only senior goal for Albion – and it was a crucial one at that, a decisive 74th-minute equaliser against Wolves at The Hawthorns. Winger Jimmy Prew later struck the winner (2–1).

Billy, who had missed the previous four matches with a knee injury, made his 352nd and last appearance for Albion at Bolton on 20 March 1937. He was sold to Swindon Town for £200 at the end of that season and when World War Two broke out in September 1939 he moved back home to sign on a free transfer for Dudley Town, assisting Vono Sports during the 1940–41 season before retiring. Later an Albion scout for three seasons (1950–53) Billy lived in Hill Top, West Bromwich until his death in the summer of 1985 at the age of 77.

Only one other player – John Wile – has appeared in more games at centre-half for Albion than Billy Richardson. And in the mid-1930s, when Billy's accompanying wing-halves were Jack Sankey and Jimmy Edwards, the trio was called 'salt, pepper and mustard.'

SAMMY RICHARDSON

'A thick set wing-half whose bustling approach made him such a valuable member of the team.'

Born:	11 August 1894, West Bromwich
Died:	23 September 1959, West Bromwich

Albion senior record:

Appearances:	League 191, FA Cup 15, FA Charity Shield 1, Others 6
Goals:	League 1, FA Cup 0, FA Charity Shield 0, Others 0
Senior debut:	League, 16 January 1915 v Sheffield United (a) lost 2–0
Also played for:	Greets Green Prims, Great Bridge Juniors, Great Bridge Celtic, Oldbury Town (guest), Coventry City (guest), Newport County, Aldershot, Kidderminster Harriers, Football League (1 app), FA XI (1 app), England international trialist

Sammy Richardson was a proud man, and very proud to be a Throstle (an Albion player). Born in Whitehall Street, West Bromwich, he moved with his family to Tipton as a young boy and attended and played for New Road School with another Albion legend, Fred Morris. At the age of 14 he began working as a pipe-screwer while turning out at weekends in the Smethwick League for Greets Green Prims. Here he bumped into yet another Albion legend, Claude Jephcott, a pacy right-winger from the Mount Pleasant team, and amazingly all three players – Morris, Jephcott and Sammy – were to feature prominently in Albion's League Championship-winning team of 1919–20.

Albion first spotted Sammy playing as a wing-half for Great Bridge Celtic with Jackie Mann, who also joined the Baggies, in the Final of the Albion Cup at The Hawthorns in 1911. Monitoring his progress carefully, they eventually signed him as a full-time professional in February 1913 and, after seeing him perform exceedingly well in a number of second-team games in the Birmingham & District League, he was handed his debut in the Football League in January 1915, in the away fixture at Sheffield United, deputising for the injured Frank Waterhouse in a 2–0 defeat.

During World War One Sammy worked on munitions in the Midlands and when off duty played as a guest for Oldbury Town and Coventry City. Available for selection when the Midland Victory League was introduced in March 1919, he played for Albion in all six games in that competition, collecting a winners' medal for his efforts, along with his best mate Fred Morris.

Then, in 1919–20, he turned out to be a key member of Albion's League Championship-winning team. Appearing in 40 of the 42 First Division matches, missing only the away clashes at

Middlesbrough and Burnley, he was the anchorman in the centre of the park, the defensive midfielder, in front of reliable full-back Joe Smith, centre-back Sid Bowser and strongman Bobby McNeal.

A totally committed right-half, Sammy gave nothing away. He tackled hard but fair, passed the ball with good pace and precision and proved to be a terrific link between his defence and attack, and he was also a wonderful aide to right-wingers Jack Crisp, initially, and later his good friend Claude Jephcott.

Like a lot of people associated with football at the time, Sammy knew Albion had a team good enough and strong enough to win the League title. With eight games to go, he told one newspaper reporter: 'I cannot imagine any rival thwarting Albion in the race for the Championship. With the Baggies so far ahead,' he said 'it is all over bar the shouting.' And so it was. In the end Albion won at a canter, finishing nine points ahead of runners-up Burnley (60–51).

A fitness fanatic who often trained on his own, Sammy was lucky not to suffer any serious injuries during his career. A player who always gave a good account of himself whatever the game, no matter what the circumstances, he continued to perform with great efficiency over the next two seasons, missing only eight League games in total, four in each campaign. He also scored his only competitive goal for the club, a well-struck effort in a 3–0 home win over Sheffield United in March 1922, and he also came mighty close to winning an England call-up when he represented the Football League against the Irish League.

Then, perhaps surprisingly, he lost his place in the first team to Tommy Magee who, for practically the whole of the 1921–22 season, had occupied the outside-right position, standing in for the unfortunate Claude Jephcott who was sidelined with a broken leg, suffered in the away League game at Middlesbrough in early September.

A fighter to the last, and a dedicated club man, Sammy nevertheless strove gamely in the reserves and he helped Albion's second string win back-to-back Central League titles in 1922–23 and 1923–24, appearing in 69 of the 84 matches overall. 'No way could he be left out of the first XI,' said one supporter – and that was quite true. After appearing in just three games during the first half of the 1924–25 season, when Bobby McNeal and Harry Dutton were both unavailable, Sammy was brought back into the team in the left-half position in place of McNeal in late December. McNeal was now nearing retirement age and would actually call it a day at the end of the season.

Sammy went on to make 23 appearances and collected a runners'-up medal as Albion finished second behind Huddersfield Town in the League Championship, edged out by just two points, and reached the quarter-finals of the FA Cup. Switching over to the right-half berth at the start of the 1925–26 campaign, Sammy ended up on the opposite flank once more, but when left-half Nelson Howarth was signed from Bolton Wanderers, and with Tommy Magee now firmly established on the right side of the middle trio, Sammy knew, deep down, that his career with Albion was nearing an end.

His younger brother, centre-half Bill Richardson, joined him at The Hawthorns in November 1926 and they actually played together a few times before Sammy made his 213th and final senior appearance for the club in a 2–2 draw with Sheffield Wednesday at The Hawthorns on 26 February 1927.

Six months later he was sold to Newport County for a fee of £450 and, after having three pretty good seasons with the Welsh club, he switched his allegiance, on a free transfer, to Aldershot in August 1930 before playing out the last four years of his football career with Kidderminster Harriers, retiring in May 1935 after being a professional for more than 22 years. Sammy, who attended The Hawthorns whenever possible, lived the rest of his life in West Bromwich, where he died in 1959 at the age of 65.

STAN RICKABY

*'Stan found his powerful frame useful as very few wingers got the better of him.
A reliable kicker, he was an expert in the art of positioning.'*

Born: 24 March 1924, Stockton-on-Tees

Albion senior record:

Appearances: League 189, FA Cup 15, FA Charity Shield 1
Goals: League 2, FA Cup 0, FA Charity Shield 0
Senior debut: League, 29 April 1950 v Manchester City (h) drew 0–0
Also played for: Stockton & District Schoolboys, Middlesbrough Crusaders, South Bank, Middlesbrough, Poole Town (player-manager), Weymouth, Newton Abbot Spurs, England (1 full cap), Football League (1 app), Combined Services (5 apps)

In the official players' booklet produced for the 1954 FA Cup Final, *Sports Argus* reporter Charles Harrold wrote this about Albion's right-back Stan Rickaby: 'Cool, calm and consistent – one of the outstanding players since he joined the club. Easily six feet tall and over 13 stone, there must be times when an unsuccessful winger wonders just why there had to be so much of him and most of all why it had to be around at the same time as he.'

After representing Stockton & District Schools, Stan took employment as a wages clerk at the Teesdale ironworks of Head Wrightson and Co. Ltd in 1940. Playing regularly for the works team and also for Middlesbrough Crusaders, he was spotted by a Middlesbrough scout who invited him, and four of his teammates, for a trial at Ayresome Park. Stan did well and played for the club's nursery team, South Bank, before signing as an amateur in July 1941. His progress was rapid and in March 1942 he made his senior debut at outside-right against Newcastle in a Wartime League (North) game at St James' Park. Stan remembered: 'I received a telegram that read "Can you play at Newcastle on Saturday?" What a silly question! I hardly slept a wink on the Friday night…and the next day I was so nervous, I was trembling while eating my pre-match lunch. Here I was in the same team as Scottish international Bobby Baxter and the legendary Bill Forrest.'

Stan did alright and played in a few second XI matches before joining the General Service Corps as a soldier. Promoted to sergeant, he was involved in the Normandy breakout and the liberations of Amiens, Brussels, Antwerp, Eindhoven and Arnhem. He figured in the Battle of the Bulge, fought in the Ardennes and Reichwald Forest, crossed the Rhine and did night patrols in Bremen, hearing that the war was over when 300 metres from German lines. Stan also ventured into Hitler's bunker, did house-to-house searches for hidden weapons, played football for his unit whenever possible and found time to marry a German girl, Leni.

Demobbed after five years of service, Stan returned to Middlesbrough and signed professional forms in July 1946. However, the competition for places at Ayresome Park was intense and over the next four years he made only 10 League appearances. During the 1949–50 season several clubs were keen on signing Stan, who revealed: 'I was unhappy at not being in the first team and asked for a transfer several times.

'Suddenly my manager David Jack told me that the club had agreed to sell me to West Bromwich Albion. I didn't really want to go to the Midlands because I knew that Sunderland had enquired about me and that would have been a good move for me. However, I was told, in no uncertain terms, that if I didn't join Albion, I would finish up playing in Middlesbrough's fourth team.

'Harry Ashley, an Albion staff member, met me when I arrived at Birmingham's Snow Hill station. We went by taxi to The Hawthorns where I was introduced to manager Jack Smith, who offered me the maximum wage for winter and summer whether I played in the first team or not. I accepted his offer, signed the transfer forms and became an Albion player on 16 February 1950.'

Stan continued to train at Middlesbrough (until he moved house) and, after a handful of reserve-team games, made his Baggies debut on the last day of the season against Manchester City. Then, after Jim Pemberton had been injured in the first match of 1950–51, Stan took over at right-back. Settling down immediately, he made 143 consecutive League appearances, the run ending when he was called up by England in November 1953.

In his book *Upover and Downunder,* published in 2003, Stan wrote: 'I knew I had been playing well and I always considered myself better than Alf Ramsey. We had played at Blackpool and were staying over a couple of days when my selection was announced. We beat Northern Ireland 3–0 at Goodison Park and I played well, considering that I'd never appeared with any of the other players before. It was a thrilling occasion and, although I was nervous at first, as soon as I got involved I felt confident. The National Press wrote well of me, indicating that I should make the position my own for a long time to come. How wrong they all were. Shortly afterwards, England played Hungary at Wembley. Ramsey was back and I was out.'

Stan's next representative call-up was for the Football League against the League of Ireland at Maine Road. He didn't put a foot wrong in a 9–1 win and was told by skipper Billy Wright that he was the best right-back in England. Sadly Stan never won another cap and he also suffered the bitter disappointment of missing the 1954 FA Cup Final through injury, which many feel denied him a place in England's World Cup squad that same year.

Stan said Albion were 'the best team in the world' in 1953–54. 'We finished runners-up in the League to Wolves and beat Preston in the Cup Final and with my teammate Norman Heath, who also missed the Cup Final through injury, we both received Cup-winners' medals, having played in the previous rounds.'

Stan made 205 appearances for Albion, scoring two League goals – the first at Bolton Wanderers on Christmas Day 1951, the second a blockbuster in a 4–2 home League win over Sheffield Wednesday in February 1954.

Unfortunately he left The Hawthorns an angry man. The only player dropped after a poor team display against Sheffield United in March 1955, he was never recalled. He said: 'Chairman Major Keys had a lot to say in this matter. I was treated like a leper. I was deeply hurt. I will never know why manager Vic Buckingham, whom I had always greatly respected, allowed me to be so miserably treated.'

Joining Poole Town as player-manager in June 1955, Stan assisted Weymouth (1960–61) and Newton Abbot Spurs, retiring in July 1964. Taking up golf, he played tennis and badminton, worked in a pub and was a representative for an ice cream company (Eldorado) before moving from Devon to West Hagley via Cambridge and working for an insurance company which he later ran (International Life). Stan emigrated to Australia in 1975 and today lives at North Beach, Perth.

BOB ROBERTS

'Usually sound and competent in all aspects of the goalkeeper's craft, although at times he showed undue agitation.'

Born:	9 April 1859, West Bromwich
Died:	20 October 1929, Byker, Newcastle-upon-Tyne

Albion senior record:

Appearances:	League 49, FA Cup 35
Goals:	League 0, FA Cup 1
Senior debut:	FA Cup, 10 November 1883 v Wednesbury Town (h) lost 2–0
Also played for:	George Salter's Works, Sunderland Albion, Aston Villa, England (3 full caps), Football Alliance (1 app), England international trialist

'Big' Bob Roberts, also known as 'Long Bob,' was well over six feet tall, weighed a good 12 stone of muscle and bone and wore a size 13 boot. He began his Albion career as an outfield player, occupying the right-half and all three central forward positions. For most of the time he proved to be the square peg in a round hole and never really looked the part in any of those roles. Then someone came up with the bright idea of trying him in goal. Bob took to it like a duck to water and became Albion's first international footballer, being honoured by England against Scotland in 1887 and later adding two more caps to his collection when playing against Ireland in 1888 and 1890. Thereafter he never failed to wear one of those three caps and became a great local hero.

Bob also helped Albion reach three successive FA Cup Finals in 1886, 1887 and 1888, gaining a winners' medal at the third attempt (2–1 v Preston North End). He was, however, partly blamed for the defeat by Villa in 1887 when he failed to play to the whistle. Assuming Dennis Hodgetts was offside, he made no attempt to save the winger's shot and was mortified when referee Major Marindin awarded a goal. An irate Bob then had to be restrained by his teammates as he confronted the official.

Bob, who was rarely out of action through injury or illness, also played in the club's first-ever FA Cup tie v Wednesbury Town in November 1883 and the first Football League game at Stoke in September 1888. Only Ezra Horton achieved this same feat.

A former pupil at Christ Church School and one of seven employees from the George Salter's Spring Works in West Bromwich who became footballers with the Albion, Bob was in goal when Albion played their first-ever game, a friendly against a team representing the local Hudson's soap factory, in November 1878. He kept a clean sheet in a 0–0 draw.

The following season he began to show his undoubted ability as a goalkeeper and throughout 1881–82 he played superbly as Albion reached the semi-finals of the Birmingham Cup. Still in great form, the very next season, 1882–83, he helped the Baggies win their first domestic trophy, the Staffordshire Cup, when Stoke were eclipsed 3–2 in the Potteries.

However, after playing in 40 of Albion's first 44 Football League games, Bob stunned the club and its supporters by leaving to join Sunderland Albion on a free transfer. Unhappy in the north-east (despite meeting his future wife) he was only away from the Black Country for one season, rejoining the Baggies in May 1891. Remaining with the club for another year, he was unable to dislodge his successor Joe Reader and subsequently switched his allegiance to nearby Aston Villa in May 1892, eventually announcing his retirement the following summer with well over 400 club appearances (at various levels) behind him.

Usually a sound and competent executor of all aspects of the goalkeeper's craft, although sometimes showing undue agitation towards the rough and ready forwards, Bob nevertheless proved a wonderful 'last line of defence' for Albion. He commanded his area with authority and his long reach enabled him to collect high balls comfortably. Although hesitant on his line at times, generally speaking he was a highly efficient performer, certainly one of Albion's best-ever 'keepers, who might well have gained more international recognition had he not moved to Wearside.

One reporter, covering Albion's 3–0 home League win over rivals Aston Villa in September 1889, wrote: 'Roberts guarded his goal splendidly. He maintained a high standard of performance throughout the match and was sound and courageous when dealing with ground shots and melees in and around his goal area. One particular save from Allen was outstanding and on this form, he deserves another chance with England.'

After retiring (at the age of 34) Bob returned to the north-east after his wife had become homesick. He worked in a local council office for many years and quite often made the trip down to the Midlands to watch a game at The Hawthorns. He was an invited guest at the club's celebration dinner following the League championship triumph in 1920.

*In an FA Cup tie against Derby Junction in November 1886, Bob was officially credited with a goal when, following a scrimmage in front of the Derby goalmouth, the ball suddenly squirted between the posts – giving him the honour of being the first Albion goalkeeper to score from open play.

ALLY ROBERTSON

'A resilient and dogged, determined and robust defender – a great player to have in your side' (Tony Brown)
'He could mix it and was certainly the brains of the Robertson-Wile partnership.'

Born:	9 September 1952, Philipstoun, Lothian

Albion senior record:

Appearances:	League 504+2, FA Cup 34+2, League Cup 53, Europe 12, Others 19
Goals:	League 8, FA Cup 0, League Cup 3, Europe 1, Others 0
Senior debut:	League, 25 October 1969 v Manchester United (h) won 2–1
Also played for:	Linlithgow Academy, Uphall Saints, Wolverhampton Wanderers, West Bromwich Albion All Stars, Scotland (4 Schoolboy, 6 Youth caps)
Managed:	Worcester City, Cheltenham Town

After joining Albion as an apprentice in July 1968, Ally Robertson made rapid progress and played in 16 Central League games in his first season as well as helping the third team reach the FA Youth Cup Final. Such was Ally's 'rise to the top' that in October 1969, at the age of 17, and just a month after becoming a professional, he made his senior debut against Manchester United, replacing the injured John Kaye at left-half.

Ally remembered: 'I was nervous, very nervous, but before the game experienced "pros" like John Talbut, 'Hopey', Jeff Astle and Doug Fraser gave me encouragement and once out on the pitch, I was fine…until I saw their line-up! Kidd, Charlton, Best, Aston – and those were only the forwards. Tony Brown told me to forget who I was playing against…just go out and play your own game, you'll be fine.'

Ally did himself proud and played his part in a 2–1 victory in front of 45,000 spectators. Another nine appearances followed that season, one at Goodison Park when Everton won the League Championship. 'The ground was packed and it was a tough game,' said Ally. 'Although we lost 2–0, we matched them kick for kick and afterwards Alan Ball came up to me, patted me on the back and said "I haven't seen you before but I'm certain we'll meet again; well played anyway." That gave me a massive boost and I knew there and then, I was a footballer!'

Albion reached the League Cup Final in 1970, but Ally, still a reserve, sat and watched from the Wembley stand as Manchester City won 2–1 after extra-time. 'That was a big occasion for me,' he recalled. 'Manager Alan Ashman took most of us along that day and told us to "enjoy the occasion…you might be out there yourselves in the future." I thought to myself, I'll be here one day…but unfortunately it wouldn't be with Albion, as much as I tried.'

After appearing in just four games early in the 1970–71 season, Ally had the misfortune to break his leg in a League Cup tie at home to Charlton Athletic. He was out of action for six months. By the time he had recovered John Wile had joined Albion and he and Ally would become one of the greatest centre-back partnerships the club has ever known.

They first played together in a 2–0 League win at Crystal Palace in October 1971 and amazingly, except for the odd interruption here and there for various reasons, they occupied the two central defensive positions for 12 years. In all they partnered each other over 570 times between October 1971 and May 1983 (404 in the League). Ally went on to accumulate a total of 626 senior appearances for Albion, making 729 in the first team overall, second only to Tony Brown (826). In fact, Ally is one of only three players in the club's history to make over 600 competitive appearances; fellow defender John Wile is the other with 619.

In the early 1970s Ally, along with the rest of his teammates, was bitterly disappointed when Albion suffered relegation at the end of the 1972–73 season. 'It was hard to take,' said Ally, 'but we knew, deep down, there was enough spirit within the club and everyone simply buckled down to the business of trying to gain promotion as soon as possible.'

In November 1972, Ally became Albion's youngest-ever captain when he led the side out at Norwich. Don Howe was in charge at the time and he told Ally 'You're our skipper today – all you have to do is toss up, the rest stays as normal.'

It took Albion three seasons to regain their top-flight status. And it came in some style under player-manager Johnny Giles in 1976. 'He was a great bloke,' said Ally. 'He knew the game inside out and he got us playing a lot of "keep ball." He even got myself and Wiley to pass to each other...that took some doing!

'We clinched promotion on the last day of the season at Oldham. What an occasion. The ground was two-thirds full with Albion fans; the atmosphere was terrific and we knew we weren't going to lose. I dread to think what might have happened had we lost, or even drawn!

'The journey home down the M6 afterwards was magic...we passed hundreds of cars with the blue and white and green and yellow scarves hanging out of the windows. Everyone was over the moon. That was one of the greatest moments of my Albion career. What a day.'

An ever-present that season, and likewise in 1976–77 and 1977–78, Ally made a club record 171 consecutive League appearances for Albion between April 1975 and May 1979, beating the previous record of 166 held by Jimmy Dudley (1952–56). Goalkeeper Tony Godden later topped it with 180 First Division outings on the trot between 1977–81. In fact, over a period of five years from 1975–80, Ally missed only seven League games out of a possible 210.

Ally played in four Cup semi-final matches for Albion and was never on the winning side, losing 3–1 to Ipswich and 1–0 to QPR in the 1978 and 1982 FA Cup and drawing 0–0 and losing 1–0 to Spurs in the 1982 League Cup. 'We were so close, mighty close, to Wembley on those occasions, but in the end we just weren't at our best when it mattered most. It was so disappointing to lose to QPR in 1982; their goal went in off my shin...it was a lucky rebound that went their way, and not ours' said Ally.

Ally served under seven different managers during his 18 years with Albion. The last was Ron Saunders, whom he loathed. 'Ron Atkinson and Gilesy were by far the best of the lot,' admitted Ally, who never played under Saunders. The former Aston Villa and Birmingham City chief let Ally join Wolves on a free transfer in September 1986. Over the next four years he helped the Wanderers win the Fourth and Third Division championships and captained the side to victory in the 1988 Sherpa Van Trophy Final at Wembley – he said he would get there sometime. He also made 136 appearances for the Molineux club before entering non-League football as manager of Worcester City in 1990, later taking a similar position with Cheltenham Town (1991–92). Now resident in Walsall, Ally works as a car salesman and is a member of Albion's former players' association.

SIR BOBBY ROBSON, CBE

'As a player Bobby was terrific — as a manager he was absolutely marvellous!'

Born:	18 February 1933, Sacriston, County Durham
Died:	31 July 2009, Newcastle upon Tyne

Albion senior record:

Appearances:	League 239, FA Cup 18
Goals:	League 56, FA Cup 5
Senior debut:	Football League, 10 March 1956 v Manchester City (home) lost 4–0
Also played for:	Langley Park Juniors, Chester-le-Street, Middlesbrough (amateur), Southampton (trial), Fulham, Vancouver Royals (player-coach), England (one B, one Under-23 and 20 full caps), Football League (5 apps), FA XI
Managed:	Oxford University, Fulham, Ipswich Town, England B, England senior team, PSV Eindhoven (2 spells), Sporting Lisbon, FC Porto, CF Barcelona, Newcastle United

Sir Bobby Robson was a colossus of football who bestrode the beautiful game for more than six decades. As a player he scored 141 goals in 627 games for just two League clubs, Fulham and West Bromwich Albion, gained 20 England caps and appeared in the World Cup Finals of 1958. As a manager he won the FA Cup, UEFA Cup and Texaco Cup and twice finished runners-up in the First Division in 13 seasons with Ipswich Town, led PSV to two successive Dutch League titles, won the League twice and the Portuguese Cup once with FC Porto, guided Barcelona to European Cup-winners' Cup and Spanish Cup glory and took England to the quarter-finals and semi-finals of the World Cup in 1986 and 1990 respectively, beaten with the help of the 'Hand of God' in the former and on penalties in the latter.

Raised in hard times by decent folk in a Durham mining village, Bobby was an amateur with Middlesbrough in 1948 and had a trial with Southampton before a Fulham scout saw him scoring goals for Langley Park. Cottagers boss Bill Dodgin was informed and in April 1950 he pipped Newcastle United for Bobby's signature, securing him as an amateur before giving him a professional contract a month later.

Linking up superbly in attack with Bedford Jezzard and then Johnny Haynes, Bobby remained with Fulham until March 1956 when Albion signed him for a record £25,000. 'This player is something special. He's got ability, stamina, drive and he can score goals,' said Baggies boss Vic Buckingham.

However, Bobby didn't have the greatest of starts to his Baggies career. The first two games he played in both ended in 4–0 defeats, but he quickly found his feet, scored his first goal in a 3–1 win at Cardiff and for the next six years produced some outstanding performances in a very good Albion team. His teammate Derek

Kevan recalled: 'Bobby had something special. He was tall, well built, could shoot, mainly right-footed, and was a decent header of the ball. He covered acres of ground during a game and because of his gentlemanly deportment was very popular in the dressing room, on the team coach and certainly on the field.'

In his first full season with Albion, Bobby partnered Frank Griffin on the right-wing and had Ronnie Allen and Kevan alongside him. Between them they scored 58 goals as the team finished 11th in the League and reached the FA Cup semi-finals. Unfortunately Bobby missed the two games with Aston Villa through injury, and although his replacement, Brian Whitehouse, scored both goals in the first clash at Molineux, Bobby was sorely missed as Villa won the replay 1–0 to go through and meet Manchester United in the Final.

Bobby scored twice in a thrilling 4–3 victory over the Busby Babes in a League game at The Hawthorns in October 1957. His first was a delicate lob over 'keeper Ray Wood in the 15th minute and his second a close-range shot from 12 yards. However, a goal eluded Bobby in a sixth-round FA Cup tie against the Reds as Albion lost 1–0 in a replay just a week or so after the Munich air disaster.

Albion netted 112 goals in 1957–58, Bobby claiming 27, the best-ever scoring season of his career, and he also bagged his first League hat-trick, a four-timer, in a 5–1 home win over Burnley. His form was rewarded with his first England cap and he celebrated by notching two goals in a 4–0 win over France at Wembley. This set him up nicely for the World Cup Finals in Sweden, where he played in all three drawn pool matches, although he had a 'good' goal disallowed against Russia. The referee said he handled the ball, but TV footage clearly shows that it hit Bobby in the stomach. This meant that England had to face Russia again in a play-off for a place in the quarter-finals. Unfortunately, with Bobby out injured, they lost 1–0.

In 1958–59, Bobby was switched from inside-right to left-half, Ray Barlow having moved to centre-half in place of Joe Kennedy. He did well and he also starred on a summer tour to Canada and North America, grabbing 12 goals including six in a 15–0 win over Alberta All Stars in Calgary.

Bobby missed very few games over the next three seasons as Albion finished fourth, 10th and ninth in the First Division, but then, surprisingly, he left The Hawthorns in April 1962, returning to Fulham for £20,000.

Continuing in League football until June 1967, he then started on the path to becoming a truly great manager. After grinding his teeth with Oxford University and with Vancouver Royals in Canada, he was appointed Fulham's boss in January 1968, only to be sacked after 10 months. 'I went into the centre-circle and cried when I was told,' said Bobby.

But he quickly bounced back. After scouting for Chelsea, he was given the manager's job at Ipswich Town in January 1969. Remaining at Portman Road until July 1982, he did wonders with the Suffolk club, twice coming close to adding League championship glory to his Cup triumphs.

After a spell as England's B team manager, Bobby took charge of the national team in January 1982 and he once again did a splendid job, following up with more success around Europe. Awarded the CBE in 1991 and knighted 11 years later, he was made honorary president of Ipswich Town in August 2006 but was taken ill at dinner that same day. Two weeks later it was announced that he had a small tumour on his brain. Diagnosed with cancer in May 2006 he vowed to 'battle as I've always done.'

Following his retirement from football in November 2007 due to poor health, Bobby received a 'Lifetime Achievement' award on BBC TV's *Sports Personality of the Year* show, was handed the Freedom of Ipswich and also of Durham and, having undergone a third operation for lung cancer, he helped raise over £1 million for his cancer charity, the Sir Bobby Robson Foundation, which he set up personally in March 2008.

After making his last appearance in public, at St James' Park ahead of the charity game for his charity between England and Germany over-35s in front of 33,000 fans, Sir Bobby died at his home in Durham aged 76.

His passing stunned many people. Ex-Albion player Don Howe, his best pal for many years, said: 'He was a standard man who loved the game. He mixed well with the players, but never hesitated to show them that he was the boss.' Manchester United boss Sir Alex Ferguson added: 'I was never too big or proud to ask Bobby for advice which he gave freely and unconditionally. And I'm sure I am speaking for a lot of people when I say that. The world, not just the football world, will miss him. Let's hope it won't be long before another like him turns up because we could never get enough of them.'

BRYAN ROBSON, OBE

'A real powerhouse in midfield for club and country, Bryan was one of the great players of the 1980s.
He was as good at 21 as he was at 28.' (Ron Atkinson)

Born: 11 January 1957, Witton Gilbert, Chester-le-Street

Albion senior record:

Appearances: League 194+4, FA Cup 10+2, League Cup 17+1, Europe 12, Others 9
Goals: League 39, FA Cup 2, League Cup 2, Europe 2, Other 1
Senior debut: Football League, 12 April 1975 v York City (away) won 3–1
Also played for: Burnley (trial), Coventry City (trial), Newcastle United (trial), Sheffield Wednesday
                  (trial), Happy Valley (Hong Kong, guest), Manchester United, Middlesbrough
                  (player-manager), England (6 Youth, 2 B, 7 Under-21 and 90 full caps)
Also managed: Bradford City, Sheffield United, Thailand national team

Bryan captained Birtley South Secondary Modern and Lord Lawson of Beamish Comprehensive Schools and also skippered the Washington & District Boys team before signing as an apprentice with Albion under manager Don Howe in 1972. Progressing through the ranks, he became a professional in August 1974 (receiving a £250 signing-on fee) and eight months later caretaker manager Brian Whitehouse gave him his League debut in a Second Division match at York. Bryan did well, scored against Cardiff on his home debut a week later and never looked back.

A strong player, Bryan worked hard at his game but faced stiff competition for a place, not least from Albion's new player-manager Johnny Giles. The Irishman believed that Bryan was more than a midfield player and used him at centre-half and left-back when promotion was gained in 1975–76.

Now an established member of the senior squad, and playing well, Bryan suffered a set-back in October 1976 when he fractured his left leg against Tottenham Hotspur. Amazingly, two months later he was back in action, only to break the same leg again in a tackle with the Stoke defender

and future Baggies manager Denis Smith in a reserve-team match. After another swift recovery Bryan returned inside two months and enjoyed a good run in the side, scoring a hat-trick in a 4–0 win over Ipswich. However, disaster struck again in April 1977 when he broke his right ankle against Manchester City, an injury which cost him an England Under-23 cap.

Former Albion player Ronnie Allen replaced Giles in June 1977 and immediately selected Bryan as his central midfielder, but when he quit and John Wile took temporary charge, Albion's performances slumped and Bryan was dropped. However, Ron Atkinson – described by Bryan as 'A down-to-earth, fair-minded, regular bloke' – took over as boss in January 1978. Making changes, he didn't select Bryan regularly until the last six weeks of the season, leaving him out of the FA Cup semi-final defeat by Ipswich. The following season Bryan became one of Atkinson's star players. Inspirational week in, week out, he helped the team finish third in the First Division (their highest placing since 1954) and reach the UEFA Cup quarter-finals.

The following season was disappointing for Albion despite Bryan's never-say-die performances, which earned him his first full England cap against the Republic of Ireland in February 1980. After Albion had claimed fourth place in the League in 1980–81, Atkinson left to become boss of Manchester United and speculation mounted that Bryan would follow him to Old Trafford.

Albion offered their star midfielder a £1,000 a week contract, but he turned it down and signed for United in September 1981 for a record £1.5 million, his colleague Remi Moses following him soon afterwards. Said Bryan: 'Money wasn't my main motivation for leaving. I simply wanted to be a winner.'

His career flourished and although he missed the 1983 League Cup Final due to torn ankle ligaments, he recovered in time to score twice when the Reds beat Brighton 4–0 in the FA Cup Final replay. This was his first major prize…with more to come. And a year after turning down a £3 million move to Juventus, Bryan captained United to another FA Cup victory, this time over Everton.

Retaining the captain's armband after Atkinson was replaced by Alex Ferguson in November 1986, it was not until 1990 that Bryan won his third medal, helping United beat Crystal Palace in another FA Cup Final replay. After a deserved testimonial, Bryan struggled with injuries in 1987–88, but was fit enough to collect a European Cup-winners' Cup medal when Barcelona were eclipsed in the Final, and during this same season he won his 90th and last cap for England. Replaced as captain by Steve Bruce in 1992–93, Bryan won his first Premiership medal, but with Eric Cantona and Roy Keane around, his midfield place came under pressure, although he did make enough appearances in 1993–94 to win a second Premiership prize. Bryan's 13-year spell at Old Trafford ended in May 1994 after 465 appearances and 100 goals. The longest-serving captain in the club's history, he had skippered England 65 times, and only Bobby Moore and Billy Wright have led their country more often. On leaving Old Trafford, Bryan became player-manager of Middlesbrough, combining his duties with that of assistant to England boss Terry Venables. He was even linked with the manager's job when Venables quit after Euro '96, but ruled himself out of the running due to his limited experience.

In seven years at the Riverside, Bryan guided 'Boro to three Wembley Cup Finals, all lost, and twice gained promotion to the Premier League. In November 2003, he was set to become Nigeria's national coach but the appointment was blocked by the country's sports minister due to Bryan's wage demands. After acting as a part-time coach at Old Trafford and spending seven months in charge of Bradford City, Bryan returned as Albion's manager in November 2004. He successfully kept the Baggies in the Premiership with a last-gasp win over Portsmouth at the end of that season – achieving something which previously had never been done. Bottom of the table on Christmas Day, Albion amazingly pulled off the 'great escape' when least expected to stay in the top flight for another term. Unfortunately Bryan couldn't keep the Baggies up and after a poor start to the 2006–07 Championship campaign he was replaced by Tony Mowbray.

Out of the game for eight months, at one point Bryan was in line to become England's Under-21 manager, but Stuart Pearce got the job instead. After a short-lived, uneasy spell in charge of Sheffield United and the talk of a job with Iranian giants Persepolis FC, Bryan returned to Manchester United in March 2008 as an ambassador, alongside Sir Bobby Charlton, helping 'promote the club's commercial and charitable aims'. Then, in September 2009, he was appointed manager of the Thailand national team, initially signing a three-year contract.

Awarded the OBE in January 1990 and named in the list of 100 Football League Legends in 1998, Bryan was an inaugural inductee of the English Football Hall of Fame in 2002 and is also listed as one of West Bromwich Albion's greatest-ever players.

The subject of the TV programme *This Is Your Life* in 1985, he formed a specialist sports company, Robson Lloyd Consultancy Ltd, in 1987, aiming to build community sports academies with long-lasting benefits for small football clubs. Bryan, whose book *Robbo: My Autobiography* was released in May 2006, has two footballing brothers, Gary and Justin. Gary made 256 appearances for Albion between 1981 and 1993. Bryan is now deeply involved with Robson Lloyd, who are committed to helping clubs build for the future – ensuring that the grass roots of UK sport will flourish and grow. Said Bryan: 'I had the good fortune of being able to achieve so much throughout my football career. My aim now is to use my knowledge and expertise to the benefit of community sports.'

REG 'PADDY' RYAN

'The Human Dynamo...whose wholehearted work was appreciated by players and fans alike.'

Born:	30 October 1925, Dublin
Died:	12 February 1997, Sheldon, Birmingham

Albion senior record:

Appearances:	League 234, FA Cup 20, Wartime 17, FA Charity Shield 1
Goals:	League 28, FA Cup 2, Wartime 0, FA Charity Shield 1
Senior debut:	Football League (South), 10 November v Millwall (away) won 4–1
	Football League, 7 April 1947 v Chesterfield (home) won 3–2
Also played for:	Nuneaton Borough, Jaguars Cars FC, Sheffield United (trial), Nottingham Forest (trial), Coventry City (2 spells), Derby County, Republic of Ireland (17 caps), Northern Ireland (1 cap), The North v South (1 app)

Around The Hawthorns during the late 1940s and early 1950s, Reg Ryan was known as the 'Human Dynamo' because he was always on the move. A utility player with laughing Irish eyes, he was here, there and everywhere, puffing and pressing from either of the two wing-half positions or as an inside-forward. During that time he also occupied six different positions on the international scene.

'Paddy', as he was also called, left his native Dublin with his parents when he was eight years of age. The family settled in Blackpool before moving south to Coventry, where his father took employment in a local car factory during the war. By that time Reg had already begun to leave his mark in football. Just before leaving the seaside resort he had starred for Blackpool Boys in the English Schools Trophy competition and on his arrival in the East Midlands it was easy enough for him to get a game.

He signed up to play left-back for Nuneaton Borough on a Saturday and centre-half for Jaguars Cars FC on a Sunday. However, after unsuccessful trials with Sheffield United and Nottingham Forest, he joined Coventry City as an amateur. He did well at Highfield Road and in August 1943 graduated to the semi-professional ranks, but refused to sign as a full-time professional because he still enjoyed playing

works football. He was given four outings at left-half by the Sky Blues in the Football League (North) First Competition in 1944–45 before he was signed by West Bromwich Albion for £750 in April 1945. Six months later he was upgraded to the club's professional ranks.

Reg continued to live in Coventry and travelled to The Hawthorns every day for training. 'It wasn't too bad,' he said. 'Sometimes I came in by bus and occasionally by train with my teammate Glyn Hood who also resided in Coventry.'

Occupying his preferred left-half position, he appeared in 17 League (South) matches in the transitional season of 1945–46, at the end of which he went on his first overseas tour to Belgium and Luxembourg. The following season – the first full League and FA Cup campaign since 1938–39 – he made only five appearances due to his National Service commitments and in 1947–48 was utilised 15 times, including an FA Cup debut in front of almost 72,000 spectators at Tottenham.

Still not quite a first-team regular, Reg added another 14 League appearances to his tally in 1948–49 and scored his first Albion goal in a 3–0 win at Lincoln City. He celebrated at the end of that season when promotion was achieved back to Division One.

With the prospect of playing against some of the best footballers in the game, Reg worked overtime on the training field and at long last won a regular place in the Albion team, completing a half-back trio alongside his fellow countryman Jack Vernon and first his buddy Glyn Hood and later Joe Kennedy.

Now at the peak of his form and as fit as a fiddle, the tough and stocky Irishman battled away resolutely in midfield, playing in the hole behind the main strikers, plying his wingers with decisive passes. His colleague Ray Barlow thought he was 'a marvellous competitor – just the sort of player every team wants. He was a great forager.'

Reg, who got an enormous amount of fun out of life – he was a real joker at times who loved horse-racing and golf, acquiring a handicap of 16 in 1953 – was, in effect, a workaholic on the football pitch, covering acres of ground every game he played. In 1949–50 he had 36 League and Cup outings and over the next five seasons made a further 184, helping Albion finish runners-up in the League and win the FA Cup in 1954.

Back in the early 1970s I asked Reg what he remembered of that Wembley triumph. He told me, in a gruff Irish accent: 'It was fantastic. The build-up to the Final was hard work but enjoyable and on the day I thought we played pretty well. I was given the dual-purpose job of stopping Preston's wing-half Willie Forbes and their play-maker Jimmy Baxter from creating things in centre-field. I think I did well and I also found time to trek back and help out in defence. It was a wonderful day, especially as we won – and I had the pleasure of setting up Frank Griffin's winning goal with just three minutes remaining.'

Following that success Reg had just one more season at The Hawthorns before moving, reluctantly, to Derby County for £3,000 in June 1955. He went on to skipper the Rams, helping them win the Third Division North title in 1957 before transferring back to Coventry City in September 1958. He retired as a player in November 1960 having scored 70 goals in a total of 432 League games for his three major clubs. He also represented The League North v The League South in the annual challenge match in 1955 and gained a total of 17 caps at full international level (16 for the Republic of Ireland and once for Northern Ireland).

During 1960–61 Reg worked as a Pools Organiser at Highfield Road and did a similar job with Albion in 1961–62 before taking over as the club's chief scout, later working as a Midlands-based scout for Aston Villa, Derby, Hereford United and Leeds United. Poor health eventually forced him to give up football and, having undergone a brain operation, Reg sadly died in Sheldon, Birmingham, in February 1997.

Reg's father was an excellent Gaelic footballer who also kept goal for the Bohemians while his uncle played as a wing-half for Shamrock Rovers.

JIMMY SANDERS

'A sound and brave goalkeeper, an expert in the art of saving penalties.'

Born:	5 July 1920, Hackney, London
Died:	11 August 2003, Tamworth, Staffordshire

Albion senior record:

Appearances:	League 327, FA Cup 36, Wartime 27, FA Charity Shield 1
Goals:	None
Senior debut:	FA Cup, 10 November 1883 v Wednesbury Town (h) lost 2–0
Also played for:	North London Boys, Longlands FC (London), Charlton Athletic; Chelsea, Fulham, Liverpool, Southampton and West Ham United (as a World War Two guest), Coventry City and Hinckley Athletic

Jovial London-born goalkeeper Jimmy Sanders certainly had his ups and downs in life. One of his worst 'downs' came in the autumn of 1942 when, as a serving RAF sergeant-gunner, his plane was shot down by enemy fire during an operational flight in the Middle East. Invalided out of the services following lengthy hospital surgery, he was told that he had a bullet and shrapnel buried in his spine and that to remove both could well cause paralysis. In fact, the doctors informed him, reluctantly, that he would never be able to play football again.

But Jimmy was a born fighter, and would not accept the decision. 'Nonsense,' he said and returned to his club, Charlton Athletic, confident he would regain full fitness and play again at the top level. Training incessantly and undergoing hours of physiotherapy, he amazingly beat all the odds by returning to action with the Addicks in January 1944, just 15 months after being shot down over a foreign country.

Known around the Valley as 'Sanders of the River' (because his boss Jimmy Seed spotted him playing down by the River Thames) he went on to make 42 wartime appearances for the London club as well as assisting six top-line clubs, including Albion, as a guest. However, with the brilliant Sam Bartram now firmly bedded in as first choice 'keeper at the Valley, Jimmy desperately wanted regular first-team football and, as a result, he joined Albion on a permanent basis in November 1945, signed for what was to prove a bargain fee of £2,250.

After his 'downs' (in more ways than one during World War Two) he was now on the 'up' and this time he never looked back, celebrating plenty of good things in his 13 years at The Hawthorns. He played in 30 competitive games for the Baggies in 1945–46 and over the next two seasons added a further 44 senior appearances to his tally when he was pressurised for the number one spot by first Tom Grimley and then Norman Heath.

However, Jimmy held firm and was an ever-present in 1948–49, helping Albion gain promotion from the Second Division. Indeed, he was quite brilliant during the course of this season, conceding less than a goal a game (39 in 42 League matches), but more importantly he saved six penalties, earning Albion a total of nine vital points in the process. In fact, Jimmy was a dab-hand at saving spot-kicks. During his lengthy career he saved no fewer than 25 penalties (so he said), including 18 for Albion.

An ever-present again in 1949–50, Jimmy, now a model of consistency, had an excellent run of 109 consecutive League and FA Cup appearances before losing his place, again, to the fast-improving Heath. He regained it before the end of 1950 and then surprisingly fell completely out of favour with manager Jack Smith. New manager-coach Jesse Carver moved in and he tended to side with Heath, so much so that when he was replaced by Vic Buckingham in February 1953, Jimmy was firmly bedded into the second team.

Heath duly held his place before tragedy struck the Wolverhampton-born goalkeeper during a League game at Sunderland in March 1954, only four days after Albion had qualified for the FA Cup Final. Heath was seriously injured diving at the feet of the home striker Ted Purdon and was taken off on a stretcher and driven to a nearby hospital. Sadly he never played again. Up stepped Jimmy once more, and with Albion Wembley-bound and still on course to complete the coveted League and Cup double, he grabbed the opportunity with open arms.

Jimmy performed very well during the last few weeks of the season and went to Wembley (for the second time in his career), where he joyously collected his Cup-winners' medal after Albion had defeated Preston North End 3–2 with a late goal from Frank Griffin. So proud was he of his medal, that he wore it on a chain round his neck for the rest of his life – along with a smart bow tie. His previous trip to the Empire Stadium had been in 1935–36 when he starred for North London Schools against South London Schools in front of barely 2,000 spectators.

Taking full advantage of Heath's misfortune, Jimmy, despite a brief challenge from Fred Brown in 1956, held his place in the side for the next four years, seeing Albion play some terrific attacking football, almost reaching their second Cup Final in three years, only to lose narrowly to rivals Aston Villa in a replay, share the Charity Shield with Wolves and become the first professional League team from Great Britain to win in Russia.

At one point he was playing so consistently well that he was in line for an England place, manager Walter Winterbottom writing his name on his list of 'possibles' in 1956–57. His manager, Buckingham, believed he was: 'As good as any First Division goalie in the Football League and would certainly not let his country down. He is one of the bravest I have ever seen and he's a fine shot-stopper. He deserves a chance.' Unfortunately Jimmy didn't make it, Winterbottom choosing Alan Hodgkinson from Sheffield United and Reg Matthews of Chelsea instead.

At the end of the 1957–58 season, and by now a fully-qualified FA coach, Jimmy was transferred to Coventry City, having made almost 400 appearances for Albion, 327 in the Football League. He also lined up in a further 101 second-XI matches and had the pleasure of scoring a goal direct from a corner-kick for the 'stiffs' against Derby County in December 1946 when he was a hobbling left-wing passenger.

His first-class tally of appearances remained a club record until Stuart Naylor bettered it in 1995.

One of three ageing goalkeepers with the Sky Blues, Jimmy spent just one season at Highfield Road before ending his career with a two-year spell with Hinckley Athletic. He announced his retirement in June 1960, just a month before his 40th birthday. In later years he ran successful pubs in Derby and Birmingham and was also an hotelier near Solihull. Confined to a wheelchair from 1986 onwards, he resided in Tamworth with his wife for many years before his death in the Staffordshire town in 2003, aged 83.

TEDDY SANDFORD

'An excellent inside-left and later a useful centre-half, Teddy was of the quiet type, never flashy.'

Born:	22 October 1910, Handsworth, Birmingham
Died:	11 May 1995, Great Barr, Birmingham

Albion senior record:

Appearances:	League 286, FA Cup 30, FA Charity Shield 1
Goals:	League 67, FA Cup 8, FA Charity Shield 0
Senior debut:	League, 15 November 1930 v Preston North End (a) won 3–2 (scored once)
Also played for:	Tantany Athletic, Overend Wesley, Birmingham Carriage Works, Smethwick Highfield, Sheffield United, Morris Commercial FC, England (1 cap)

Raven-haired Teddy Sandford made an impressive League debut for Albion against Preston North End at Deepdale when he was just 20 years of age. Lining up at inside-left, he scored that afternoon in front of 15,000 spectators and it must be said 'he never looked back after that.' Indeed, six months later he celebrated with his teammates at Wembley after the Baggies had defeated Birmingham 2–1 in the FA Cup Final and then, a week after that, he was again in party mood when promotion was clinched from Division Two.

Strong, well-built and blessed with boundless energy, for such a young player he produced some wonderful displays during the unique double-winning season of 1930–31, when he scored seven times in 28 League games and once in nine FA Cup matches while partnering Stan Wood on the left-wing.

Described by his 1930s teammate Joe Carter as being 'a vital cog in an Albion football machine', Teddy was certainly a key player and his boss, Fred Everiss, writing in the *Sports Argus* during World War Two, said 'He was a terrific footballer who gave the club tremendous service both as a forward and centre-half. He was one of the best players I have signed.'

Born within 50 yards of The Hawthorns, Teddy attended Wattville Road Junior and Holyhead Road Senior Schools in Handsworth and was a very keen Albion supporter as a lad, attending most home matches with his father. Initially a centre-half, he was spotted playing in that position for Smethwick Highfield, one of the Midlands' better-known junior clubs and a fine nursery for the Albion over many years. Signed as an amateur in October 1929, he turned professional in May 1930 and remained at the club until March 1939.

A get-on-with-it type of player, not flashy or clever, Teddy did things the simple way. He could be aggressive when required and, in fact, was a very strong and positive tackler, especially when playing at the centre of the defence. Completely out of context, he had the ill-luck to become the first Albion player ever to be sent off twice – wrongly dismissed for a robust but seemingly fair 50–50 challenge on Arthur Cunliffe against Blackburn Rovers in 1932 and for kicking Willie Hall on the head during a League game at Tottenham in 1934. Although it was a 'foul', Teddy received sympathetic applause from the Spurs fans as he walked from the pitch.

Teddy played in three Central League games in 1929–30 and 14 at the start of the following season, during which time he was switched from a defender into an inside-forward. Then, with the first team struggling to score goals, changes were made up front. W.G. Richardson was brought in to lead the attack, while Teddy was introduced alongside him. From that point on, Albion looked promotion material and Teddy went on to play a massive role in securing that famous double.

In 1931–32 he missed only two League games and scored another eight goals and the following season was also selected to play for England against Wales at Wrexham – his only international honour. The game ended goalless and, in his own words, Teddy admitted: 'I didn't do all that well.'

Continuing to perform for Albion, he was very impressive in 1932–33 and again in 1933–34, being an ever-present for the first time in his career in the latter campaign, when he also reached double figures in the goal charts, including a winning penalty in the 6–5 victory over Sunderland in March and a brace in a 5–1 home win over Stoke City.

Teddy had his best-scoring season in 1934–35 when he notched a total of 24 goals, 20 of them in the League. By now the club's main penalty-taker, he netted from the spot in the FA Cup semi-final replay against Bolton Wanderers to seal a place in the Final against Sheffield Wednesday. And although he scored at Wembley, on this occasion Albion failed to lift the trophy, losing 4–2 to the Owls.

In February 1937, Albion's first-choice centre-half Billy Richardson got injured and, with no reliable replacement as such, Fred Everiss asked Teddy to take over as pivot. He did a superb job in the six matches he played, producing a quite magnificent display when Albion defeated the FA Cup holders Arsenal 3–1 in a sixth-round clash on a snowbound Hawthorns pitch in front of a record crowd of almost 65,000. Captaining the side that afternoon, he completely blotted out the goal threat of Ray Bowden, Alf Kirchen and Alex James.

After this thrilling victory, thousands of Albion fans assembled in front of the main stand, chanting Teddy's name, begging him to come and say a few words. The Albion boss (Everiss) recalled having to drag the half-clad captain, with towel wrapped round his waist, up the stairs so that he could speak to the fans via a megaphone. Unfortunately Teddy was badly injured against the Gunners and missed the 4–1 semi-final defeat by Preston at Highbury when Alf Ridyard was asked to deputise at centre-half.

An ever-present in 1937–38, when Albion struggled and were subsequently relegated, Teddy made only six appearances the following season (all at inside-left) before leaving the club for Sheffield United, the Blades paying just £1,500 for his signature. Teddy, whose departure was due to him putting on weight, had given Albion 10 years of dedicated service, during which time he had scored 75 goals in 317 first-class appearances.

He hardly had time to settle in at Bramall Lane before World War Two intervened and in 1941 he went to work (and play) for Morris Commercial. In May 1950 he became an Albion coach, a position he held for seven years, and from 1961 to 1967 he was employed as the club's Midland-based scout while running his own café right next to the Woodman Corner, where many of the players and indeed supporters (I was one) used to call in for their daily chat.

The nephew of Abe Jones, who also played for Albion from 1896 to 1901, and Billy 'Bullet' Jones, who starred for Birmingham and Brighton & Hove Albion in the early 1900s, Teddy lived until he was 84.

GEORGE SHAW

'A reliable, two-footed full-back, rangy in build and a strong kicker.'

Born:	13 October 1899, Swinton
Died:	10 March 1973, Doncaster

Albion senior record:

Appearances:	League 393, FA Cup 31, FA Charity Shield 1
Goals:	League 11, FA Cup 0, FA Charity Shield 0
Senior debut:	League, 4 December 1926 v Sheffield United (a) lost 2–1
Also played for:	Bolton-on-Deane FC, Rossington Main Colliery, Doncaster Rovers (2 spells), Gillingham, Huddersfield Town, Stalybridge Celtic, Worcester City (player-manager), FC Floriana, Malta (player, coach, manager), England (1 full cap), Football League (1 app), FA (2 tours, 8 apps), international trialist

After doing exceptionally well in schoolboy football as a full-back and centre-half, George Shaw worked down the pit for a while and played for the colliery team, joining the Navy in 1915, based at Chatham. Immediately after World War One he returned 'nearer home' and signed for Doncaster Rovers as a professional. However, while in the Navy George had made friends with William Groombridge who, at the time, was secretary-manager of Gillingham. Anticipating that the Gills would gain election to the Football League (which they did) Groombridge contacted George and asked him if he would like to join the Kent club.

A meeting was set up and in March 1920, to the surprise of his family and friends, George moved nearly 300 miles south to sign for Gillingham, whom he served for two-and-a-half years before returning to Doncaster in September 1922. Then, in February 1924, the manager of Huddersfield Town, Herbert Chapman, who was searching for a reliable deputy for the injury-prone Ned Barkas and looking to strengthen his squad, made enquiries about George. Within a matter of days an agreement was drawn up, and George moved to Leeds Road for a fee of £1,000.

Basically a reserve to full-backs Barkas and England internationals Roy Goodall and Sam Wadsworth, George did a useful job with the Terriers, helping them win three successive League Division One championships, although he failed to make enough appearances in either campaign to qualify for a medal. However, the club rewarded him with a gong following the 1924–25 triumph when he played in 11 games as Huddersfield claimed the title ahead of Albion.

After making 29 appearances for the Yorkshire club, George was snapped up by Albion, who paid out a record fee of £4,100 for his signature in November 1926. At first Huddersfield were reluctant to let any of their full-backs go, but eventually Albion's chief Fred Everiss and chairman Billy Bassett persuaded them to agree to a fee. Even this was not easily settled. In fact, an argument ensued in a local hotel which went on until the small hours of the morning, before George finally put pen to paper and became a Baggie.

Two-footed, strong and rangy in build, with strong kicking power, George was just the player Albion needed. If the truth be known, there hadn't been a commanding left-back since Jesse Pennington four years earlier. In fact, no fewer than five different players had lined up in that position following Pennington's retirement and George's arrival, among them Dicky Baugh, Arthur Perry and Billy Adams. After acquiring George's services Albion chief Fred Everiss said: 'George will play for England, mark my words.'

Settling well into the side, George had Bill Ashurst as his full-back partner before Bob Finch was brought in at the start of the 1927–28 season. They played splendidly together for three seasons before George switched over to allow Bert Trentham to come in on the left. During that time George was chosen to go on the FA tour to Belgium, France and Spain; a second tour would follow in 1931.

In fact, George, it must be said, was extremely lucky not to suffer any serious injury. Indeed, he was hardly ever side-lined, only occasionally through illness and once when he gained his only England cap (in front of his club colleague, goalkeeper Harold Pearson) in a 3–0 win over Scotland at Wembley in 1932.

The Daily Mail reporter James Freeman wrote: 'The England team played with fine keenness – smoothly, harmoniously and with a fair measure of accuracy. The defenders, Shaw in particular, who was making his first appearance for his country, defended stoutly and showed a real zest for the task. He is a cool and resourceful player.'

George missed only three Albion games out of a possible 302 between his debut at Sheffield United in December 1926 and September 1933, being an ever-present on four occasions. In 1930–31 he was brilliant at times as Albion strode on to complete the unique double, gaining promotion from Division Two and lifting the FA Cup.

In the home sixth-round Cup tie against Wolves he completely lost his bearings and headed the ball into his own goal for an equaliser, but he soon overcame that disappointment by playing splendidly in the replay, likewise in the semi-final against Everton and again in the Final against Birmingham.

At the end of that season George accompanied his Albion teammates Tommy Magee and Jimmy Cookson on the FA's tour to Canada, following this up two years later with an appearance for the Football League against the Scottish League in 1933–34.

In 1935, Albion once again reached the FA Cup Final, but this time they weren't so lucky, losing 4–2 to Sheffield Wednesday, George blaming himself for one of the Owls' goals. George spent three more seasons at The Hawthorns, during which time he upped his first-team appearance tally to 425.

In May 1938 he joined non-League Stalybridge Celtic before taking over as player-manager of Worcester City. After World War Two he went over to Malta to play for, then coach and later manage FC Floriana, bringing his team over to play Albion in a Festival of Britain game in May 1951. He retired after that game and returned to England, taking a job at Hamworth Colliery, Doncaster, while enjoying his hobbies of mat-making and singing. George, a strict teetotaller, was nicknamed 'Teapot' by his colleagues, simply because he was always wanting a cuppa and often had to make tea for everyone else.

He was 72 when he died in March 1973.

FRED SHINTON

'A direct centre-forward, always charging through the middle — a centre-half's nightmare!'

Born:	7 March 1883, Wednesbury
Died:	11 April 1923, Leicester

Albion senior record:

Appearances:	League 64, FA Cup 4
Goals:	League 46, FA Cup 0
Senior debut:	League, 22 April 1905 v Bolton Wanderers (h) lost 1–0
Also played for:	St James' School (Wednesbury), Hawthorn Villa, Moxley White Star, Wednesbury Old Athletic, Hednesford Town, Leicester Fosse (2 spells), Bolton Wanderers

Centre-forward Fred Shinton was signed by Albion in April 1905 from once-prolific colliery club, Hednesford Town. Times were bad for a coal-miner in those days and Fred jumped at the chance of regular employment – that of just kicking a ball around instead of using a pick-axe. He had scored over 30 goals in two seasons for Hednesford and prior to that had found the net regularly for each of his junior clubs, once bagging a double hat-trick for Wednesbury Old Athletic in a Birmingham Cup tie. He was 'over the moon' when Albion signed him, telling one local reporter: 'I can't believe what's happened. Last week I was as black as the ace of spades, now I'm as clean as a whistle and a professional footballer at that. I am going to make the most of my opportunity.'

Prior to Fred's arrival, Albion had already used six different players in the centre-forward position. They were simply missing a top-class goalscorer and believed Fred was the man for the job. And so it proved over the next two-and-a-half years as he averaged a goal every 133 minutes, scoring 46 in just 68 League and FA Cup games, including 28 in 1906–07 when he was joint leading marksman (with Alex Young of Everton) in the entire Football League.

When Fred turned up at The Hawthorns for his first morning's training, although displaying a collar and tie, he was wearing a rather tatty-looking dark grey suit. Albion director Billy Bassett and the club's secretary-manager Fred Everiss took Fred into town after training and bought him some new clothes. 'We want you to look the part,' they told him, and when Fred paraded for duty next day, Albion's trainer Bill Barber thought he was a visiting director on a social call!

A little over a year later, prior to an away League game at Gainsborough, Barber said to the team: 'Now, the first player to score three goals can come off!' 'Really?' said Fred, who went out with great determination and promptly cracked in a hat-trick. As he proceeded to walk off the field, with a broad smile on his face, an irate Barber, with a soggy sponge in his hand, was waiting for him on the touchline. As Fred got there, Barber said: 'What's the matter with you?' Fred replied: 'I've got my three goals, I'm coming off.' Hoist with his own petard the annoyed trainer nearly had a fit and told Fred to go back out there and score three more. 'I was only joking, you fool.' Albion won the game 4–0.

A well-built lad (5ft 11in tall and weighing 12st 6lb) Fred – as hard as nails with a rather reckless style which often saw him go headlong at defenders and even goalkeepers – was a danger to most teams and quite frequently he would go in and shoulder-charge an opponent when the ball was some distance away – just to let him know he was around. Blessed with a powerful right-foot shot, he always played with great determination, total commitment and will-power. A never-say-die competitor, he certainly gave Albion wonderful service for two and a half years.

With Freddie Buck and Adam Haywood his inside-partners, Fred scored 18 goals in 32 senior games in his first full season at The Hawthorns (1905–06) and followed up by netting 28 times (including three fours) in 33 starts in 1906–07. Unfortunately he was plagued by an ankle injury after that (from which he never really recovered) and made only two more appearances before being transferred to Leicester Fosse for £150 (plus Harry Wilcox) in November 1907. The ardent Albion fans weren't too happy when they heard the news that Fred had been sold – and hundreds of them demonstrated outside the ground.

Around this time Albion were desperately in need of a replacement for Fred and no fewer than eight different players lined up at centre-forward that season. The former Aston Villa player Billy Garraty eventually came in to fill the gap.

Fred did very well with Leicester, his 10 goals (in 24 games) helping the East Midlands club gain promotion to the top flight as runners-up in 1907–08. His goal-tally endeared the 'enthusiastic bustler' to the Filbert Street supporters, who immediately made him their new goalscoring hero. Strangely Fred was given few chances to enliven a rather weak Leicester front-line in the First Division and relegation ensued. However, in 1909–10 he top scored with 34 goals in 42 games – a new club record, which lasted until 1928.

Fred always parted his hair neatly down the middle. He had film-star looks – making him a firm favourite with female supporters – and he had a splendid singing voice. Nicknamed 'Appleyard' and 'Tickler' by his Albion colleagues and 'Nutter' by his Leicester teammates, he was sold to Bolton Wanderers for £1,000 in August 1910 but failed to settle at Burnden Park. Returning to Filbert Street in January 1911 for £750, Fred failed to regain his goalscoring technique and, after struggling with his health, he was forced to retire at the end of the 1911–12 season.

Remaining in Leicester, Fred was only 40 years of age when he died in 1923. His younger brother, Arthur, signed for Leicester in 1918 but never made the first team.

CHARLIE 'CHIPPY' SIMMONS

'Tall and elegant, perhaps not powerful enough, but nevertheless a fine centre-forward.'

Born:	9 September 1878, West Bromwich
Died:	12 December 1937, Wednesbury

Albion senior record:

Appearances:	League 178, FA Cup 15
Goals:	League 75, FA Cup 6
Senior debut:	League, 19 November 1898 v Burnley (a) drew 1–1
Also played for:	Trinity Victoria, Oldbury Town, Worcester Rovers, West Ham United, Chesterfield Town, Wellington Town, Royal Rovers (Canada), Professionals XI (1 app), England international trialist

An inside-right or centre-forward, Charlie 'Chippy' Simmons had the pleasure of scoring Albion's first goal at The Hawthorns. He gleefully fired home the equaliser 12 minutes from the end of the opening League game at the new ground on 3 September 1900, after Cradley Heath-born Steve Bloomer had given Derby County the lead with a close-range header on the half-hour mark.

Dark-haired, tall and slim, a brilliant ball-player with a splendid body-swerve, Chippy was only kept out of the England team by the aforementioned Bloomer, whose greater shooting powers gave him preference. Named as reserve to the national team at least three times – including sitting on the bench at the ill-fated game against Scotland at Ibrox Park in 1902 when terracing collapsed, killing 25 spectators – in the end Chippy was presented with a multi-coloured consolation cap by the Albion directors.

A pupil at Beeches Road School, West Bromwich, Chippy played and scored for Trinity Victoria, Oldbury Town and Worcester Rovers before joining Albion as a professional in April 1898. He had to wait seven months before making his League debut at Burnley in late November, lining up at inside-right in a changed attack after Ben Garfield had cried off with an injury. Albion went behind in that game but hit back to equalise from the spot following a bizarre decision by the referee, who denied Chippy what seemed a legitimate goal and awarded a penalty instead! This was converted by Billy Williams.

Chippy went on to make a total of 13 appearances that season without scoring, but in 1899–1900, with Billy Richards as his main strike-partner, he at last got going, top scoring with 12 goals in 38 games and bagging a brace in an 8–0 victory over Nottingham Forest – Albion's last-ever game at their Stoney Lane ground.

Joined in attack by former England star Fred Wheldon for the next season, and despite that flying start against Derby, Chippy's form dipped alarmingly. In fact, an article in the *Sports Argus* stated: 'Simmons has recently taken unto himself a wife, and while everybody will wish him every happiness, he will have to improve considerably if he is to maintain the good impression he created last season. He is now so easily knocked off the ball, falls down at the least touch by an opponent, and seems unable to dash forward and score in that electrifying manner which seemed to indicate he was a budding international. He has fallen off unaccountably, and the only thing is to try someone else and give Simmons a rest, which may have the desired effect.'

Eventually axed from the team, he was subsequently brought back but mustered only five League goals in his 20 games as Albion slipped out of the top flight for the first time in the club's history. Thankfully, after a summer's hard training, Chippy was back to his best in 1901–02, blitzing his way to a total of 24 goals (23 in the League) as Albion won the Second Division championship at the first attempt.

His haul included a brilliant hat-trick in a 7–3 home win over Blackpool and five twos, one coming in the 4–0 victory over Chesterfield when he almost tore a hole in the net with a bullet-like penalty. His form throughout this season was exemplary and it resulted in an international trial.

There followed two not-so-good campaigns, although he did have a problem at times with his right knee, which would trouble him again later in his career. He notched only nine goals in 22 starts in 1902–03 and nine more in 30 outings the following season, when once again Albion suffered relegation. In his own words Chippy said: 'I have lost it…something's missing.' To make things worse, he knew he was becoming injury-prone and, after a disagreement with the club regarding his fitness, he somewhat reluctantly moved out and joined West Ham United in July 1904 for a fee of £700.

He recovered his fitness with the Hammers and scored eight times in 34 Southern League games and represented the Professionals against the Amateurs, before being persuaded to return to The Hawthorns in May 1905 for a reduced fee of £600. In season 1905–06 Chippy played alongside Adam Haywood and Fred Shinton in Albion's attack and between them the trio scored a total of 56 goals, Chippy weighing in with 16, including his second Baggies hat-trick in a 5–3 home win over Barnsley. 'That was one of my best-ever performances for the club,' he said in a newspaper interview soon after that game.

Twice during the course of that season Chippy went out with his right knee heavily bandaged, once helping his side whip Blackpool 5–0. Unfortunately he took a nasty knock in the fixture with Grimsby Town at The Hawthorns in late March and was ruled out for the rest of the season.

He struggled after that and made only seven starts in 1906–07 (three goals scored) and he even missed Albion's FA Cup semi-final defeat against Everton. He eventually left Albion for good in March 1907, joining Chesterfield Town, for whom he scored seven times in 32 appearances. Next he joined non-League club Wellington Town, where he stayed for a little over two years, from August 1908 to October 1910. Chippy then, surprisingly, decided to try his luck in Canada with Royal Rovers, based in Toronto. He retired as a player in the summer of 1912, after his dodgy knee finally gave up on him. Chippy chose to remain in North America until after World War One, taking on various coaching positions as well as teaching PE at a local school.

Almost 44 years of age when he returned to England early in 1922, Chippy took over a pub in West Bromwich which he ran for 10 years. He also battled against illness and was hospitalised for a short time. He was only 59 when he died in Wednesbury in 1937.

JOE SMITH

'Long-serving right-back, justifiably regarded as one of the best in the country in 1919–20.'

Born:	10 April 1890, Darby End, Dudley
Died:	9 June 1956, Wolverhampton

Albion senior record:

Appearances:	League 434, FA Cup 30, Others 7
Goals:	None
Senior debut:	League, 2 September 1910 v Bolton Wanderers (a) lost 3–1
Also played for:	Netherton St Andrew's, Darby End Victoria, Cradley St Luke's; Everton and Notts County (World War One guest); Birmingham, Worcester City (player-manager), England (1 Victory, 2 full caps)

Joe Smith was a stocky little right-back, skilfully dour in style, whose remarkable high level of performance over a long period of time is illustrated by the number of first-class appearances he made for Albion. Between March 1919 and February 1926 he played in 291 out of a possible 311 competitive matches – quite a record.

In fact, he missed only seven League games in the first six and a half post World War One seasons, being an ever-present on three occasions and playing in 117 consecutive League games from October 1922 to September 1925. Amazingly, during his 16 years at The Hawthorns, Joe never scored a goal in a grand total of 471 senior appearances.

'Well,' said his former teammate, Bobby Blood, 'he never went over the halfway line. I think the only time he saw that was when we stood around the centre-circle for a minute's silence before a home game.'

One of the most popular sporting figures in the Dudley area before, during and after World War One (when he served in the Army, based in Bootle, Liverpool), Joe found everlasting fame as a professional footballer. Educated at Halesowen Road Council School (Netherton), he played for Netherton St Andrew's from the age of 12 and, after assisting Darby End Victoria, he joined Cradley St Luke's in 1908. A year later he represented England in a Junior international v Scotland and soon afterwards he was snapped up for 'peanuts' by Albion, signing as a full-time professional in May 1910.

Five months later, at the age of 20, he made his League debut in a Second Division match at Bolton, playing at left-back in the absence of the legendary England international Jesse Pennington, who, over the next 12 years, would become his full-back partner. And what a partnership it turned out to be – one of the finest anywhere in club football.

They played together no fewer than 240 times at senior level between 1910 and 1922 (when Jesse retired). And if it hadn't been for Jesse's England call-up then the pairing could easily have gone past the 250 mark.

At the end of his first season in professional football (1910–11) Joe was presented with a Second Division championship-winners' medal, but despite appearing in 32 League games the following season, he missed the FA Cup Final defeat by Barnsley, Arthur Cook taking his place at right-back. In fact, Joe never played in a single round of the competition. He was injured against Bury on Boxing Day and it transpired that he was never 100 per cent for the remainder of the season. No disrespect to his deputy (Cook), but he was sorely missed in the Final.

Sidelined for the opening seven games of the 1912–13 season, Joe regained full fitness and was in excellent form right up until the outbreak of war. During the hostilities he played as a guest for Everton (1915–18) and Notts County (1917–18) and helped Albion win the Midland Victory League, the tournament taking place during March and April 1919.

Then came glory for Albion and, of course, for Joe when the Football League championship was won for the first time in the club's history. Joe missed only two games – both due to international calls – and actually played the last three games of the season with strapping to both ankles and his right knee. He was determined to celebrate with the rest of the lads. He was a really dedicated footballer.

In the away game at Derby County he was brilliant, completely 'bottling up' the England left-winger Alf Quantrill as Albion romped to a resounding 4–0 victory. He was also outstanding in the home match against the subsequent runners-up Burnley, never allowing the clever Eddie Mosscrop 'a decent kick' in a 4–1 win, and was superb against Bolton Wanderers, also at The Hawthorns, when Welsh international left-winger Ted Vizard was 'shackled throughout by the the Albion full-back Smith who played a very clever game.'

As an England player, Joe starred in the 2–0 Victory international win over Wales at Stoke's Victoria Ground in mid-October 1919 and a week later, along with his Albion teammate Sid Bowser, he featured in a 1–1 draw against Ireland in Belfast.

Secretary-manager Fred Everiss accompanied the Albion duo to Belfast, thus missing the home League match with Notts County. While sitting down for dinner after the game, Fred received a message from The Hawthorns giving him the result – 8–0 to Albion. When the score was passed on to the players, Joe said: 'Wow, we must have strengthened the team by being out of it.'

Joe's second full cap followed two years later, when, in front of his own supporters at The Hawthorns, he helped England beat Ireland 2–0, future Albion star Harry Chambers scoring both goals. In 1920–21 he again missed two matches but was an ever-present in 1921–22 when he partnered Jesse Pennington for the final time. Thereafter, and for the next four seasons, Joe was joined at full-back by first Billy Adams, then Arthur Perry and also by Dickie Baugh.

Joe's final game for the Baggies came in a 2–0 defeat by Bury at Gigg Lane on 24 February 1926. All told, adding together his appearances for the first and second teams, in friendlies and in local Cup competitions, Joe played in more than 500 games for Albion – an excellent record. From The Hawthorns he moved the short distance to St Andrew's. He remained with the Blues for three years and then spent the next three in non-League football as player-manager of Worcester City.

Retiring in May 1932, Joe took over the Red Lions pub in Darby End, retaining his position as landlord until 1936 when he took employment at Lloyds Proving House, eventually becoming Chief Tester.

Joe was taken ill early in 1956 and after spending some time in Wolverhampton's Royal Hospital he died in June of that year, aged 66.

RICHARD SNEEKES

'An inspirational, all-action midfielder who put new life into Albion.'

Born:	30 October 1968, Amsterdam, Holland

Albion senior record:

Appearances:	League 208+19, FA Cup 7, League Cup 14+3, Others 2
Goals:	League 31, FA Cup 2, League Cup 2, Others 0
Senior debut:	League, 12 March 1994 v Watford (h) drew 4–4 (scored)
Also played for:	DWS (Holland), Ajax Amsterdam, FC Volendam, Fortuna Sittard, Lugano, Bolton Wanderers, Stockport County, Hull City, Herfølge BK (Denmark), Hinckley United, West Bromwich Albion over-35s, Holland (22 Schoolboy and 2 Under-21 caps)

A junior with the DWS club (who later became FC Amsterdam) and a youth team player at Ajax, Richard made 22 appearances for the Netherlands national Schoolboy team (youth standard really) and in 1983, as a 15-year-old, played in front of a crowd of 63,000 at Wembley against England. He made his senior debut for Ajax (under manager Johan Cruyff) at the age of 16 years and five months – the youngest-ever player for that club at that time. Fellow countryman Clarence Seedorf took over that mantle later.

Richard then broke into the Dutch Under-21 team, but unfortunately he never quite fulfilled his potential and, after a season-long loan spell with FC Volendam, he was transferred to Fortuna Sittard in August 1989. He spent four years there and, after assisting the Swiss club FC Lugano, also on loan, he returned briefly to Fortuna before having a trial at the Reebok Stadium. He was successful and joined Bolton Wanderers for £200,000 in August 1994.

A key player in manager Bruce Rioch's team that won promotion to the Premier League and reached the League Cup Final (beaten by Liverpool) in his first season in English football, Richard was a casualty the following term when Bolton struggled in the top flight and was subsequently sold to Albion for £400,000 in March 1996.

Alan Buckley was in charge at The Hawthorns at that time and he declared the Dutchman a 'key signing for the club,' adding 'He's a talented footballer with an intelligent brain; he's a good passer of the ball who can also score goals and he's got a tremendous shot,' although he then said that it would be a while before he made any difference.

He was wrong. Richard almost immediately became a cult hero, quite literally an overnight sensation, and many of the fans took to wearing long blond wigs in honour of their new idol. Even the club shop sold them by the box load. Richard ended that season with 10 goals from just 13 games, and was arguably the main reason that Albion stayed up.

When he arrived the Baggies were languishing in 22nd position in the First Division table and only three wins had been recorded in their previous 21 matches. A new spark was required to ignite the Albion flame – and that came from the flying Dutchman. He scored a splendid 15th-minute goal on his debut in the 4–4 home draw with Watford and from that point onwards, until the last ball was kicked in earnest that season, Richard did the business in more ways than one. Albion lost only once in their last 13 League matches, rose 11 places up the ladder to finish above halfway and it was all down to Richard's presence.

Richard netted important goals in the home games against Barnsley (won 2–1), Millwall (1–0, an 88th-minute strike to make it six goals in seven games), Grimsby Town (the clincher in a 3–1 victory) and the champions Derby County (3–2) and was on target in the away fixtures at Birmingham City (the opener in a 1–1 draw), Leicester City (won 3–2) and Norwich City (2–2) as well as at Portsmouth where he scored twice, one a real beauty from outside the area, in a 2–0 victory.

The following season Richard claimed only eight goals in 48 appearances, mainly because he played a little bit further back than usual, as Albion had Andy Hunt, Paul Peschisolido and Bob Taylor as their main strikers. Still holding centre stage, however, and remaining a huge favourite with the fans, Richard struck six times in 49 outings in 1997–98, but managed only four goals in 43 games the following season and as few as three in 1999–2000, but one of them, against Charlton Athletic, on the last day of the League programme, effectively helped keep Albion up…again.

Richard spent one more term at The Hawthorns and his efforts (three goals in 45 League appearances) helped confirm a sixth-place finish and a place in the Play-offs against his former club, Bolton Wanderers. Unfortunately it wasn't a happy occasion. After a 2–2 first-leg semi-final draw, Albion failed to turn up at the Reebok Stadium and were whipped 3–0. That was the end for Richard.

Released by Gary Megson, he joined the manager's former club Stockport County on a free transfer in September 2001, but stayed at Edgeley Park for just two months before switching to Hull City, teaming up with his ex-boss Brian Little again. That move didn't work out either and he left the Tigers in May 2002. The next 12 months were spent with the Danish club Herfølge BK before he announced his retirement at the age of 34.

However, Richard was persuaded to come out of retirement following a chance meeting with Hinckley United manager Dean Thomas at the Hong Kong Sixes tournament in July 2007. He initially trained with the Conference North club before agreeing to sign for them. He made his debut in a 4–2 FA Cup win over Grantham Town two months later but was released after playing only three games. At that point he 'retired' for a second time, saying 'the fact that I was not really enjoying it meant that it became too much of a chore to do it'.

He subsequently became a finance services agent and started Total Football UK with another ex-Albion star, Daryl Burgess, and the former Walsall player Chris Marsh, which offers coaching courses to youngsters. He also coached local junior club Castlefield Athletic himself (2003–04).

Richard runs his own Italian restaurant, Angelo's in Wylde Green, and is a partner in Biddle & Sneekes, Mortgage Consultants, based in Sutton Coldfield. When fit and available he turns out for Albion's over-35s team in various six-a-side indoor tournaments.

In October 2007 Richard's daughter, Melissa, was crowned Miss Netherlands, thus qualifying for the next Miss World beauty contest.

DEREK STATHAM

'Derek was miles better than Kenny Sansom.' (Ron Atkinson) 'In terms of pure football, "Dekka" was exquisite; his touch was fantastic and his delivery was perfect; a great overlapping left-back.'

Born: 24 March 1959, Whitmore Reams, Wolverhampton

Albion senior record:

Appearances:	League 298+1, FA Cup 26, League Cup 34, Europe 12, Others 2
Goals:	League 8, FA Cup 2, League Cup 1, Europe 0, Others 0
Senior debut:	League, 18 December 1976 v Stoke City (a) won 2–0 (scored)
Also played for:	Southampton, Stoke City, Aston Villa (trial), Telford United, King's Lynn, West Bromwich Albion Old Stars, England (3 full, 2 B and 6 Under-21 caps)

In December 1976, West Bromwich Albion's player-manager Johnny Giles handed Derek Statham an early Christmas present by selecting him for his first-team debut against Stoke City. It was a big occasion for the 17-year-old, who earlier in the year had helped the Baggies beat his local team, Wolverhampton Wanderers, in the FA Youth Cup Final.

For Derek, his big day turned out to be something special. Besides playing very well, he had the pleasure of scoring a brilliant individual goal against one of the best 'keepers in the world, England international Peter Shilton, as the Baggies won 2–0 at the Victoria Ground.

Although not the fastest player around, Derek's all-action approach to the game, his skill with the ball (he used to dribble past opponents inside his own penalty area), his attacking prowess and his ability to out-jump much taller opponents made him one of the best left-backs in the First Division during the late 1970s.

Manchester United approached him twice but each time Derek turned them down, reluctant to leave The Hawthorns. Why should he? At that time Albion had a terrific team under manager Ron Atkinson and Derek was a vital cog in the mechanism. 'I believed we would win something under Big Ron, that's why I stayed with Albion,' said Derek, who added: 'I was encouraged to get forward at every opportunity by the boss. He loved to attack and so did I. We had some great attack-minded players like Tony Brown, Laurie Cunningham, Cyrille Regis, Bryan Robson and Willie Johnston, as well as our other full-back Brendon Batson. I loved playing behind Willie, a great crowd pleaser, fast and clever. Several times I ended up in front of him and he didn't appreciate that!'

Derek was Albion's first choice left-back from the day of his debut right through until November 1979 when he was struck down with knee ligament damage, suffered in a League Cup replay at Norwich. Out of action for nine weeks, he regained full fitness and won back his first-team place, but was he brought back too soon? Some say he was as on his return in mid-January he twisted his knee against Nottingham Forest. Back in action just a fortnight later, he had the misfortune to injure the same knee again, this time against Crystal Palace, was carried off and missed the rest of the season.

Derek recalled: 'I got injured when both myself and the team were playing some superb football. I was devastated and I wanted to play as soon as I could after that first injury against Norwich. I had the necessary treatment but on reflection I wish I'd had another couple of weeks with the physio. I probably came back a week too soon. I remember Garry Pendrey stepping into my position first time and when I was injured again the following season Barry Cowdrill occupied the left-back position. They both did well.'

Thankfully for Derek he regained his fitness and his form, and helped Albion reach the FA Cup semi-final for the second time in four years. But, as it had been in 1978 when they were defeated 3–1 by Ipswich Town, the Baggies failed to make it to Wembley, losing 1–0 to QPR. Also in 1982 they succumbed at the same stage in the League Cup, beaten by Tottenham Hotspur.

Derek played in 48 games in 1981–82 and 35 the following season – his best sequences for some considerable time. His form was excellent and he was rewarded with three England caps, lining up against Wales in February 1983 and twice against Australia on a summer tour Down Under. He deputised for the injured Kenny Sansom each time – and there is no doubt that Derek deserved more international calls.

Early in 1980, Albion boss Ron Atkinson was in discussion with his Manchester City counterpart Malcolm Allison. The topic of conversation was Derek Statham and Kenny Sansom…who was the better full-back? Allison thought that Sansom was the best in the country. Atkinson responded by saying that Statham was the best in Europe. The discussion went on until 2am and in the end the men agreed that Sansom wasn't in the same class as Statham and was only in the England team because he played for Arsenal. Ron won the debate and his last words were: 'Statham was miles better than Sansom. End of discussion, England caps or not.'

Sadly for Derek, he returned home from that Aussie trip with a serious pelvic injury, which kept him out of action until February 1984. Being the club's top wage-earner, Derek's absence from first-team duty was costing Albion around £6,000 a week, and with the team failing to live up to expectations out on the pitch, things didn't look rosy.

Relegation was suffered at the end of the 1985–86 season (Albion's worst ever), and although Derek was still the best player at the club, in truth Second Division football didn't appeal to him. Liverpool boss Kenny Dalglish offered £250,000 for him, but the move was called off at the last minute following a medical check up which revealed a hole in his left leg from an earlier operation.

With manager Ron Saunders under pressure to reduce the wage bill, Derek was transfer-listed at the end of the 1986–87 season. Southampton moved in and a week into the new campaign one of Albion's finest attacking defenders moved to the Dell for £100,000.

Playing alongside Matt Le Tissier, Alan Shearer, Jimmy Case, Andy Townsend and Danny Wallace, Derek spent two seasons with Saints before joining Stoke City for £50,000 in July 1989. He later had a trial with Aston Villa, assisted Walsall for two years (he appeared for the Saddlers against Albion in the Auto-Windscreen Shield in 1990), played non-League football for Telford United and King's Lynn and also turned out for the Albion All Stars charity team before retiring in 1995. He amassed a total of 488 League appearances for his four clubs.

In 2004, Derek was named as one of West Bromwich Albion's 16 greatest-ever players, in a poll organised as part of the club's 125th anniversary celebrations. A member of the former Albion Players' Association, Statham now sells hot tubs from Estepona near Marbella on Spain's Costa Del Sol.

BOB TAYLOR

'A 1990s Albion legend without a doubt – a goalscoring genius. How many goals would "Super Bob" have netted if Hope and Giles were around to feed him?'

Born: 3 February 1967, Easington, County Durham

Albion senior record:

Appearances: League 256+68, FA Cup 6+4, League Cup 21+1, Others 16+5
Goals: League 113, FA Cup 4, League Cup 6, Others 8
Senior debut: League, 1 February 1993 v Brentford (h) won 2–0 (scored)
Also played for: Horden Comrades Welfare, Peterlee Juniors, Hartlepool United (trial), Newcastle United (trial), Horden Colliery Welfare, Leeds United, Bristol City, Bolton Wanderers, Cheltenham Town, Tamworth, Kidderminster Harriers

Known to every Baggies supporter as 'Super Bob', Bob Taylor is a true West Bromwich Albion legend. The son of a miner, he attended Dene House School, Peterlee and captained the team from full-back and centre-half before becoming a striker. He played for Horden Comrades Welfare and Peterlee Juniors, for whom he scored 60 goals in one season, and had trials at Newcastle and Hartlepool before joining Horden Colliery Welfare in 1984. Continuing to score goals, he was recommended to Leeds United by his manager Dick Malone, who had helped Sunderland beat Leeds in the 1973 FA Cup Final. 'I went to Elland Road on a month's trial,' recalled Bob. 'Billy Bremner was the manager and he saw me score a hat-trick in my first game against York City in the Northern Intermediate League. We won 5–4 and I finished the season with 12 goals in 15 games and was offered a professional contract.'

In 1985–86, Bob scored 20 goals for Leeds' second XI, made his League debut against Millwall and had his contract extended by two years. The following

season he struck another 26 goals and played in the second leg of the Division Two Play-off Final against Charlton but missed the replay, which Leeds lost.

Claiming 11 goals in 1987–88, Bob made a moderate start to the 1988–89 campaign before learning that Bremner had been sacked and replaced by Howard Wilkinson. 'I became surplus to requirements,' said Bob. 'Wilkinson wanted immediate success and brought in experienced players in order to achieve this.'

Bob nevertheless hung in there before moving to Bristol City for £175,000 in March 1989, Carl Shutt joining Leeds in the same deal. An instant success at Ashton Gate, Bob scored eight times in the last 12 games of the season and a year later helped City win promotion as the Third Division's top marksman with 27 goals (34 in total). He was also voted City's Player of the Year.

Early in 1992, Albion's manager Bobby Gould, forced to sell Don Goodman, made an offer for Bob that City couldn't refuse. Bob recalled: 'My boss Jimmy Lumsden said "Albion want to sign you; they have made an offer of £300,000; do you want to go?" I said yes straightaway – it was a spur of the moment thing…so I went for it.' Bob scored on his Baggies debut in a 2–0 win over Brentford and added two more to his tally in his next game at Birmingham. He had arrived in style.

Nicknamed 'Trigger' after the character in the TV comedy *Only Fools and Horses*, Bob soon became 'Super Bob' after netting eight times in 19 games that season. The following campaign he benefited from the attacking style adopted by new manager Ossie Ardiles and top scored in Division Two with 30 goals (37 in all competitions).

Andy Hunt, signed in March 1993, quickly forged a lethal partnership with Bob that would last several seasons, helping Albion beat Port Vale in the Play-off Final at Wembley to secure promotion. In fact, with the scores level, Bob was brought down by former Leeds teammate Peter Swan, who was sent off. This proved the turning point as Albion went on to win 3–0.

Bob top scored again in 1993–94 with 21 goals, but the team struggled in Division One, only avoiding relegation on the last day. Bob had a lean time the following season, netting only 11 times, but he was back to his best in 1995–96 with a haul of 23, including his 100th goal for Albion in a 3–2 win over Derby. He also notched his only hat-trick for the club, in a 4–4 draw with Watford.

Affected by an ankle injury, he scored 10 goals in 25 appearances under two managers, Alan Buckley and Ray Harford, in 1996–97. Bob never got on with Smith, and after scoring in a League Cup tie at Luton and being dropped, he joined Bolton Wanderers on a month's loan in January 1998. He played in four top-flight matches and scored at Old Trafford before returning to The Hawthorns, only to go back to the Reebok Stadium in a vain attempt to try and save Bolton from relegation.

Signed on a free transfer, Bob helped the Lancashire club reach the Division One Play-off Final in 1999, but unlike his triumph with Albion six years earlier, this time it was Wembley gloom as Watford won an awful game 2–0.

With Albion struggling near the foot of Division One, new boss Gary Megson delighted the fans by re-signing Bob for £90,000 in March 2000. His return paid dividends. He scored five goals in eight games, one in a last-match 2–0 win over Charlton to keep the Baggies up, while his strike against former club Bolton – a terrific overhead kick in a 4–4 draw – was voted goal of the season.

In 2000–01, Albion themselves reached the Play-offs, but it all ended in disappointment again for Bob as his old club, Bolton, won the semi-final 5–2 on aggregate. A year on, and having become the 100th player to be sent off in a first-team game for the club (dismissed at Barnsley in October), Bob scored vital goals at the end of 2001–02, including the clincher against Crystal Palace, to steer Albion into Premiership for the first time.

Unfortunately the team struggled in the elite division and Bob, who made only one start before March, was unhappy about his lack of first-team action. Training with the youth team, he didn't speak to Megson for four months and, by the time he made his final appearance for the club, in a 2–2 draw with Newcastle, Albion were down.

Bob left the pitch after the Newcastle game to a standing ovation, having scored 131 goals in 377 appearances for Albion, and he said his diving header against Wolves in March 1995 was 'the best goal of my career.'

Over 12,000 fans attended his testimonial match in May 2003, which marked the end of an era for Super Bob. He spent a season with Cheltenham, played for Tamworth in 2004–06 and Kidderminster Harriers in 2006–07 before retiring to set up his own promotions company, Super Bob Events.

BERT TRENTHAM

'Astute in positioning, stylish to a degree, at times Bert played with nonchalant authority.'

Born:	22 April 1908, Chirbury, Shropshire
Died:	10 June 1979, Ward End, Birmingham

Albion senior record:

Appearances:	League 246, FA Cup 25, FA Charity Shield 1
Goals:	None
Senior debut:	League, 5 March 1930 v Blackpool (a) lost 1–0
Also played for:	Knighton Town, Knighton Victoria, Knighton United, Hereford United (2 spells), Aston Villa (trial), Darlaston, England (junior international), Football League (1 app)

In March 1929, Albion were tipped off about a promising young defender in the Hednesford Town team. So chairman Billy Bassett and secretary-manager Fred Everiss arranged to go and watch Hednesford play Hereford United in a Birmingham & District League game. The only player of note was a lively, quick-tackling full-back in the Hereford side who had a white handkerchief in his withered right hand, following a fire accident at home when he was just six. That player was Bert Trentham, an England junior international who, four months earlier, had been on trial with Aston Villa. 'We liked the look of him and at the age of 21 he was just beginning to thicken out,' said the chairman.

Bert actually knew the two Albion representatives. He had seen them both at a hotel where the Albion party had stayed prior to a 1924 charity match against a Montgomeryshire XI in aid of the County Infirmary. At the time Bert was working as a delivery boy for the local greengrocer and was delivering some requisitions to the hotel in Aberystwyth. Negotiations took place and on 16 April 1929 Bert joined Albion for a fee of £500.

Signed initially as cover for full-backs Bob Finch, George Shaw and

Hugh Foulkes, Bert appeared in one Central League game at the end of the 1928–29 season and 35 the following term when he also made his senior debut in a Second Division match at Blackpool, standing in for the injured Shaw.

However, with Finch and Shaw already bedded in as Albion's regular full-back pairing, Bert had to bide his time in the reserves before finally gaining a regular place in the first XI six weeks into the 1930–31 season – and what a season that turned out to be.

Lining up at left-back, with Shaw to his right, Bert produced some superb displays as Albion powered on towards the 'unique' double, which they achieved in style, gaining promotion with a last-match win over Charlton Athletic and defeating Birmingham in the FA Cup Final at Wembley.

In the early 1970s, I met Bert at his Ward End home in Birmingham and, although he wasn't too well at the time, he was able to recall some great times he had with Albion, especially that double-winning season. 'We played some good stuff. We had a settled team and we all got on well together,' said Bert. 'I loved travelling and on long distances often played cards with goalkeeper Harold Pearson and centre-half Bill Richardson. We argued at times, but we were all good mates, especially on the football pitch.

'I will admit that I never really wandered away from my side of the pitch, and on one occasion, against Manchester City, just after Albion had won promotion, I had to mark Ernie Toseland. He was a fast, direct, hard-shooting winger. I tried to get close to him but he was too clever with the ball and I asked if I could swap positions and move to the right. I changed places with George Shaw but to my surprise, Toseland switched from the right-wing to the left and he continued to give a tough time.

'I loved playing against a line-hugging winger. I always seemed to cope with the threat posed by Joe Hulme of Arsenal, Sammy Crooks of Derby County and even Stan Matthews, then of Stoke City. Stan was certainly one of the greatest players I ever saw and after one game at The Hawthorns, which Albion won, he came up to me and said, well played Bert…but next time I will score; I never got a look in today. You did good.' Keeping true to his word Stan did find the net in his next game against Albion, helping the Potters win 3–2.

Bert also remembered when he bought his first car and picked Harold up on his way to a morning training session. 'It was a decent day so we had the top open, but as we approached The Hawthorns, Stan Wood was just going inside. He turned round and shouted out, presumably to a colleague, "Hey, watch out, I think there's a couple of new directors or a new manager coming to see us." Harold and I were both wearing our trilby hats and that's perhaps why we weren't recognised, but as soon as we got into the ground, the rest of the players, and the trainers, all wanted a ride! I recall Tommy Glidden asking me if I wouldn't mind taking him home to see his parents…fine, I replied…but then he said, they live in Newcastle!'

Sure-footed, a stern tackler and a good user of the ball, Bert was a model professional. He was a regular in Albion's defence for six years, from October 1930 until December 1936, and during that time played in 268 games out of a possible 268, was never dropped and only missed the action through illness and injury. He also represented the Football League against the Irish League in 1934.

He helped Albion reach the 1935 FA Cup Final, which they lost 4–2 against Sheffield Wednesday, and recalling that day at Wembley, Bert said: 'We should never have lost that game. We gave away four goals, yes all four. We were level at 2–2 and were in control. We lost concentration and it cost us dear. Still, two Cup Finals in four years wasn't bad really.'

Bert – whose nickname was 'Corker' – eventually lost his place at left-back to Cecil Shaw and after 272 appearances for the club (and not one single goal scored, although he did concede two own-goals) he finally left in May 1937, rejoining Hereford United on a free transfer. Later with Darlaston, Bert retired in April 1942 and shortly after the war opened an ironmonger's shop in Ward End. He was 71 years of age when he died.

JACK VERNON

'Belfast's darlin' boy, Jack Vernon, was the best centre-half in Europe in the late 1940s.'

Born:	26 September 1919, Belfast
Died:	24 August 1981, Belfast

Albion senior record:

Appearances:	League 190, FA Cup 10
Goals:	League 1, FA Cup 0
Senior debut:	League, 15 March 1947 v West Ham United (a) lost 3–2
Also played for:	Springfield Road Juniors (Belfast), Spearmint FC, Dundela Juniors, Liverpool (amateur), Belfast Celtic, Shamrock Rovers (guest), Crusaders, Ireland (17 full and 3 Victory caps), Republic of Ireland (2 caps), Great Britain (1 app), United Kingdom (1 app), Irish FA XI (6 apps), Irish Regional League XI (12 apps)

At the age of 64, a Justice of the Peace and a legend in his own lifetime, Fred Everiss, it must be said, 'could spot a good player a mile off,' and one of his last duties as Albion's secretary-manager was to go out and sign one of the greatest centre-halves the club has ever seen: Irishman Jack Vernon, a brilliant defender, who was to go on and give the Baggies five years of magnificent service.

Jack had already gained two Irish Cup-winners' medals (in 1941 and 1943), five League championship medals (1941, 1942, 1943 and 1944, with another to follow in 1947), two County Antrim Shield winners' prizes (1943 and 1945), had represented the Irish FA on six occasions and starred for the Irish Regional League 12 times between 1941 and 1946. He was a fine player who now wanted to win something with Albion.

Following the resumption of League football in August 1946, Albion had selected the ageing George Tranter at centre-half, and although the defence, on the whole, was decent enough, occasionally it leaked goals – conceding five at home to Barnsley, another five at Manchester City and four at Bury, plus several twos and threes.

So it was imperative that a change be made and, after seeing the former Liverpool amateur play brilliantly for Ireland against Scotland in Glasgow, when he never put a foot wrong, Fred Everiss knew there and then he had seen a star player in action. However, Jack's club, Belfast Celtic, would not sell him and with Glasgow Celtic also interested, it was a long time before his manager and former Liverpool goalkeeper Elisha Scott, who had actually recommended Jack to Anfield, agreed to a deal with Albion. This was eventually completed on 8 February 1947 when a club record fee of £9,500 was paid for his signature, Jack agreeing a contract which would keep him at The Hawthorns until the summer of 1952.

Interviewed by a *Birmingham Gazette* reporter in 1949, Fred described auburn-headed Jack as follows: 'He was perfectly proportioned, tackled cleanly, was dominant in the air, despite being on the small side and above all he was a wonderful captain who led by example. He had a neat style of play, his passing was precise when given time on the ball and very rarely would you see him thump it downfield willy-nilly, in the hope that one of his colleagues would manage to get on the end of it. Signing Jack was money well spent.'

Jack was the son of a Belfast butcher and used to work in his father's shop when he could. He stood 5ft 11¼in tall yet wore size 5½ boots and as a result was called 'Twinkletoes' by his colleagues. In truth, that was not just because of his small feet, far from it – he was pretty clever with the ball for a defender, so much so that occasionally he would dribble it outside his penalty-area, much to the annoyance of his manager and, indeed, his teammates.

After moving to The Hawthorns, it was quite a while before Jack could make his debut for Albion. This was due to the Arctic weather conditions which had gripped the country and very few games were actually being played. Albion didn't figure in a single League or Cup game between 9 February and 14 March. Jack was signed on the day before the shut down.

At long last Jack finally played in his first English League game on 15 March 1947 – five weeks after joining Albion. He lined up at centre-half in the away fixture at West Ham and had a tough time against a very useful centre-forward named Frank Neary, who scored a hat-trick as the Hammers won a tight game 3–2.

Jack, as he always did, put that performance behind him and set about the task in hand – that of trying to help Albion regain their First Division status, which they had surrendered at the end of the 1937–38 season. Jack played in the last 14 League games of the 1946–47 season, missed seven matches in 1947–48 and was absent from just four Second Division fixtures in 1948–49 when Albion at last won promotion, finishing runners-up to Fulham (56 points to 57).

Another moment of joy for Jack came in Albion's home League game against Sheffield Wednesday on Christmas Day 1949. Going up for a corner, he had the pleasure of scoring his first and only goal in England, and it proved to be the winner as the Baggies edged out the Owls 1–0 in front of almost 35,000 spectators.

International call-ups were the main reason why Jack missed certain Albion matches. He was a regular in the Irish team and, as time passed by, he collected 20 senior caps for Ireland, captaining the side on 17 occasions, won two for the Republic of Ireland and also played for Great Britain against the Rest of Europe in front of a 135,000 crowd at Hampden Park in May 1947 and for the United Kingdom v Wales in December 1951. His appearance for the Great Britain team confirmed that he was the best centre-half in the game at that time.

With Albion back in the top flight, Jack continued to produce his best form. He missed only two League games in 1949–50 and one the following season before a tedious knee injury sidelined him for half of the matches in 1951–52. At this point Jack was fast approaching his 33rd birthday and he admitted that he wasn't as fast as he had been in previous years. With Joe Kennedy and Les Horne ready to step into his position when required, he appeared just once during the last five months of the campaign.

In July 1952, after exactly 200 first-team appearances, Jack bid farewell to Albion, joining Crusaders (Belfast). He went on to win the Ulster Cup in 1954 before retiring to start a full-time job in his father's butcher's shop. He remained there right up until his untimely death in 1981, two years after he had attended Albion's centenary celebrations. The following day Jack's wife of 38 years also passed away.

DAVE WALSH

'Dave scored a goal every 156 minutes for Albion — some record for a brilliant centre-forward.'

Born: 28 April 1923, Waterford, Ireland

Albion senior record:

Appearances: League 165, FA Cup 9
Goals: League 94, FA Cup 6
Senior debut: League, 31 August 1946 v Swansea Town (a) won 3–2 (scored twice)
Also played for: Mount Sion (Gaelic football), The Corinthians, Shelbourne Juniors, Glen Rovers, Shelbourne, Limerick, Linfield, Aston Villa, Walsall, Worcester City, (Northern) Ireland (9 full and two Wartime caps), Republic of Ireland (20 caps), Irish League (2 apps), FA of Ireland (1 app)

Interviewed for the *Albion News* in 2007, Dave confessed he played Gaelic football and hurling as a youngster. 'My father was a great Gaelic man and as far as he was concerned it was taboo to play soccer, soccer was an English game,' he said. 'You couldn't really play both games – it wasn't allowed.'

Yet Dave loved his sport and once competed in two different 'sports' on the same Saturday. In the morning he played for the Corinthians at soccer and in the afternoon helped Mount Sion win a Gaelic Cup semifinal. Unfortunately, in the newspaper on the Monday, a photograph showed Dave playing in the soccer match. The opposition objected, the result was overturned and both Dave and a teammate were suspended from playing Gaelic football for six months.

That didn't bother Dave. He continued to play soccer as an outside-right and when his team's centre-forward was called up for a rugby game, Dave led the attack. And what an impact he had – he scored eight goals. Dave was on his way and the goals continued to flow. He ended the 1938–39 season with over 40 to his name, and he scored 30 more the following term.

World War Two didn't disrupt sport in Ireland and several scouts turned up to watch weekend junior matches. One of them, a Limerick player, spotted Dave and asked him if he would like to come and have a game with his club 'just to see how you get on?' Initially Dave said 'no', but realistically he wanted to go and eventually changed his mind. He recalled: 'I was still at college, it was in October 1942, and I travelled 80 miles by taxi to Limerick. I played in a game against St James' Gate and scored twice, was signed up and helped Limerick reach the semi-final of the Inter-City Cup that season.'

Loaned out to Shelbourne in 1943–44, Dave met future Albion captain and centre-half Jack Vernon for the first time when he played against Belfast Celtic in a Cup tie. Said Dave: 'Jack was a brilliant centre-half, one of the best I've ever seen. I did okay against him but his team was good, very good, and they knocked us out of the competition. Jack and I became great friends and we played together for both Albion and Ireland for many years.'

In August 1943, Dave was transferred to Linfield but broke his collarbone twice in six months and it was touch and go whether or not he would be retained for the following season. Thankfully he was and over the next two years he scored more than 100 goals, including 73 in 1945–46 (61 in major competitions) and gained successive Irish Cup-winners' medals, netting twice in the 1946 Final against Distillery.

Towards the end of the 1945–46 campaign Albion were looking for a replacement for W.G. Richardson. Secretary-manager Fred Everiss and director Claude Jephcott heard about Dave's scoring ability and crossed the Irish Sea to watch him net twice for Linfield against Bohemians in a Cup tie. Immediately they asked him if he would like to play for Albion. Dave – after serious thought – said 'yes' and a fee of £3,500 secured his transfer to Albion in May 1946.

He made a terrific start to his Baggies career, scoring in each of his first League games, all at the start of season 1946–47, a record unequalled in the history of the game. He finished with a total of 29, and to show it was no fluke cracked in another 22 the following season.

Then, in 1948–49, alongside Jackie Haines, Dave bagged 28 more, 23 coming in the League, including two hat-tricks (against Lincoln and Bradford Park Avenue) as Albion clinched promotion to the First Division. In the FA Cup his splendid treble knocked out Chelsea in the fifth round.

Ideally built for a centre-forward, he was blessed with a powerful shot and could head as well as most – and he continued to hit the net from all angles. By now an established international, having represented Northern Ireland and the Republic of Ireland, he actually helped the latter pull off a major upset by beating England at Goodison Park in September 1949.

Dave remained on international duty until 1954, gaining a total of 29 full caps (nine for Eire) and scoring 10 goals. The pundits feel that he would have gained more honours had injuries not interrupted his game in 1946–47. He missed two internationals in a row after being clattered by Birmingham City's bruising centre-half Arthur Turner and in 1948 was sidelined again after some more rough treatment from another Blues defender, Ted Duckhouse. 'Duckhouse was a real toughie,' said Dave. 'He kicked everything and anything that moved.'

In his first season of top-flight football Dave did well, netting 15 goals in 37 appearances, but then, surprisingly, having scored six times in 14 games during the first half of 1950–51, including his 100th goal for Albion in a draw with Liverpool in October, and just hours after a superb headed goal for Ireland against Norway in Dublin, Dave was told he was 'on the transfer list' by the chairman of Shamrock Rovers. 'I couldn't believe it,' said Dave. 'I had been injured but I was still only 27. I had lost my scoring touch, but so had a lot of other players, and, in fact, I was dropped, but it certainly knocked me for six when I found out that manager Jack Smith didn't want me.'

'So off I went, sold for £25,000 to Aston Villa. There I teamed up with my Irish colleague Con Martin, and I enjoyed almost five years of football with Villa before moving to Walsall in an exchange deal involving Billy Myerscough.'

Dave netted 40 goals in 114 appearances for Villa and nine in 23 for Walsall. After a spell with Worcester City he retired in June 1957 to concentrate on his sports-outfitter's business in Droitwich, which he bought in 1953.

In 1976, Dave and his wife agreed to buy a hotel in Thurlestone, Devon, which was being converted into holiday apartments – and it was right next to a golf course. That suited Dave to a tee. They moved south, ran the apartments and Dave became president of the golf club. One of the oldest former Albion players alive today, he still enjoys nine holes and when I caught up with him on the course, he said, smiling: 'You can't get much better than this at my age.'

JOHN WILE

Johnny Giles said (about John Wile): 'If he could play football from nine in the morning till nine at night, seven days a week, 52 weeks a year, he still wouldn't be satisfied.'

Born: 9 March 1947, Sherburn, County Durham

Albion senior record:

Appearances: League 180, FA Cup 23, Others 5
Goals: League 8, FA Cup 2, Others 2
Senior debut: League, 19 December 1970 v Blackpool (h) drew 1–1
Also played for: Eppleton & Hetton Juniors, Durham City, Sunderland, Peterborough United (2 spells, one as player-manager), Vancouver Whitecaps (guest), Rotherham United, Sutton United, West Bromwich Albion All Stars

John Wile was a professional with Sunderland and played over 125 games for Peterborough United before joining Albion for £32,000 in December 1970. Replacing John Talbut at centre-half, he quickly settled into the team, initially playing alongside John Kaye.

Three months into the 1971–72 season, Ally Robertson took over from Kaye to begin a 10-year partnership with John at the heart of Albion's defence. John was disillusioned after relegation in 1973 but after three years hard graft in the Second Division he helped Albion become one of the best-equipped teams in the top-flight.

He had six different managers – Alan Ashman, Don Howe, Johnny Giles, Ronnie Allen (twice), Ron Atkinson and Ron Wylie – and skippered Albion throughout the glorious Atkinson era and beyond, forming an almost impenetrable centre-back pairing with Ally Rob. They played together 573 times between October 1971 and May 1983 – 404 in the League, 35 in the FA Cup, 39 in the League Cup, 12 in European competitions and 83 in 'other' games.

John played 719 times for Albion's first XI (all levels). He made 619 appearances in senior competitions – the fourth highest in the club's history – and 449 of his 500 League games were at centre-half. In fact, only two players have made more League appearances for Albion than John – Tony Brown (574) and Ally Robertson (506).

John also had a run of 224 consecutive appearances during the 1970s (172 in the League), was an ever-present a record seven times between 1971–72 and 1981–82 and in 1978–79 played in 75 of Albion's 76 first-team matches. His last League game for Albion was against his former club, Sunderland, in May 1983.

After floundering in the Second Division for two seasons (1973–75) John recalled the day the former Leeds midfielder Johnny Giles moved in: 'When he arrived, he was fresh to the job and it took quite a while to sort things out. Leaving Brian Whitehouse to do the coaching, nothing changed much from what we had been doing under his predecessor, Don Howe. In fact, results were poor, I remember losing badly at Southampton and Fulham. But he slowly got things in order and changed our style of play. He asked us all to try and pass the ball, rather than hoofing it around the park, emphasing that possession is nine-tenths of the game. If you can pass it accurately, then that's even better. He got us to close opponents down quickly, made the midfielders track back as often as possible and more importantly he encouraged us to play football. He used to say to me and Ally Rob "You tackle, win the ball, that's your strength. Pass it to me and we'll play from there." My game improved enormously. I grew in confidence and we were soon on our way...back to the First Division.'

John admitted: 'I was once dropped by Gilesy when I wasn't playing well. Fair enough, I thought, but I told him, neither are you gaffer...so why don't you leave yourself out? "I'm the manager and I pick the team" was his reply. We gained promotion that season – after a dramatic last-match win at Oldham – which was one of the greatest moments in my career. Shortly after that triumph J.G. told us that he was leaving, but we persuaded him to 'stick with it' for another season and we finished a creditable seventh in the table. Ronnie Allen took over and then it was Ron Atkinson. Well, what can I say about Big Ron. What a guy. He was terrific and for three years we played some brilliant attacking football.'

Albion were on course to win the FA Cup in 1978 but didn't perform against Ipswich Town in the semi-final at Highbury and lost 3–1. Everyone associated with football will recall that John played on in that game with blood pouring from a head wound after clashing with future Albion player and manager Brian Talbot. 'He simply didn't want to let his teammates down,' said midfielder Mick Martin, 'he played with great courage and determination well into the second-half before finally trudging off.' At the end of that season Albion toured China, where John acted as a marvellous ambassador, not only for Albion, but also for English football in general.

Moving on to 1978–79, Albion were bang on course to win the League Championship and they also reached the quarter-finals of the European Cup-winners' Cup. 'The weather didn't do us any favours that season,' said John. 'After going top early in the New Year, we played only one League game in six weeks. We lost our momentum and in the end had to settle for third spot. It was disappointing, but it turned out to be my best-ever season in top-flight football, especially that epic 5–3 victory against Manchester United at Old Trafford. What a game that was, one of the best I ever played. And the goals scored by Len Cantello and Cyrille Regis were two of the finest I've ever seen on a football pitch.'

The following season wasn't great for Albion, but in 1980–81 they took fourth place in the League. Then Atkinson left, taking with him Bryan Robson. 'That was a disappointment,' said John, 'but we knew he would become manager of Manchester United one day.'

Albion suffered two semi-final defeats in 1981–82, losing to Tottenham Hotspur in the League Cup and QPR in the FA Cup. 'We were unlucky against Spurs,' said John. 'We should have beaten them at home – and we never got going against Rangers who won with a lucky ricochet off Ally Rob. I would have loved to have played at Wembley – but it wasn't to be. Sad, but that's football.'

John spent one more season at The Hawthorns before returning to his former club Peterborough as player-manager, retiring as a player in March 1986 and quitting as manager six months later. In the late 1980s he took charge of the Solihull Indoor Cricket Centre and was also chief executive of Walsall and Cradley Heath Indoor Cricket schools while also playing briefly for Sutton United before returning to The Hawthorns as chief executive in March 1997, remaining in office until 2002.

BILLY WILLIAMS

'Billy showed a praiseworthy, never-say-die spirit — and stuck to his opponent like glue.'

Born:	20 January 1876, West Smethwick
Died:	11 January 1929, West Bromwich

Albion senior record:

Appearances:	League 180, FA Cup 23, Others 5
Goals:	League 8, FA Cup 2, Others 2
Senior debut:	League, 1 September 1894 v Sheffield United (a) lost 2–1
Also played for:	West Bromwich Hawthorn, West Smethwick, Hawthorn Villa, Old Hill Wanderers, England (6 caps), Football League (5 apps), The Professionals (3 apps)

A write-up in the official programme issued for the England v Scotland international at Celtic Park, Glasgow in April 1898, stated: 'Williams is an efficient, reliable full-back. He has a most effective tackle and shows a praiseworthy never-say-die spirit in sticking to an opponent after having been momentarily beaten.'

In the *Daily Mail*'s report of that match, which England won 3–1, the journalist praised the 'fine combination play' of the two full-backs Williams and Oakley (from the Corinthians), and added: 'England's final goal came after a splendid bout involving Scotland's Doyle and the big, English back, Williams. The latter won the ball fair and square and sent a long pass to Wreford-Brown who transferred it to Forman. He then passed the ball forward to Bloomer who scored with a side-shot that Anderson could not reach.'

In the newspaper report covering his international debut against Ireland at Nottingham in February 1897, a game England won 6–0, it stated that: 'Williams, the young West Bromwich full-back, was full of resource…only stern tackling and positive defence kept the Irish at bay on several occasions…he was always watchful and alert.'

Billy Williams, at 5ft 10in tall and 12st 4lb in weight, was certainly a well-built, physically strong defender, a stern tackler,

sound and resolute in his all-round play who could kick a dead ball with immense velocity and accuracy. And he was a pretty useful penalty-taker as well, hardly ever missing from the spot.

In the 1892 FA Cup semi-final second replay encounter with Nottingham Forest at Derby, Billy scored a goal from near the halfway line in Albion's emphatic 6–2 victory. Some reporters thought that the goal was scored from 60 yards. His mid-air volleying of the ball was also a feature of his game and he would shoot at goal from quite a long distance.

He was also a dedicated club man, who once turned down an invitation to play for the Football League side in order to turn out for Albion in an FA Cup tie against Liverpool. He received a medal for his loyalty.

Sadly Billy's career ended all too soon due to a cartilage injury, suffered initially during a home League game against Newcastle United in September 1900. He was only 27 years old. In those days the treatment for a knee, or indeed an ankle problem, was rough and ready. Billy's right knee was simply set in a plaster-of-paris cast, which was removed after a few weeks.

Returning to first-team duty against Nottingham Forest at The Hawthorns on 20 October, Billy's knee seemed to be okay, but he complained of some discomfort in the next match at Blackburn, yet manfully and bravely battled on, as he always did. Unfortunately he broke down again in the next home fixture with Stoke a week later, and although he underwent intense treatment, and played in a couple of second-team games, he was forced to call it a day in May 1901 – a great playing loss to the club.

Billy had given Albion nine years excellent service, scoring 12 goals in 208 first-class matches. He played in the 1895 FA Cup Final defeat by Aston Villa, gained six full caps for England (three v Ireland, two v Wales and one v Scotland), represented the Football League on five occasions (against the Scottish twice and the Irish League three times) and played three times for The Professionals against The Amateurs in international trials.

Signed as an 18-year-old professional from Old Hill Wanderers in May 1894, Billy replaced 'Mark' Nicholson at right-back and was initially partnered by Bob Crone before linking up with Jack Horton. At the end of that season he had appeared in an FA Cup Final and, in fact, between his debut on the opening day of the 1894–95 campaign and his final appearance against Stoke in November 1900, Billy missed only 19 competitive matches out of a possible 227, being an ever-present in season 1895–96 when he scored in two vital Test Match victories over Manchester City and Liverpool which secured Albion's top-flight status.

Unfortunately his absence was a severe blow to Albion, who were relegated at the end of the 1900–01 season – their first at The Hawthorns.

One of the highest-paid players at the club in the late 1890s, Billy was earning £4 10s a week. And along with goalkeeper Joe Reader, defender Tom Perry, wingers Billy Bassett and Ben Garfield and centre-forward Billy Richards, he was one of Albion's star players.

Albion's former secretary-manager Fred Everiss said: 'Billy Williams was a strong and powerful full-back who, if the truth be known, was certainly in the same class as the better-known Jesse Pennington and Bob Crompton of Blackburn Rovers.'

In an article written for *Association Football and The Men Who Made It*, by co-author Alfred Gibson, Billy was described as 'one of the stoutest defenders of his time,' while in the same publication, William McGregor, founder of the Football League, stated that 'Williams of West Bromwich was one of the finest full-backs in the First Division, even in the country.'

After announcing his retirement, Billy remained at The Hawthorns as a trainer, later taking over as a coach and nurturing along a certain Jesse Pennington, who joined the club in 1903.

In the summer of 1906 Billy quit football for good and took over a pub at the Smethwick end of Halfords Lane. This was often packed when Albion were at home, with supporters having a pre-match drink – although many just wanted to call in and chat with a Baggies legend who one feels might well have gone on playing for club and country for at least another 10 years.

GRAHAM WILLIAMS

*'Graham was a fine leader, who could certainly look after himself. It was great to have him in the team,
and I was glad he was on my side and not playing against me!' (Jeff Astle)*

Born:	2 April 1938, Hellan, North Wales.

Albion senior record:

Appearances:	League 308+6, FA Cup 25, League Cup 15, Europe 5, FA Charity Shield 1
Goals:	League 10, FA Cup 0, League Cup 1, Europe 0, FA Charity Shield 0
Senior debut:	League, 19 November 1955 v Blackpool (h) lost 2–1
Also played for:	Flintshire Boys, Burnley (trialist), Rhyl Athletic, Weymouth (player-manager), Wales (26 full caps)
Also managed:	Poole Town, Cardiff City, FC Rovaniemen (Finland)

Graham Williams joined Albion from the Welsh League club Rhyl as an outside-left in September 1954. Turning professional in April 1955, he made his first two League appearances on the wing against Blackpool (home) and Huddersfield Town (away) seven months later, replacing the injured George Lee, but it wasn't until April 1958 that he got another chance in the senior side – this time as a strong-tackling left-back.

He replaced his namesake Stuart Williams in the local derby at Villa Park, and played three times more before the end of the season, partnering Stuart twice. He played in four League matches in 1958–59 before bedding down at left-back in late December 1959, as partner to Don Howe.

Gordon Clark was Albion's manager at the time and he gave Graham a decent run in the side, through to the end of season 1960–61. Then Scotsman Archie Macaulay took over and he relegated Graham to the reserves, using him sparingly, mainly when Stuart was on international duty.

Graham won the first of his 26 Welsh caps against Northern Ireland at Wrexham in April 1960, partnering Stuart in a 3–2 win. The two players played together for their country just once more, in another 3–2 victory, this time over the Republic of Ireland in Dublin five months later. Graham remained a valuable member of the Welsh team for nine years and scored one goal, in a 5–0 win over Northern Ireland in Belfast in March 1965, when he played behind future Albion winger Ronnie Rees. He is also one of the few Albion players to captain both club and country.

From March 1962 to September 1966, Graham was Albion's regular left-back, and he was given the job of marking George Best when he made his Manchester United debut in 1963. After Albion had lost 1–0 and Graham had been given a tough time, he said to the Irish winger: 'Will you stand still for a minute so I can look at your face?' 'Why?' asked Best. 'Because all I've ever seen of you,' replied Graham, 'is your backside disappearing down the touchline.'

After recovering from a cartilage operation, Graham was appointed Albion skipper in 1965, by his fourth manager Jimmy Hagan, and the following year he lifted the League Cup when Albion beat West Ham 5–3 on aggregate in the Final. Albion lost the first leg 2–1 at Upton Park but thrashed the Hammers in the second, Graham scoring the fourth goal from the left-half position where he had been playing for just three matches. At the end of that season he had a well-deserved testimonial.

It was all doom and gloom, however, in 1967 as Albion lost in the Final of the League Cup, beaten at Wembley by Third Division side QPR. Graham recalled: 'That defeat was a real sickener. None of us could believe what had happened. We were cruising, 2–0 up at half-time and playing well, very well, but after the gaffer had made a couple of changes, it all went pear-shaped.'

Thankfully, 12 months on it was a completely different story as Graham led Albion out at Wembley for the second season running, this time in the FA Cup Final against Everton. Now aged 30, but still sublimely fit, he was on top of his game and had broken through the 300 appearance barrier for Albion. Defending with great energy and commitment, he played his part in the 1–0 extra-time victory over the Merseysiders and admitted 'I was absolutely delighted, over the moon, when the final whistle went. Tears were in my eyes as I went up to receive the Cup.'

Earlier, in a fourth-round replay at Southampton, John Osborne suffered concussion in the third minute but stayed on the pitch. At half-time manager Alan Ashman told Graham to put on the goalkeeper's jersey. Graham, whose boyhood hero was the great Frank Swift, had already kept goal for Emmanuel Secondary School, on the training ground and for the reserves when Clive Jackman was hurt. So he was no stranger to the position.

'We were leading 2–1 and everyone expected 'Bomber' Brown to go in goal,' recalled Graham. 'We were unsure of ourselves at the back as Ossie was struggling to see the ball! But I had something of a nightmare in the dressing room during the interval trying to put Ossie's kit on. He was 6ft 2in tall and I was 5ft 7in and there wasn't a spare jersey available. You can imagine what I looked like in an over-sized top – it was huge, especially round the shoulders. And I also had his gloves on – they didn't fit either!'

Saints equalised early in the second half but Albion held on. Stand-in 'keeper Graham produced a couple of 'brilliant' saves before Jeff Astle grabbed a last-minute winner. At the start of the next season, Graham took over from Ossie again – this time in the Charity Shield game against Manchester City. Unfortunately, it wasn't a happy story on this occasion as Albion lost 6–1!

Soon after their '68 Cup win, Albion toured East Africa where Graham was sent off for the second time in his career, dismissed against the Ugandan National XI. 'They were kicking chunks out of us,' said Graham, 'I had a go back and although my tackle was considerably milder than the ones they were dishing out, the ref said off!' Four years earlier Graham had taken an early bath at Villa Park for laying out Tony Hateley.

With Ray Wilson pushing for a place in the team, Graham made 26 appearances in 1968–69 (when Albion lost in the FA Cup semi-final and in the Cup-winners' Cup quarter-final) and the following season he was used 20 times, but missed a third visit to Wembley when Albion lost to Manchester City in the League Cup Final.

After two seasons as player-coach (during which time his Central League appearance tally rose to 229) Graham was released by his former playing colleague Don Howe in 1972.

Reflecting on his career, 1960s teammate Tony Brown said: 'If you weren't pulling your weight, "Willy" would be the first one on your back. A good captain, a good leader, a good full-back, he was as hard as nails. The ball might get past him, but not many opponents did.'

Taking over as player-manager of Weymouth, he later coached in Kuwait, Greece, Nigeria and Dubai, managed Poole Town, Cardiff City and FC Rovaniemen, scouted for Cheltenham Town, Newport County and Newcastle and was Wales's assistant manager (under ex-Albion boss Bobby Gould). He is now chairman of the West Bromwich Albion former players' association.

STUART WILLIAMS

'Two-footed, Stuart had pace and was able to match the speed of most wingers. He was a first-class player, a wonderful club man who perhaps was hard done by at times.'

Born: 9 July 1930, Wrexham

Albion senior record:

Appearances: League 226, FA Cup 20
Goals: League 6, FA Cup 3
Senior debut: League, 16 February 1952 v Huddersfield Town (a) lost 3–0
Also played for: Wrexham Boys, Victoria Youth Club, Wrexham, Birmingham City (trialist), Southampton, Wales (43 full caps)
Managed: Payhaan (Iran), Stavanger (Norway)

Stuart Williams won more international caps with Albion than any other player. Over a period of 11 and a half years he represented Wales on 43 occasions, 33 during his time at The Hawthorns. He made his debut for the Principality against Austria in Vienna in May 1954 when his teammates included John Charles, Trevor Ford and Ivor Allchurch, and collected his last cap against Denmark in his home town of Wrexham in December 1965 when Allchurch was again in the team along with Terry Hennessey, future Albion winger Ronnie Rees and Roy Vernon.

A confident footballer throughout his career, Stuart, the son of a Wrexham director, started as a forward and once scored four times in one match for his local youth club. He signed for Wrexham as an amateur on his 16th birthday, and also had a trial with Birmingham City, although at the time it was common knowledge that his father didn't want his son to become a professional footballer. 'Remain an amateur – that means you won't be tied down to a specific club and you get a job outside the game,' said Mr Williams.

Continuing as a forward, Stuart spent two years in Wrexham's second team and two years doing National Service while appearing in only one League match – a 1–0 defeat at Carlisle in September 1949. He was not making much progress at all, and just prior to the start of the 1950–51 season his father found him full-time employment with an insurance company in the centre of Birmingham – clearly believing that his son could soon be out of a job.

Then, in November 1950, an Albion scout spotted Stuart 'having a fine game' for Wrexham reserves in the Welsh League. Invited down for a trial at The Hawthorns, he impressed everyone present with his enthusiasm and commitment and, after serious consideration, manager and fellow countryman Jack Smith signed him as a professional in February 1951.

Stuart made rapid progress, and a year later played his first senior game for Albion, deputising for Ronnie Allen at centre-forward, away at Huddersfield. Then, just a fortnight later, he took the place of injured left-half Ray Barlow against Chelsea. The following season Stuart wore the number three, five and six shirts in different League games and also made his FA Cup debut at inside-right at West Ham, while in two of the four fourth-round Cup games against Chelsea he occupied both full-back positions.

Now respected as being one of the Albion's most 'versatile' players, Stuart still couldn't gain a regular place in the first team, due to the excellent form of full-backs Stan Rickaby and Len Millard, Barlow and the three inside-forwards, Reg Ryan, Allen and Johnny Nicholls. Agreeing that right-back was his best position, Stuart modelled himself on Rickaby, and it was an unfortunate injury to the England international that led to Stuart having a decent run in the team.

In fact, he was all set to play in the 1954 FA Cup Final at Wembley – even the official programme included him at right-back – but in the end boss Vic Buckingham, who had been in charge for just over a year, chose the more experienced Joe Kennedy to partner skipper Millard, leaving Stuart to watch from the sidelines as the Baggies beat Preston 3–2.

Soon afterwards Stuart perked up when he was told he had been selected for Wales. Rickaby returned for the start of the next season and although Stuart slipped back into the reserves, he still made 27 appearances. He also scored five goals in six weeks either side of the New Year, two in the League and three in the FA Cup, when he played alongside Allen and Nicholls.

In the meantime, Don Howe was making good headway in the reserves and Stuart knew he would have to work hard to earn his place in the team. In 1955–56 he made 20 appearances, mainly sharing the right-back spot with Howe, who became first choice in 1956–57, leaving Stuart once again battling for a place in the side. But he hung in there and finally, after six years, he became Albion's permanent left-back, taking over from Millard.

Over the next five years, from August 1957 to September 1962, Stuart made 177 appearances in Albion's first team, while also starring for his country, taking part in the World Cup in Sweden in 1958 when Wales reached the quarter-finals only to lose to the eventual winners Brazil, Pelé scoring the all-important goal.

In the late 1950s, Stuart's performances were, said Dick Knight in the *Sports Argus,* 'top drawer,' while the *Birmingham Gazette* journalist Rex Bellamy wrote: 'Albion's left-back Williams is one of the finest in the First Division. He is strong in defence, crisp in the tackle, has good speed and is smart in the air.'

With his namesake Graham Williams ready to step into the left-back position, Albion did a deal with Southampton a month into the 1962–63 season, transferring both Stuart and Davey Burnside to the south-coast club, Stuart being valued at £15,000. Six months later Stuart played in the FA Cup semi-final defeat by Southampton and went on to make 167 appearances for the Saints before retiring as a player in May 1966. Two months later he returned to Albion as a trainer and was 'spongeman' at three Wembley Cup Finals in 1967, 1968 and 1970. Stuart was then employed briefly as a trainer at Villa Park before taking over as manager of Payhaan FC (Tehran). He then returned to the UK with Morton as their trainer, acted as Southampton's assistant manager/coach from 1971–73 and, after bossing Stavanger FC in Norway, and scouting for Carlisle United, he pulled out of football altogether in 1975 to become a representative for two tyre companies. Later manager of a transport company and also an hotelier, he looked after the ex-Saints XI for a couple of years and is now a member of Albion's former players' association.

JOE WILSON

'A very thrustful winger with good skill and a mean shot.'

Born:	8 January 1861, Handsworth, Birmingham
Died:	20 October 1952, Acocks Green, Birmingham

Albion senior record:

Appearances:	League 40 FA Cup 13
Goals:	League 8, FA Cup 12
Senior debut:	FA Cup, 15 October 1887 v Wednesbury Old Athletic (h) won 7–1 (two goals scored)
Also played for:	Hampstead Swifts, Aston Unity, Stoke, Walsall Town (two spells), Aston Villa, Kidderminster Harriers, Birmingham St George's

Outside-left Joe Wilson had the distinction, honour and pleasure of scoring Albion's first-ever League goal, in a 2–0 win at Stoke on 8 September 1888. Six months earlier he had gained an FA Cup-winners' medal as Albion defeated the red-hot favourites Preston North End 2–1 in the FA Cup Final at the Kennington Oval.

A smart, unobtrusive player with a dashing style, Joe was aggressive, had plenty of will-power, some good tricks, possessed a strong shot and was mainly left-footed, keeping defenders on their toes.

Twenty-six years of age when he joined Albion from Walsall Town in September 1887, he spent three excellent seasons with the club, scoring 20 goals in only 53 first-class appearances and proving to be a huge favourite with the supporters. Educated at St Mary's Council and Handsworth Grammar Schools, he played for Hamstead Swifts at weekends before starting his football career, in earnest, with Aston Unity in 1878. He didn't figure at all with Stoke,

Walsall Town (in his first spell) or Aston Villa, where for one season he acted as reserve to Richmond Davis. However, after returning to the Saddlers in the summer of 1887, he produced excellent performances in a couple of pre-season friendlies and was immediately signed by Albion who, so the reference books say, had watched him off and on for over a year.

Making his senior debut at inside-left in a first-round FA Cup tie at home to Wednesbury Old Athletic in mid-October 1887, Joe scored twice in a resounding 7–1 victory. At around the same time he was also helping Albion make steady progress in two local competitions, the Birmingham Cup and the Staffordshire Senior Cup.

Switching places with Pearson on the left wing, he was in good form in the next round of the FA Cup as Albion defeated Mitchell's St George 1–0 and then scored again in a 2–0 third round home victory over Wolves before going out and laying on two of centre-forward Jem Bayliss's four goals when his former club Stoke were thrashed in round five.

In the quarter-final clash against the 1881 Cup-winners, Old Carthusians, Joe was on target twice in an excellent 4–2 victory and then, in the semi-final encounter with Derby Junction, he scored yet again in a 3–2 win which took Albion into their third successive Final.

Unfortunately, in the Final he came up against Preston's redoubtable England international right-back Bob Howarth, a strong tackler who in the very first minute sent Joe sprawling. He was shaken up and thereafter played well below his best, never really threatening. A report of the Final in *The Birmingham Post* stated: 'In the second-half, the Albion forwards, who seemed fresher than their opponents, with the exception of Wilson who played very indifferently throughout, were now seen to greater advantage than in any part of the game.'

Bayliss had scored early on but Dewhurst had equalised soon after half-time and this is when Albion started to gain the upper-hand. Joe, although hardly seeing the ball, still had to be marked closely. He moved inside occasionally and made a nuisance of himself, especially late on, and it was his presence inside the goal area which enabled George Woodhall to steal in unnoticed and bag the winning goal in the 77th minute.

Albion unfortunately lost in the finals of both the Birmingham and Staffordshire Cup competitions in 1887–88, going down 3–2 to Aston Villa and 2–1 in a second replay to Wolves respectively, but they did go out and win the West Bromwich Charity Cup, defeating Great Bridge Unity 10–1 in a rather one-sided final when Joe scored twice and assisted in three of the other goals.

In the first season of League football, 1888–89, Joe scored four times in 20 games, missing the 4–3 home win over Burnley and the 2–1 defeat at Accrington through injury. His other goals, after his opener at Stoke, came in the home games against Notts County (won 4–2), Accrington (drew 2–2) and Stoke (won 2–0).

Joe also played in four FA Cup ties that season, scoring a hat-trick – the first of his career – in a 10–1 demolition of Chatham in round three. Albion went through to the semi-final stage, but lost 1–0 to Preston at Sheffield. He did, however, gain a Staffordshire Cup-winners' medal this term, scoring in a 2–0 final win over Leek at Stoke.

On target four times in 20 League games for the second season running in 1889–90, including a real beauty in a 3–0 home win over Aston Villa, Joe also scored in the first FA Cup game against Accrington, but this was to be his last campaign as an Albion player. He wasn't getting any younger and by now had lost a bit of his zest for the game.

In May 1890 he joined Kidderminster Harriers on a free transfer. Remaining at Aggborough for one season, he scored 10 goals in 25 games before switching his allegiance to Birmingham St George's, who at the time were members of the Football Alliance. Retiring through injury in the summer of 1892, Joe immediately qualified as a referee and, after two years officiating at intermediate and non-League levels, in 1894 he was accepted onto the Football League List, initially running the line in Second Division matches before moving into the middle in 1895.

He continued to referee First and Second Division League matches, and also FA Cup ties, right through to 1910, at which point he chose to quit football for good.

Gaining employment as a goldsmith in Birmingham's jewellery quarter, having learnt that trade as a teenager, he continued in this line of work until 1935 when, at the age of 64, he called it a day and retired to live out the remainder of his life in Acocks Green, attending his last Albion match in 1950.

Joe was 91 years of age when he died in 1952.

STAN WOOD

'Chubby-cheeked Wood turned out to be a great little winger who struck up an almost inseparable partnership with Teddy Sandford in the 1930s.'

Born:	1 July 1905, Winsford, Cheshire
Died:	22 February 1967, Halifax, Yorkshire

Albion senior record:

Appearances:	League 256, FA Cup 24, FA Charity Shield 1
Goals:	League 58, FA Cup 8, FA Charity Shield 0
Senior debut:	League, 3 September 1928 v Notts County (h) lost 3–1
Also played for:	Whitegate Victoria, Winsford United, Halifax Town, Huddersfield Town (guest), Football League (1 app)

Albion have been blessed with some splendid outside-lefts and Stan Wood is one of them. Described as 'wiry and slippery' in one matchday programme, he scored 66 goals in 281 games for Albion, whom he served for 10 years.

In April 1928, in between matches, Albion's secretary-manager Fred Everiss, along with club director Lou Nurse and trainer Fred Reed, went along to watch a Cheshire County League game between Winsford United and Runcorn. Having received glowing reports about the Winsford outside-left from former goalscorer Bobby Blood, who was playing in the same forward line, it was imperative that they took a closer look at the chubby-faced, dark-haired Stan Wood.

The Winsford secretary told the Albion representatives that 'Wood was very green…and had not been playing all that well,' but that didn't deter them. What they had seen of the left-winger meant that they quickly made their minds up. Albion wanted him and an agreement was reached that Stan would sign for the Baggies at the end of the season for a fee of £400. A post-dated cheque for £200 was handed over immediately, with a similar one to follow in due course.

Winsford didn't have to wait too long for the rest of the money as Stan was quickly into his stride at The Hawthorns. He took over from Arthur Fitton in the first team just four games into the 1928–29 season and went on to retain the left-wing position for five-and-a-half years, only injury and illness causing him to miss out on the action.

In fact, from his debut in September 1928 until December 1933, Albion completed 250 first-team matches and Stan was absent from just 39 of them. He had his worst spell on the sidelines during season 1932–33, missing out on 14 fixtures due to a severe knee strain suffered initially in the home League encounter with Portsmouth in mid-March.

In his first season with Albion, Stan scored four goals in 33 League and Cup appearances, breaking his duck in his fifth outing to set up a 2–0 win at Blackpool. With Frank Cresswell as his inside partner in 1929–30 he netted seven times in 36 games and then, in 1930–31, he was outstanding alongside Joe Carter and then Teddy Sandford as Albion stormed through to complete the unique double of gaining promotion and winning the FA Cup in the same season.

Stan – who was nicknamed 'Splinter' and the 'Singing Winger' – recorded his best goal-tally this season, netting 13 times in Division Two and on four occasions in the FA Cup. In the League he weighed in with crucial strikes against Burnley (h), Nottingham Forest (h), Preston North End (a), Reading (h) and Wolves (a), while in the Cup, after scoring in two of three third-round games with Charlton Athletic, he struck the only goal of a hard-fought fourth-round tie with Tottenham Hotspur – a wonderful left-footed drive from fully 20 yards – and then netted the opener on 20 minutes in the 2–1 quarter-final victory over Wolves at Molineux.

In the semi-final against Everton he gave his marking full-back, Welsh international Ben Williams, a testing time and did likewise in the Final when opposed by George Liddell of Birmingham. After all the excitement of that double-winning season, Stan hit the headlines again in August 1931 when he scored the only goal of Albion's opening League game at Arsenal. This was, of course, Stan's first appearance in top-flight football and one match report of this tight contest at Highbury stated: 'Wood was always a threat down Albion's left flank. He was tireless, always probing and over the 90 minutes certainly gave Tom Parker, Arsenal's veteran right full-back, plenty to think about.'

As enthusiastic as anyone on the training pitch, Stan sometimes started doing laps around The Hawthorns' pitch half an hour before the rest of the players arrived, and on the odd occasion would return for an extra hour's work in the afternoon. 'He was a fitness fanatic,' said his teammate Joe Carter, who added: 'Sometimes when we had to sprint up and down the pitch, Stan would be miles ahead of us, even passing us on the way back to the centre-circle!'

One of the quickest movers in Albion's team, Stan missed only two League games in 1931–32 and, before injury struck, appeared in the first 28 matches the following season when he also represented the Football League and was named as a reserve for England. By this time Welshman Walter Robbins had joined the club and he was a very capable deputy. So too was Walter Boyes in 1933–34. In fact, he eventually replaced Stan on the left wing and appeared throughout the 1934–35 campaign when Albion again reached a Wembley Cup Final, but this time without Stan, who in the meantime had helped the reserves win the Central League championship.

Boyes was injured three months into the 1935–36 season, which meant a return to first-team action for Stan, who went on to score eight goals in 33 games before following up with nine more strikes in 24 games in 1936–37, by which time yet another outside-left, Lol Coen, was pressing hard for a place in the side.

After 11 outings and two goals in season 1937–38, Stan was replaced as first-choice outside-left by Joe Johnson, who had been signed from Stoke City. In May 1938, he left The Hawthorns for Halifax Town, turning out for the Shaymen in every wartime season as well as guesting for Huddersfield Town in 1941–42. Retiring as a player immediately after the war, Stan took over as the Yorkshire club's trainer, a position he retained until May 1949.

Remaining in Halifax for the rest of his life, enjoying his fishing and bowls, Stan Wood was a guest at the celebration dinner following Albion's 1954 FA Cup final victory. He was exceptionally fine footballer, one of the best in his position.

GEORGE 'SPRY' WOODHALL

'Woodhall was so good on the right-wing, he was fast and clever – a real handful.'

Born:	5 September 1863, West Bromwich
Died:	9 September 1924, West Bromwich

Albion senior record:

Appearances:	League 44, FA Cup 30
Goals:	League 10, FA Cup 10
Senior debut:	FA Cup, 25 October 1884 v Junction Street School, Derby (a) won 7–1
Also played for:	West Bromwich All Saints, Churchfield Foresters, Wolverhampton Wanderers, Berwick Rangers (Birmingham League), Oldbury Town, England (2 full caps)

George 'Spry' Woodhall was singularly well-nicknamed for he was, indeed, a sprightly footballer, who occupied three different positions in the front line, those of outside-right, inside-right and centre-forward, during his nine-year stay with Albion. Signed in May 1883 from the local Churchfield Foresters club in West Bromwich, in his first season with Albion George shared the outside-right berth with Dennis Smith, Harry Aston and Jack Whitehouse.

The following season he made the right-wing position his own, producing some brilliant performances and scoring plenty of goals as Albion destroyed defences all over the Midlands with their tremendous attacking flair. In fact, George 'ran rings round' Bloxwich in a Birmingham Cup tie which Albion won 15–0, bamboozled the defenders of Stoke, Leek Town and Burton Swifts in Staffordshire Cup matches and also played pretty well on his FA Cup debut, scoring once and setting up two more goals in an emphatic 7–1 win over the Derby team Junction Street School.

George also played in the very first game at Stoney Lane, helping Albion beat Scottish club Third Lanark Rifle Volunteers 4–1 in early September 1885. In 1885–86, and having by now turned professional, George, who was still comfortably holding down the right-wing position, scored around 20 goals in more than 40 first-team appearances, helping Albion reach the finals of three tournaments – the FA Cup (for the first time), the Birmingham Cup and the highly-competitive Staffordshire Cup. Unfortunately, and despite George having a fine game, Albion succumbed 2–0 to rivals Aston Villa in the FA Cup. The other two finals were both won, and George scored in each one, against Walsall Swifts and Stoke respectively.

Around this time it transpired that George wasn't always the nice guy he seemed. Quite often he went in to a 'mood all of his own' and quite regularly, during a game, boycotted younger men around him, simply refusing to pass to a colleague whom he believed was usurping his position as Albion's star performer. He had several arguments with his teammates about this and was certainly reprimanded more than once by the club's committee members. George was a wonderful player, the best in the club at that time – and he knew it.

An FA Cup finalist once again in 1886–87, when Blackburn Rovers won the trophy after a hard-fought replay, George was also a loser in the Birmingham Cup, although he more than made up for those disappointments, helping Albion lift the Staffordshire Cup by scoring in a 4–0 win over Walsall Swifts. He also managed his 'fair share' of goals in another 40 or so other matches, having a hand in four of the eight which were scored against Hednesford Town in a Staffordshire Cup tie.

After collecting successive losers' medals in FA Cup finals, George at long last collected a winners' prize in 1887–88 after his 77th minute goal (from Billy Bassett's exquisite pass) earned Albion a thoroughly deserved 2–1 victory over the pre-match favourites Preston North End. He also represented England on two occasions during the second half of this season, having the honour of scoring on his international debut in a 5–1 victory over Wales at Crewe in the February before putting in an outstanding performance in a 5–0 drubbing of Scotland in Glasgow a month later.

After the Scotland match, the *North British Daily Mail* reporter wrote: 'England's right-wing pair of Woodhall and Goodhall combined cleverly throughout. Woodhall was a constant threat, his speed and centring, and his general all-round play catching the eye on several occasions…Lindley headed home an accurate Woodhall corner for the opening goal…and Goodhall scored a fifth goal after fine approach work by Lindley and Woodhall.'

Unfortunately a spate of irritating injuries to his right ankle and knee, and also his left hip, restricted George to just 10 first-class appearances for Albion in 1889–90 and, after he had reluctantly moved inside to accommodate Billy Bassett on the right wing, he was given 17 starts in 1890–91, followed by just seven in 1891–92 when, effectively, he was acting as a reserve to England's number one winger Bassett and the main two 'front men' of Sammy Nicholls and Billy Richards. As a result, he missed Albion's FA Cup Final win over the Villa, having to sit and cheer on his colleagues from the stand.

George's last senior appearance in an Albion shirt came in the 2–2 draw with Stoke at home (Stoney Lane) on 11 April 1892. He had been with the club for nine years and had scored 20 goals in 74 League and FA Cup matches, plus another 50 goals in more than 100 other games, including well-taken hat-tricks in 12–2 and 23–0 Staffordshire Cup victories over Burton Wanderers in October 1887 and Burton Swifts in February 1890.

Transferred to neighbours Wolves in July 1892, George spent two years with the Wanderers during which time he scored once in 18 appearances. After decent-enough spells in the Birmingham League with first Berwick Rangers and then Oldbury United, George announced his retirement in May 1898. He remained in football, to a certain degree, by visiting local schools, while at times he also called in on Albion to assist with training (when the regular men were unavailable).

George lived until he was 61 years of age, having made his final visit to The Hawthorns as a guest of his former playing partner Billy Bassett when England played Ireland in an international match in October 1922.

*Telford-born British middleweight boxing champion Richie Woodhall, a bronze medallist at the Seoul Olympics in 1988 and a Commonwealth Games gold medal-winner in Auckland, New Zealand in 1990, is a relative of the former Albion player.